# The changing Labour Party

In the 1992 General Election the Labour Party presented a substantially changed programme to the electorate. *The Changing Labour Party* presents the first analysis of the fundamental changes to Labour policy which occurred during the 1980s. It examines in detail the ideological and political context of the Policy Review undertaken by the Party following its third consecutive electoral defeat in 1987. It also traces changes in Party organization and analyses Party members' views of the new policies.

In recent years the Labour Party's policies have been accused of representing an acceptance of a 'Thatcherite agenda'. By focusing on a number of key policy areas including defence, economic policy, trade union policy, the EC and the environment, the contributors assess whether the Party's policies have really changed. Can the Party's policies be seen as a return to those of the Wilson/Callaghan era or do they suggest the development of a new form of socialism for the differing circumstances of the 1990s?

**Martin J. Smith** is Lecturer in Politics at Sheffield University. His publications include *The Politics of Agricultural Support in Britain* and *Pressure, Power and Policy*, and articles in *Public Administration, Political Studies* and *Parliamentary Affairs*. **Joanna Spear** is Lecturer in Politics at Sheffield University. She specializes in British and American foreign policy and will shortly publish *Carter and Arms Sales*.

# The changing
# Labour Party

Edited by
Martin J. Smith and Joanna Spear

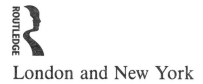

London and New York

First published in 1992
by Routledge
11 New Fetter Lane, London EC4P 4EE

Simultaneously published in the USA and Canada
by Routledge
a division of Routledge, Chapman and Hall, Inc.
29 West 35th Street, New York, NY 10001

© 1992 Martin J. Smith and Joanna Spear

Typeset in Times Roman by
Falcon Typographic Art Ltd, Fife, Scotland
Printed and bound in Great Britain by
Biddles Ltd, Guildford and King's Lynn

*British Library Cataloguing in Publication Data*
A catalogue record for this book is available from the British Library.

ISBN 0–415–07833–4 (hb)
    0–415–07834–2 (pbk)

*Library of Congress Cataloging in Publication Data*
*has been applied for.*

# Contents

# Preface

This book was conceived of in the summer of 1990 with the bulk of the chapters being completed in the spring of 1991. In the course of preparation of the book the Department of Politics, University of Sheffield hosted a series of seminars on the theme of *Labour's Policy Review*. This provided an opportunity for several of the contributors to present papers and get feedback. The editors would like to thank the academics and graduate students who took part in the programme for their ideas and enthusiasm. A further series of papers were presented at the Political Studies Association 1991 Conference at Lancaster University. Again the editors would like to thank all those who attended the panel for their input.

The editors would also like to express their thanks to Pat Gordon Smith of HarperCollins for her initial help and support in getting the book underway and to Gordon Smith of Routledge for seeing the project through to fruition.

*Martin Smith and Joanna Spear*

# List of contributors

**Dr Pete Alcock** is Acting Head of Division, Applied Social Sciences, The School of Health and Community Studies, Sheffield City Polytechnic.

**Valerie Atkinson** is the Administrator for the Ford Foundation Project on India, Department of Politics, University of York.

**Dr Simon Bromley** is a Lecturer in Social and Economic Policy, School of Health and Community Studies, Sheffield City Polytechnic.

**Dr Neil Carter** is a Lecturer in Politics, Department of Politics, University of York.

**Dr Stuart Croft** is a Lecturer in International Studies and Deputy Director of the Graduate School of International Studies, University of Birmingham.

**Professor Andrew Gamble** is Professor of Politics, Department of Politics, University of Sheffield.

**Stephen George** is a Senior Lecturer in Politics, Department of Politics, University of Sheffield.

**Chris Guiver** is a Doctoral Student and Teaching Assistant in the Department of Politics, University of Sheffield.

**Professor David Marquand** is Professor of Politics, Department of Politics, University of Sheffield.

**Ben Rosamond** is a Lecturer in Politics, School of Business, Oxford Polytechnic.

**Dr Patrick Seyd** is a Lecturer in Politics, Department of Politics, University of Sheffield.

**Dr Martin J. Smith** is a Lecturer in Politics, Department of Politics, University of Sheffield.

**Dr Joanna Spear** is a Lecturer in Politics and Deputy Director of the Graduate Programme in International Studies, Department of Politics, University of Sheffield.

**Professor Paul Whiteley** is the Patricia Harriman Professor of Government, Department of Government, College of William and Mary, Williamsburg, Virginia.

# Part I

# 1 The Labour Party in opposition

*Martin J. Smith*

The 1980s have seen substantial changes in the Labour Party both in terms of policy and organization. To a large extent the 1980s was, for Labour, the lost decade. It was a period of intense internal fighting, electoral humiliation and even, with the rise of the Social Democratic Party, threats to its very existence. However, the 1990s has seen a reinvigorated Labour Party which appears, for the moment, to have overcome its apparently fundamental divisions, and as Seyd and Whitely show in chapter 3, reorganized its structure. There have also been, partly as a result of the Policy Review, major changes in Labour Party policy. This book will assess the nature of these changes. It will examine how much policy has changed, why it has changed and what the impact of this change might be on a Labour Government. This chapter will first provide a brief overview of the key events within the Labour Party during the 1980s.

## THE LABOUR PARTY IN THE 1980s: THE RISE OF THE LEFT

The final years of the last Labour Government were a period of economic and political crisis. The Party came to power in February 1974 with a radical manifesto committed to greater public expenditure, increased intervention in the economy, an expansion of welfare services and a radical redistribution of wealth. These policies were never implemented. This failure was due to a lack of commitment by the leadership, the absence of a parliamentary majority and the severe economic crisis which dogged Labour almost throughout its five years in power. As early as 1975 the Chancellor of the Exchequer, Denis Healey, demanded £3 billion worth of cuts in public expenditure. By 1977 the severity of the economic crisis had forced the Government to ask the International Monetary Fund for a loan which resulted in further substantial cuts in expenditure and revisions of policy (see Coates 1980).

The public expenditure cuts combined with economic crisis created increased dissatisfaction within both the party and the trade union movement. The Government attempted to deal with inflation through incomes policies of increasing severity which tested to breaking point the support of trade union leaders. In the autumn of 1978 unions demonstrated their unhappiness by voting against pay policy at the TUC conference. A number of strikes in the public and private sectors culminated in the 'Winter of Discontent'. With lorry drivers, hospital porters, refuse collectors and even grave diggers on strike, the country appeared to be in a state of chaos where the unions rather than the Government were in control. The series of strikes undermined the Government's economic strategy, the view that only it could work with the unions, and eroded much of its authority. It seemed that the party leadership was strategically and ideologically bankrupt. By cutting public expenditure, abandoning full employment, deflating the economy and pursuing monetarism, the leadership had explicitly abandoned Keynesian social democracy and seemed to have little idea, apart from financial orthodoxy, of how to resolve Britain's crises.

There was, as a consequence, an increasing divergence between the views of the party leadership and those of its active members. A largely left-wing membership became disillusioned with a Government lacking in direction and apparently challenging its supporters in the unions and the Party rather than its opponents in the city (Whiteley 1983). The strength of the left of the Party had been developing throughout the 1970s due to: the increasing dissatisfaction with Labour in power; changes in Labour Party membership and union leadership; and the development of left-wing organizations within the Party (Seyd 1987). The combination of an influx of young, radical and middle-class members with the election of a number of left-wing union leaders, enabled the left to become increasingly strong within the key policy-making bodies, the NEC and the conference. It was then able to ensure the adoption of many of its favoured policies. *Labour's Programme 1973*, committed the Party to planning agreements, the nationalization of the top twenty-five companies and a wealth tax. The failure of the Labour Government to implement these policies made the left realize that changing policies at conference was not enough. Hence a new group was formed – the campaign for Labour Party Democracy (CLPD) – with the aim of changing the party constitution (Kogan and Kogan 1982).

The CLPD working with other left-wing groups and under the umbrella of the Rank and File Mobilizing Committee began a campaign to change the Labour Party constitution. Through contacts with constituency parties and by lobbying unions, the CLPD was successful in achieving two important constitutional changes (Kogan and Kogan 1982; Seyd 1987). At the 1979 conference, the mandatory reselection of MPs was passed. This meant that within the lifetime of a parliament each Labour MP would have to go through the selection process. This was seen as a way of making MPs accountable to their constituency parties and of replacing MPs regarded as right wing with candidates of the left. Second, at the 1980 conference an electoral college was accepted as the means for electing the leader and at a special conference in January 1981 a system was agreed which gave 40 per cent of the vote to the trade unions and 30 per cent each to the constituency Labour Parties and the Parliamentary Labour Party (PLP).

Jim Callaghan resigned as leader before the new electoral system was in place. Even with election by the PLP, the veteran left winger, Michael Foot, defeated the candidate of the right, Denis Healey. Hence, by the end of 1980 the left had control of the NEC, had instituted important constitutional changes and the Party had a left-wing leader. What impact did the strength of the left have on the Party?

## THE LEFT IN CONTROL

The first consequence of the left's new found strength was to split the Party even further. The left although dominant was not hegemonic, and so the left/right battles became even more intense. The first real battle came in 1981 when Tony Benn decided to use the new electoral machinery to challenge Denis Healey for the deputy leadership of the Party. Throughout the summer and autumn of 1981 the Labour Party openly paraded its divisions before the media and, effectively, the electorate. The electoral contest was extremely bitter with the right accusing the left of bullying and undemocratic methods and the left accusing the right of distortion (Kogan and Kogan 1982). The contest also created a new division within the Party. John Silkin stood as the non-Bennite candidate of the left and so effectively split the left. This division was reinforced when certain members of Tribune, led by Neil Kinnock, abstained rather than support Benn in the final ballot (Harris 1984). These abstentions effectively resulted in Healey's victory as he won by only 0.8 per cent (Punnett 1990).

A second consequence of the left's strength was a shift in Labour Party policy. The 1982 programme which formed the basis of the 1983 manifesto could be seen almost as the left's archetypal platform. It provided the first steps in the transition to socialism with a comprehensive range of policies including a high level of state intervention, economic planning, import controls, an isolationist and neutralist foreign policy based on unilateralism, withdrawal from the EC and the removal of US military bases. Although Labour watered down some of these policies for the 1983 manifesto, it was still, according to Austin Mitchell (1983: 65) 'the most radical set of policies of any European socialist party'.

Labour's shift to the left and the subsequent constitutional changes were also a major factor in the breakaway of the Social Democratic Party (SDP). With a combination of the constitutional changes and leftward drift of policy, certain members of the Party believed that they could no longer remain within its folds. Immediately following the 1981 Wembley conference, David Owen, Shirley Williams, William Rogers and Roy Jenkins made their 'Limehouse Declaration' saying that 'the need for a realignment in British politics must be faced' and this rapidly led to the formation of a new party (Whitehead 1985: 362; Stephenson 1982).

The importance of these events for the Labour Party were twofold. It highlighted and confirmed the degree of division within the Labour Party. Although certain members of the 'outside' left were pleased that the social democrats had left (Kogan and Kogan 1982), the majority of MPs were concerned about the Party falling to pieces. It also emphasized the frailty of Labour Party support: Labour's voters seemed to be quickly deserting to the SDP. By November 1981 the SDP, in alliance with the Liberals, had a poll rating of 43 per cent, with the Conservatives at 25.5 and Labour on 28. At the local level 'the Alliance won 23 per cent of the seats they fought in the local by-elections between mid-May and mid-July, 45 per cent between mid-July and mid-October, 67 per cent between mid-October and mid-November; in these elections, the two traditional parties virtually collapsed' (King 1982: 248). The real implications of the new party were brought home by their parliamentary by-election victories. Between July 1981 and March 1982 the SDP/Liberal Alliance swept to victory in four seats with Labour suffering swings against it of between −8.5 and −13.2 per cent (King 1982).

In addition to these internal conflicts and divisions, there had also been important changes outside of the Party. The election of the first Thatcher Government in 1979 had produced a Government which was not prepared to operate within the post-war social democratic consensus. The Conservatives produced alternative solutions to the crises that had inflicted Britain in the 1970s. Rather than Keynesianism and full employment, Mrs Thatcher was committed to reducing the role of the state, cutting taxation, fiscal discipline, and reducing the power of the unions and local authorities. In so doing the 1979 Government challenged much of what Labour stood for in the post-war period. By arguing that the state did not have responsibility for employment, or the economy, and that nationalized industries should be returned to the private sector, Thatcherism changed the terms of the political debate.

Labour faced an election in 1983 with a set of radical left-wing policies, a leader not suited to the job or a modern election campaign, a poor, divided campaign and a new centre-left party which split the anti-Conservative vote. These policies, combined with the divisions in the Party, the Thatcher Government's success in the Falklands and apparent improvements in the economy, led to Labour's greatest defeat certainly since 1931 and possibly since 1900. The Party received a humiliating 28 per cent of the vote, compared to 26 per cent for the Alliance and 43 per cent for the Conservatives. Outside of London the Party only held on to three seats in the south. 'Over the Labour wastelands of the south the Party won only 17 per cent of the votes against the Alliance's 29 per cent, coming third in 149 seats and losing deposits in half the constituencies' (Mitchell 1983: 131).

## LABOUR AFTER DEFEAT

The 1983 election was the nadir of Labour's misfortunes in the 1980s. A divided and poorly led party suffered a humiliating defeat when it nearly, in terms of votes, became Britain's third party. Yet, this defeat had important consequences which were to influence the development of the Policy Review in the late 1980s.

First, it appeared to some to confirm the strength of the Thatcherite agenda. The 1979 election could no longer be seen as an aberration due to the disasters of the last Labour Government and the Winter of Discontent. The election showed that skilled working-class voters did not vote Conservative only once due to Labour's economic failure, but were prepared to vote Conservative again. With this second landslide, it also appeared that the post-war consensus had gone for good. Mrs Thatcher had won a second election without a commitment to full employment, with promises to reduce dependency on the welfare state and to shift large sections of the public sector into the private domain. It appeared that the success of Thatcherism had changed the terrain of British politics. Labour's traditional supporters were prepared to vote for a party that did not offer the policies which had been central to Labour's thinking in the post-war period. Hence, both left and right recognized that a policy rethink was necessary.

Second, this defeat severely weakened the left. The peak of the left's strength had been in 1980–1. Its successes in the early 1980s had stung the right into action. For the first time the right started a concerted fightback and with the unions they began to consider how to reverse the constitutional and policy changes. Even at the 1981 conference the right was successful in the National Executive Committee (NEC) elections. Five right wingers, with trade union support, replaced five left wingers, on the NEC (Kogan and Kogan 1982). Following this success, John Golding replaced Tony Benn as chair of the important home policy committee of the NEC and he used this position to water down some of the policies in the *1982 Programme* for the 1983 manifesto.

In addition the left was becoming increasingly divided. The constitutional and policy successes had been achieved by a very unlikely alliance of Trotskyists, the 'outside left' in the CLPD, the Labour Coordinating Committee (LCC) and the more traditional Tribunite left. This alliance held together whilst they were fighting the right and had specific goals, but once these were achieved there was little to unite these groups. Infighting between various left-wing factions developed and was personified first by the growing rift between Benn and Foot and then by the expulsion of five leading Militant supporters from the Party (Seyd 1987: 160–1). These divisions were exacerbated during the deputy leadership contest in 1981, and in 1982 the division between the 'hard' left and the 'soft' Tribunite left was formalized with the creation of the Campaign group with twenty-three left-wing MPs (Seyd 1987).

Third, and perhaps most importantly, the defeat led to the resignation of Michael Foot as leader. This provided the first opportunity to test the new electoral college for the election of the leader. Neil Kinnock with 71 per cent of the college votes for the leadership and Roy Hattersley with 67 per cent for the deputy leadership overwhelmingly defeated the left-wing candidates, Eric Heffer and Michael Meacher (Drucker 1984). The size and nature of this victory was important. Kinnock clearly had support throughout the Party and this gave him a high degree of legitimacy and authority. In addition, his alliance with Hattersley demonstrated that the leadership had the support of the left and the right. Hence, Kinnock was able to use this victory to build a new coalition within the Party. The separation between the 'soft' and 'hard' left enabled Kinnock to build support on both sides of the Party whilst isolating the hard left. With support of the centre left and centre right Kinnock secured control of the Party's three power centres – the PLP, the NEC and the conference (Curran 1987). This gave the leader the base to make the Party electable once again.

## REFORMING THE PARTY

Kinnock realized that if Labour was to achieve electoral victory it was necessary to reorganize the Party, to make policy more acceptable to the electorate and to end the internal divisions. In effect all these goals were closely related. In order to change policy central authority had to be re-established and the divisions within the Party overcome (Kelly 1991). Kinnock and his advisers set about reorganizing national headquarters, 'in a way that gave the leadership more control over campaigning, presentation and coordination of party activity throughout the country' (Kelly 1991: 6). With the appointment of Peter Mandelson as the head of a directorate of campaigns, the Party began to take public relations and the media seriously, and Labour's campaigns took on a much more professional approach (Hughes and Wintour 1990). Kinnock also attempted to reduce the power of activists by challenging the outside left and through changing the constitution. Kinnock tried, but failed, to introduce one member, one vote for reselection (Shaw 1988). At the 1985 conference Kinnock indicated his intention to rid Labour of Militant because, according to Shaw:

> His long range objective had always been to emasculate Militant as a significant political force. . . . But, secondly, the attack on Militant had a more general purpose – to allay the fears (which opinion surveys suggested had cost the Party dear in 1983) that Labour was too left wing. He wanted to demonstrate that the Party would have no truck with extremists.
>
> (Shaw 1989: 189)

Kinnock also managed to fill the NEC policy sub-committees with his supporters and so he had the ability to determine the direction of policy. However, analysis of the 1987 manifesto reveals that the degree of policy change between 1983 and 1987, although significant, was not substantial. In 1987 Labour was trapped both within the framework of 1983 and of Kinnock's left-wing roots. The manifesto confirmed that the Party's attachment to unilateral nuclear disarmament remained. It added a new promise to reduce unemployment by 'one million in two years' with a commitment to increased spending through borrowing. Labour could still be portrayed as the party of promises, of taxation, of spending and of unilateralism.

The problem for Kinnock was that although he wanted change, he was constrained by both the Party and his own past. Rather than changing policy, the manifesto was full of compromise and ambiguity. So the commitment to withdraw from the EC disappeared, but was replaced with very little explanation of Labour's view of the Community. Renationalization of privatized industries was replaced by a confusing system of 'special new securities' which 'will be bought and sold in the market in the usual way and will carry either a guaranteed return, or dividends linked to the company's growth' (Labour Party 1987a: 6). These were, in effect, a sort of non-share share. Taxation policy was interpreted differently by different spokespeople and non-nuclear defence sometimes meant US protection and sometimes did not. It appeared that the rhetoric was changing but the direction of substantive policy was difficult to discern.

Kinnock thus faced a number of problems in his first period as leader. Divisions within the Party were still apparent. The year-long and vindictive miners' strike caused tremendous difficulties for Labour by highlighting the divisions within the Party and the problematic relationship with the unions. In addition, parts of the Party, particularly in London, continued to be stuck with the 'loony left' label and so the media constantly associated Labour with the hard left.

Nevertheless, Labour did fight an effective election campaign in 1987. The Party was better organized than they ever had been and made full use of new technology in their campaign. Kinnock was also prepared to run a presidential campaign in order to directly challenge the dominant style of Margaret Thatcher. The epitome of the leadership focus was the famous 'Kinnock' party election broadcast which concentrated solely on Kinnock the man (Hughes and Wintour 1990). Undoubtedly, Labour ran a well-organized and professional campaign, the complete opposite to the performance of 1983; although there was some suggestion that it peaked too early (Butler and Kavanagh 1988). The campaign was effective enough to cause jitters within the Conservative camp on several occasions (Tyler 1987). It was not, however, effective enough to win the election.

Labour's intention was not to win, that was always unrealistic, but to remove any doubt that they were the main opposition party (Hughes and Wintour 1990). They did, nevertheless, expect to substantially reduce the Conservative majority. Despite the fact they had lost all the excuses of 1983 – there was no Falkland factor; Labour now had a new professional leadership; it had removed many of the more extreme policies from the manifesto; the divisions were much less apparent then they had been in 1983; the campaign was probably the best of all the parties – Labour still only won 31 per cent of the vote and the Conservative majority was 102 seats. Undoubtedly, part of the explanation for the Conservative victory was the success of their pre-election economic boom (Sanders *et al.* 1987), and the division of the anti-Conservative vote between Labour and the Alliance. However, poll evidence demonstrated that people were still unhappy with Labour's policies, particularly on defence, and that they saw the Party as divided. Voters did not believe that Labour was a credible governing party (Crewe 1987). In some ways the defeat in 1987 was worse than in 1983 because its scale was unexpected and there were no excuses.

The scale of Labour's defeat, despite all the party leadership had achieved between 1983 and 1987, demonstrated the need for a more fundamental review of policy. Labour's policy had changed but the contradictions and ambiguities were all too visible in the election campaign. After some discussion within the Party, it was widely accepted among the leadership that major revisions were vital. The Party could not win an election if people would not support Labour's policies. Tom Sawyer suggested that the Party had to examine its key 'themes and issues'. In July 1987, Neil Kinnock set a 'two year deadline for far reaching changes designed to match the Labour Party's policies with the needs of the electorate' (*The Times*, 14 July 1987). In September 1987 seven policy groups were set up each with a convener from both the shadow cabinet and the NEC. These groups would

> assess the policy issues and opportunities in the 1990s: make an assessment of the relevance and credibility of existing party policy matched against the need and concerns of groups of voters; and recommend broad themes of political strategy as well as policy areas in which more detailed examination is required.
>
> (Quoted in Hughes and Wintour 1990: 46)

These groups worked through 1988 and 1989 with the final Policy Review documents being passed at the 1989 conference after Neil Kinnock had ensured the necessary trade union support for success.

The policy documents also had to be passed as a whole, without amendment to individual policies, making it impossible for conference to reject particular items. Kinnock's position in this review process was strengthened by several factors. The scale of the 1987 defeat shocked the Party as a whole. There was a realization that Labour could not afford a fourth electoral defeat and so many members of the left subjected themselves to a self-denying ordinance. Hence many left wingers who were prominent in the period 1983–7 have either joined the Kinnock camp, like Margaret Beckett and Michael Meacher, or like Dianne Abbott, Tony Benn and Ken Livingstone have remained remarkably quiet. This silence on the left was further ensured by the leadership challenge in 1988. Shortly after the 1987 election, Benn and Heffer announced that they would challenge Kinnock and Hattersley for the leadership. They were substantially defeated. Kinnock won 89 per cent of the college vote and Hattersley 67 per cent (Punnett 1990). Consequently, it was clear that the hard left had little support even in their traditional CLP heartlands and this has enabled Kinnock to consolidate even further his 'soft' left/centre right coalition and so increase his control over the party machinery. With the acquiescence of the CLPs, the defeat of the left and the new policy review machinery, Kinnock was in a strong position to fundamentally change Labour policy.

The remaining chapters will assess the degree to which Labour Party policy has changed since 1987. How great are the policy changes that have occurred? Are they an acceptance of the Thatcherite agenda or a return to the Labourism of Wilson and Callaghan? Or do they offer a completely new range of policies? Chapter 2 places the policy change in its historical and ideological context, whilst chapter 3 examines the organizational changes. The following chapters then look at specific policy areas. Some focus on policy areas that have been traditionally important like the economy, defence and industrial relations, whilst others examine policies that have arrived on the political agenda more recently such as women, citizenship and the environment. Finally, the conclusion assesses the degree of continuity and change across the various policy areas and the difficulties a Labour Government might face in implementing these policies.

# 2 A return to revisionism?
# The Labour Party's Policy Review

*Martin J. Smith*

With the fall of Mrs Thatcher, commentators on both the left and the right have claimed that 'Thatcherism' has left a lasting impression on British politics. Consequently, the Labour Party's Policy Review is seen as a response to the success of Thatcherism. They claim that the Labour Party has been forced into accepting the 'Thatcherite agenda' with its adoption of 'market socialism'. To quote Peter Jenkins:

> One of her [Mrs Thatcher's] achievements was to split the Labour Party, and through her populist appeal to its working class supporters, oblige the party to rid itself of its most radical leaders and to reform itself. In the process socialism was, to all intents and purposes, abandoned.                    (Jenkins 1990)

This chapter questions the view that the fundamental change in Labour's policy in the late 1980s was merely a reaction to Thatcherism. It will demonstrate that the Policy Review was not solely the result of Thatcherism and that the policies that have emanated from the review are not Thatcherite. By placing the Policy Review in context it will be seen that the policy changes of the late 1980s derived from a whole range of factors and that the ideological position of the new policies is closer to revisionism than Thatcherism.

It has been argued that the Policy Review is the result of the Thatcher Government's success both electorally and in terms of transforming the post-war agenda (Kavanagh 1990: 304). Labour's electoral failures in the 1980s and the Conservative's ability to set the parameters of political debate has resulted in Labour moving onto this new ground. Peter Jenkins (1988: 374) maintains that Mrs Thatcher's Governments ended the socialist era and that consequently 'the Thatcher revolution is entrenched'. There is a new common ground, 'Its assumptions are individualistic rather than collectivist, preferring private to state ownership, putting the rights of the member before the interests of trade unions and sound money before priming the economy' (Jenkins 1988: 375). For Jenkins the Policy Review is an attempt to attune Labour's policies to this new agenda.

On the left, it has been argued that Thatcherism has become ideologically dominant (Hall 1985) and this has forced Labour to operate within the discourse of the New Right and 'on the terrain of the individualist appeal of neo-conservatism' (Jessop *et al.* 1987: 112; Panitch 1988: 321). From these perspectives the Policy Review is seen as a direct response to Thatcherism. On the one hand, Labour is accepting the Thatcherite agenda by appealing to individualism, the market and private ownership. Alternatively electoral opportunism, as Downs (1957) would predict, is forcing the Labour Party to the new centre ground. Thus, the new policies emerging from the Policy Review are seen as Thatcherism with a human (or social democratic) face.

However, if we look at why the Policy Review occurred it becomes clear that Thatcherism was only one impetus behind the change. Thatcherism undoubtedly created the space for a thorough examination of Labour Party policy. By being so successful electorally, it forced Labour into rethinking its policy. In addition, the Conservatives undermined the post-war consensus and so presented a new set of problems – mass unemployment, deficiencies in the welfare state, the level of taxation – which the Labour Party was forced to confront. By shifting the agenda to the right it allowed the Labour leadership to consider policy changes that otherwise would have been completely unacceptable to the Party as a whole. Yet, these were policy changes that had long been considered by the leadership. Many of the factors that led to the Policy Review were external to Thatcherism and to some extent also explain the changes that have occurred in the Conservative Party. The causes of the Policy Review are complex and come from both within the Labour Party and from wider social and economic changes.

## THE CAUSES OF THE POLICY REVIEW

### Electoral failure

As we saw in chapter 1, the immediate cause of the Policy Review was Labour's third successive defeat in the 1987 election. However, Labour's poor electoral performance is not a recent phenomenon. From 1951 to 1987 Labour's vote fell in every election except 1966.

'Between 1944–78 and 1979–88 the average Labour vote fell from
44.5 to 31.8 per cent' (Crewe 1989: 2). In the elections of 1979,
1983 and 1987 the Conservatives managed to win a majority of
the vote of certain sectors of the working class. Even amongst
unskilled and semi-skilled workers, Labour's share of the vote
declined.

There has been an intense debate as to why Labour has suffered
such a loss in electoral support. One explanation is that the nature
of the working class has changed with a decline in union membership
and an increase in home ownership (Jenkins 1988). Consequently,
people are much less likely to think of themselves as working class
and so less likely to align with the perceived working class party. It
is suggested that the working class is now much more individualist
and is prepared to vote according to perceived self-interest rather
than class (Crewe 1989; Franklin 1985). Therefore the working class
no longer automatically votes Labour. Between 1945 and 1983 class
voting fell from 62 per cent to 47 per cent and Labour's share of
the working class vote fell from 62 per cent to 42 per cent (Crewe
1986: 620).

Alternatively it has been proposed that the size of the working
class has declined and that the occupational structure has changed
as people move from manual work to the service sector (Lash
and Urry 1987; Hobsbawn 1981: 3; Marshall *et al.* 1988: 22).
Therefore, there are less working class people to vote Labour and
so Labour needs to change its policies to attract the new middle
classes. Heath, Jowell and Curtice (1985) accept that Labour has
lost about half its vote due to the decline in the size of the
working class and the rest due to political failure rather than
dealignment.

Whatever the causes of the decline in Labour Party support, the
Policy Review is an attempt to widen the appeal of the Party and
to win back some of the working class who voted Conservative in
the 1980s. To some extent there is disagreement within the Labour
Party over why Labour has done so badly. The left believes that the
working class has changed little and is still open to traditional socialist
ideas (Heffer 1986). The leadership seems to recognize the need to
attract the '£400 a week docker' and the upwardly mobile non-manual
worker. Therefore, the Policy Review was an attempt to drop some
of Labour's unpopular policies like nationalization and unilateralism
and to appeal to individualism, consumerism and privatism in order
to widen Labour's support. The electoral failure was in part a result
of the failure of social democracy and the inability of the left to

develop a popular alternative. This was also an impetus behind the review.

## The crisis of social democracy and the failure of the left

To some extent the Policy Review was also an attempt to fill the vacuum which resulted from the failure of both the revisionist social democracy that dominated the Party from the 1950s through to the 1970s and left-wing socialism that became increasingly dominant between 1973 and 1983.

Revisionists believed that through demand management economic growth could be achieved to allow the necessary public expenditure to provide for education and welfare services. This would ensure social justice. However, it became increasingly clear throughout the 1960s and 1970s that the social democratic state was unable to deal with economic problems and maintain its welfare goals. In 1964 and 1974 Labour Governments came to power committed to economic planning and the modernization of the British economy and the expansion of the welfare state. On both occasions they failed to achieve the desired economic growth and were forced into cutting public expenditure. In 1977 the economic crisis was so severe that the Government was forced to borrow from the International Monetary Fund (IMF). The conditions imposed by the IMF resulted in the Labour Government abandoning any pretence of attempting to achieve revisionist goals. The commitment to full employment was dropped and the Labour Government was the first, and perhaps only, post-war Government to cut public expenditure in real terms (see Coates 1980). In September 1977 Callaghan made his famous speech, which was seen as the burial of revisionism: 'We used to think that you could spend your way out of a recession and increase employment by cutting taxes and boosting government spending. I tell you in all candour that that option no longer exists . . .' (Quoted in Whitehead 1985: 189). Demand management was replaced by monetary control, the goal of full employment by controlling inflation and public spending by cutting taxes.

Labour had failed to control the economy and in so doing hit its own supporters hardest by trying to control their wages and cutting their jobs. For Marquand (1988: 52), 'policy-makers were trapped in an impasse, from which there was no escape. . . . The old Keynesian assumptions had collapsed'. As a result 'Labour entered the 1979 election with every major part of its post-war social and economic strategy undermined, and with a history of the recent failure of its new and *ad hoc* expedients in economic management' (Hirst 1989: 21).

As we saw in chapter 1, the undermining of Keynesianism created the space for the left to become the dominant influence within the Party. Yet, the left was hardly more successful than the revisionists. First, its strength within the Party led to internal conflicts both between various factions of the left and with the right which became more assertive (Seyd 1987: 161–6). Second, the Party with a left-wing manifesto and leader suffered its greatest electoral defeat since the 1930s. Third, the collapse of communism in Eastern Europe has delegitimized concepts of planning and state intervention which were central to the alternatives of the left. With the unpopularity of the Alternative Economic Strategy (AES) and the failure of 'actual existing socialism', the left was almost completely devoid of alternatives. By the end of the 1980s an economic policy of the left just did not exist. The policies of the left were seen to be unpopular and, in the context of the international political economy, unworkable. Consequently, the 1983 defeat led to a realignment of the left with the isolation of those organized around Tony Benn (Seyd 1987: 167).

It was apparent that the Party had to develop policies that did not repeat the mistakes of the 1970s and which would be more popular than those of the 1980s. Labour was looking for a broader appeal than the left could provide, whilst not wanting to be the party of promises, more spending and full employment that it was in the 1970s. The election of Neil Kinnock in 1983 allowed him to change policy with the support of a coalition of the 'soft left' and the right. This enabled a rejection of both the left-wing policies of the early 1980s and the Keynesian revisionism of the 1970s. After its defeats and splits in the 1980s, while continuing with some vocal opposition, the left was no longer in a position to prevent the dropping of its policies. With the failure of both left and right the leadership had to develop a new set of policies. In that sense the Policy Review was more a response to the ideological failings of the Labour Party than the ideological strength of the Conservatives. It was also part of a long-term attempt by the leadership to change the Party.

## The long-term modernization of the Labour Party

The policy and organizational changes undertaken by Neil Kinnock are not completely new but a continuation of a process initiated by Gaitskell. All Labour leaders since the 1950s, except Michael Foot, have attempted to modernize the Party by identifying it as a national social democratic party. The attempt to change policy started long before the arrival of Mrs Thatcher.

Revisionism in the 1950s was intended to relieve Labour of the policies which were seen to contribute to electoral defeat. After the third defeat in 1959 Gaitskell felt it necessary to completely repudiate the image of Labour as a 'party devoted to nationalisation' by removing clause 4 of the Labour Party constitution. In Gaitskell's view the Party needed to 'modernize itself both organizationally and doctrinally' so that it was no longer the party of class conflict and was national rather than dependent largely on working class support (Howell 1976: 222; Hamilton 1989). Gaitskell was able to ensure an almost total break with public ownership by 1959 (Coates 1975: 78) and he 'firmly wedded [the Party] to a constitutional and electorally respectable path' (Haseler 1969: 239).

This attempt to move Labour from a party of class to a party of nation was continued by Wilson. Although Wilson made no direct challenges to clause 4, he gradually removed nationalization from Labour's agenda. In the 1964 election he presented Labour as a modern, non-class party through the notion of the 'white heat of technology' by demonstrating that Labour was the party of technocracy and efficiency. Howell (1976: 248–9) suggests that Wilson 'attempted to mobilise support on the basis of national symbolism' and he used this symbolism to achieve 'the termination of a widespread identification of the party with a particular class, and its replacement by an identification with the interests of the nation as a whole'. The climax of this modernization strategy was the White Paper, *In Place of Strife*, which was an attempt to reform industrial relations by bringing trade unions within a legal framework and trying to limit the disruptive impact of their decentralized organization. 'Wilson's public criticism of trade union activity could be interpreted as an important step in his strategy of remoulding Labour as the National Party' (Howell 1976: 265).

With the failure of *In Place of Strife*, the collapse of the social democratic consensus and the increasing strength of the left, modernization stagnated in the 1970s. The failures of revisionism in the 1960s meant the right was ideologically bankrupt. A right-wing leadership no longer had the support nor the vision to change the Party. Consequently, Wilson took a pragmatic line. He allowed a left-influenced manifesto, which he tried to water down in government, as a means of holding the Party together. Under Callaghan modernization was immobilized because he lacked the loyalty of the NEC, was elected with a small majority and had little party support outside of Parliament (Haseler 1980: 116).

When Kinnock became leader he believed that the modernization of the Party had to be revived and was able to reinvigorate the process because he held advantages over previous leaders. Coming from the left he did not alienate the constituency parties in the way Wilson and Callaghan had. His attempt at reform, initially anyway, was not seen as a right-wing attack on the left. As mentioned previously, Kinnock managed to build a coalition of support which enabled him to control the NEC and was all the more effective and legitimate because of the high level of support for Kinnock in his leadership elections. Moreover Labour's electoral defeats have been a salutary lesson for the party membership and it appears that they have been prepared to accept change if this is a means of achieving a Labour Government (see Seyd and Whiteley, chapter 3).

Kinnock is in a position to continue the reform process initiated by Gaitskell by modernizing the party organization, policy and relationship with the trade unions (see Rosamond, chapter 7). In modernizing the Labour Party he is not doing anything new. However, the combination of electoral defeat, leadership support and the leader's skill has enabled Kinnock to be much more successful than any of his predecessors. In modernizing policy, the party is also recognizing that the external world has changed and that many of the policies of the past are no longer viable.

**Changing external circumstances: the world economy and the European Community**

The Policy Review was a recognition that the Party had to develop new policies because of changes in the world economy and Britain's integration into the European Community (EC). The external constraints that a future Labour Government will face mean that policies like the AES are no longer viable. Labour's acceptance of free trade, the abolition of exchange controls, the end of planning and privatization was partly a result of changing circumstances.

There have been important changes in the world economy which make it increasingly difficult for governments, and in particular British Governments, to control their own national economies. First, there has been a growth in the number of multinational corporations. Consequently production and trading is transnational and often carried out between companies rather than nations. Nations now have less control over production and trade (Lash and Urry 1987: 197–8; Gill and Law 1988). Even under the last Labour Government it was impossible to get multinationals to abide by planning agreements (Coates 1980). With greater internationalization of production, nationalization is likely to have little impact because, at best, it would just give a Government control over only part of the production process (Leadbeater 1987).

Second, financial markets and banking have expanded rapidly in the last twenty years. With the floating of exchange rates, governments have increased their currency reserves which has made financial markets more volatile and extremely difficult for governments to control (Strange 1986: 9–21). The financial sector is especially important for the British economy and now accounts for 20 per cent of the Gross Domestic Product (GDP). This means that governments have to be particularly careful about the impact that policies have on the international market. It would be almost impossible for a future Labour Government to reimpose exchange controls or to take measures seen to harm the interests of the City because of the adverse impact on the British economy. It is particularly true for Britain that:

> no nation state, not even the most powerful, can develop its own domestic or foreign economic policies on the basis of a purely self-regarding choice of the full range of options potentially available to it. An attempt to solve a balance of payments problem, for example, by imposing direct controls over the national currency, closing the border to imported goods and expropriating the assets of non-cooperative private producers, would infringe a wide range of treaty obligations organised through the international organisations and produce potentially devastating retaliation from the international community of countries and multinational firms.
>
> (Brett 1986: 17)

All Labour Governments have amended policies because of actions of the financial markets (Wilson 1974; Haines 1977) and with increased internationalization the impact of the financial markets for a future Labour Government is likely to be even greater.

The Labour leadership is now aware that a single country cannot determine its economic policy and this is why membership of the EC has become increasingly important (see George and Rosamond, chapter 12). However, membership of the EC implies further constraints on the actions of a Labour Government. Labour's acceptance of the Exchange Rate Mechanism (ERM) will constrain policy on interest rates and have an indirect impact on the level of public expenditure and taxation in Britain, because the Government will be prevented from taking action which will result in a loss in confidence in sterling (*Independent on Sunday*, 7 October 1990). British banks will also be constrained from issuing more credit than banks in Germany and France. As financial services come under EC control, many of the instruments of a national macroeconomic policy will disappear (Pelkman and Winters 1988: 65). The establishment of a Single European Market extends these constraints even further. Already, membership of the EC rules out the use of import barriers as an economic instrument. With 1992, a Labour Government would have to disallow all indirect subsidies and so would be unable to help 'lame ducks'. It will, therefore, be severely limited in the type of regional policy it could implement. The Single European Market will disallow the reimposition of exchange controls and limit discretion on indirect and excise taxes (Pinder 1989: 100). It will also mean greater regulation on the environment and a whole range of production issues coming from the community (Pinder 1989).

Labour's adoption of more market-oriented policies and the rejection of the national economic policy of the left is not a result of Thatcherism. It is rather a reflection that the world economy has changed and of Britain's need to be competitive within that economy. Moreover, Britain faces a whole range of constraints from international organizations that prevent the rejection of market policies. Changes in the world economy and the EC have greatly constrained the policy options available. Labour's policies post-review are a recognition of these constraints and a rejection of the 'socialism in one country' model of reform.

The reasons for the Policy Review were complex. The electoral success of the Conservatives was important. It highlighted the degree to which Labour's electoral base had been declining. It also allowed the leadership to continue the modernization of the Party which was necessary because of the ideological vacuum and the changes in the world that the Labour Party has to confront in the 1990s. Therefore, Thatcherism did not directly cause the change in the Labour Party but created a situation whereby it was easier for the Labour leadership to change the Party. It is now necessary to examine the ideology of these new policies and to assess whether they are on the Thatcherite terrain.

## THE IDEOLOGICAL CONTEXT OF THE POLICY REVIEW

Labour's manifestos in both 1974 and 1983 were substantially more radical than any others in the post-war era. Once sufficiently domi-- nant, the left rejected Keynesianism and the idea that there could be a middle way between socialism and capitalism (Marquand 1988).

Hence, it broke with the social democracy that had traditionally dominated the Labour Party.

The left proposed a whole range of policies intended to speed the transition from capitalism to socialism and to ensure a 'fundamental and irreversible shift of the balance of power and wealth to working people and their families' (Labour Party 1973: 7). The left's policy included a high degree of state intervention in the economy through increased nationalization, planning and import controls. The 1982 programme proposed a Department of Economic and Industrial Planning in order to produce 'agreed development plans' with management and unions. The department would have a whole range of statutory measures over price controls, credit, imports, investment and be able to issue directives on a wide range of industrial matters to ensure that 'companies participate constructively' (Labour Party 1982a: 41–3). In the 1983 manifesto there was a commitment to the renationalization of privatized companies and an extension of nationalization. Trade unions were to be given a central role in economic planning and the Conservative's employment legislation was to be repealed (Labour Party 1983a). The Policy Review saw a substantial shift from these policies.

**The Policy Review**

As far as the leadership of the Labour Party is concerned the review was neither the result of electoralism or the embracing of Thatcherism. Roy Hattersley has emphasized the importance of ideology in the modern Labour Party (Hattersley 1987) and so the Party produced a statement of principles with the Policy Review (Labour Party 1988a). The goal of the review was to adapt Labour policy to the changes that had occurred in Britain and the world in recent years. The statement of *Aims and Values* placed primacy on the 'creation of a genuinely free society' (Labour Party 1988a: 3). Yet, this freedom could not be maintained without the achievement of equality. As Hattersley (1987: 135) emphasized: 'A socialist government committed to real equality will clearly embark on a massive programme of redistribution, confident that it is more likely to improve overall economic performance rather than depress it.'

An important feature of the Policy Review is the emphasis on markets and this clearly distinguishes the position of the review from the policy position of Labour in 1983. According to *Aims and Values* (1988a: 10), 'In the case of the allocation of most . . . goods and services, the operation of the market, where properly regulated, is a generally satisfactory means of determining provision and consumption'. The final Policy Review document was if anything even more emphatic in its support for the market. The question for Labour now is not whether to accept or reject the market, but how to use it (Gould 1989: 95).

This recognition of the role of the market has had important implications for the Labour Party's economic policy (see Gamble, chapter 5). Despite talk of the need to increase social ownership in many forms and the need to renationalize the natural monopolies (Labour Party 1988a, 1989a; Gould 1989), it appears that Labour's plans for future public ownership and renationalization are limited. The Policy Review rules out renationalization that would punish existing shareholders or require 'substantial resources' (Kellner 1989a; Labour Party 1989a). The emphasis of economic policy is on 'supply-side' socialism where the state intervenes if there has been market failure or monopolization. Moreover, Labour has committed itself to containing public expenditure, rejecting incomes policy and accepting the Thatcherite priority of containing inflation above limiting unemployment (Young 1990).

The Policy Review departs further from the left's policy programme by accepting the sale of council houses (and even the extension of the right to buy), commitment to trade union reform and a recognition of the rights of shareholders. There have also been important changes in foreign and defence policy. The Labour Party is now committed to membership of the EC and it has rejected unilateral disarmament (see Spear, chapter 13; Croft, chapter 14).

Nevertheless, Labour's acceptance of a central role for the market, the importance of the individual and freedom, trade union reform and the rejection of unilateralism does not mean that it has accepted the Thatcherite agenda. Although Labour might be seen as using some of the same language as the New Right, it is apparent that the meanings they attribute are completely different. First, the Thatcherite notion of freedom is largely negative and individualistic. Freedom is to be achieved by removing oppressive state institutions and rules, and various intermediate bodies so that the individual can achieve the greatest possible self-fulfilment. For Labour, freedom can only be achieved through greater equality because equality is necessary for people to have real choice. 'Economic power and liberty are inextricably linked. Being free to make a choice is only the beginning of liberty' (Labour Party 1988a: 4). Labour's belief in equality and the need to redistribute wealth creates a fundamental difference between the Labour and Conservative views of freedom.

This divergence leads to a completely different view of the role of the state and community. The New Right believes that the role of the state should be limited to its smallest possible extent: the provision of the conditions for a free market and the maintenance of order (Gamble 1988). This is essential for the creation of greater freedom. Therefore, the individual and the community are important as alternatives to state and collective action. For Labour, 'Real freedom can only be extended by cooperative action, by participation in democratic institutions at work, in the community and in public life and by collective provision to gain and sustain individual liberty' (Labour Party 1988a: 5). Thus the role of the state is positive. To enable the individual to gain greater freedom, choice and welfare within society the state must intervene. By contrast, the New Right views individualism as an alternative to the collective which can be harmed by, and be in conflict with, the goals of the state.

The Policy Review and Thatcherism have equally divergent views on the role of the market. In New Right thinking the market is morally right and economically efficient and, to some extent, social and political problems are caused by interventions in the market which distort its outcomes (Hayek 1979; Olson 1982). In the Policy Review the market is essentially morally neutral. It is an efficient means of distributing certain goods, but there is a danger of it producing distortions and inequalities particularly where there are monopolies or it is necessary to provide public goods. So the new Labour view of the market differs from the left – who see it as bad – and from the Thatcherites – who see it as good. They take a pragmatic approach recognizing that it is often efficient and fair but also that, 'a socialist administration should intervene in the market as a matter of conscious policy and for defined purposes. It should first monitor and regulate the market so as to prevent market abuse and the unfair exploitation of market dominance' (Labour Party 1988a: 10).

Thatcherism and David Owen's social market (see Brack 1990), see the state and the market as separate. The economy should be left to the market whereas the state operates within a distinct sphere of the social. In Labour's view the market can only work effectively *with* the assistance of the state. Hence the Policy Review document contains a whole range of policies which involve the state intervening in the market, from industrial policy, environmental regulation, regional policy, training, competition, control of natural monopolies through to much greater tripartite discussion. Consequently, Labour has not completely abandoned the use of public ownership. As with Crosland, Labour rejects the view that nationalization is a goal in itself or indicative of socialism. Yet party leaders recognize the need to nationalize the basic utilities (Hattersley 1987: 179) whilst proposing new forms of social ownership – ESOPs, coops, local enterprise agencies, public ownership of firms rather than industries – for other areas of the economy (Hattersley 1987; Gould 1989; Labour Party 1989a).

Labour's policy post-review is substantially different from the policy of the Labour left up to 1983. Nevertheless, Labour's view of the state, equality and the role of the market-place is within the context of social democracy and not the New Right. It has not adopted the position of the New Zealand Labour Party or some US Democrats of accepting a New Right economic policy within the framework of a liberal social policy. Hence, it is ideologically closer to revisionism than Thatcherism.

## Labour and revisionism

Revisionism has certain similarities with the Policy Review in the sense that it was an attempt to reformulate Labour's ideology and policy in the face of social change, electoral defeat and the apparent success of capitalism. Foote points out:

> When Labour was forced into opposition in the 1950s, the Labour Right took the initiative in attempting to force the party to sever its connections with the cloth cap image of British Socialism and present itself as a 'modern' national party.
>
> Foote (1985: 189)

The ideological and theoretical framework of this revisionism was provided by Anthony Crosland (1956 and 1974). He argued that the Marxist predictions about the collapse of capitalism have been disproved and that despite the continuation of capitalism, 'the capitalist business class has lost its commanding position' (Crosland 1956: 26). Crosland believed that capitalism had been substantially reformed and that nationalization and planning had failed to achieve the desired goals. Nationalization did not equal socialism and detailed planning was often 'economically inefficient' (ibid.: 500). Like the Policy Review, he recognized the importance of the market: 'The price mechanism is now a reasonably satisfactory method of distributing the great bulk of consumer goods and industrial capital goods' (ibid.: 504).

As capitalism had reformed and could provide economic growth, the role of the state should be to concentrate on the provision of social welfare and social equality (ibid.: 518). The goal of socialism was to achieve greater equality through economic growth. Growth provides more people with access to goods; it allows the better off to accept greater equality without a decline in their living standards and it provides the public expenditure to pay for the necessary social welfare (Lipsey 1981: 27). Equality remained a fundamental belief of Crosland and he proposed radical measures to achieve it. He called for an anti-poverty programme, the redistribution of wealth through wealth and inheritance taxes and the recognition of the need to increase levels of taxation generally (Crosland 1974; 44–55).

There are important similarities between Crosland's revisionism and Labour's Policy Review. Like Crosland, the Policy Review accepts that the market and capitalism exist and that the goal of a future Labour Government is not to abolish them but to use them to ensure that the goal of greater social equality is achieved (Gould 1989: 95). Consequently, the Policy Review and revisionism share a certain scepticism towards nationalization and detailed planning in the economy. Kinnock has moved towards Gaitskell's goal of abandoning clause 4, by maintaining that nationalization is only appropriate in certain circumstances and it is not the first priority of an incoming Labour Government. Crosland in fact favoured the nationalization of development land, private-rented housing and the creation of a state oil company (Crosland 1974: 43). The Policy Review also shares with Crosland, despite its apparent environmentalism (see Carter, chapter 9), a commitment to economic growth. Again this is part of a Croslandite belief in the importance of achieving social equality through economic growth rather than relying solely, or even mainly, on redistribution (Labour Party 1989a: 7–8).

In terms of principles, the review and revisionism have strong similarities. The Policy Review is revisionist in its view of capitalism. Capitalism can be reformed to achieve public goals, the market is a useful means of distribution and nationalization is only desirable where it can provide the means to particular ends. Yet the Policy Review is not merely the re-establishment of revisionism; there are some important differences.

Central to the revisionist vision was Keynesianism and in keeping with the optimism of the *Future of Socialism*, it was believed that governments could iron out the fluctuations of capitalism through demand management. Crosland wanted 'a Keynesian state, commit- ted to using the controls at its disposal, whether regulatory, fiscal or monetary to sustain growth and secure full employment' (Lipsey 1981: 29). The Policy Review, as well as being a response to the failure of the left, was also a response to the failure of Keynesianism and the inability of the 1974–9 Labour Government to maintain economic growth through traditional methods. The Policy Review is an attempt to develop a post-Keynesian revisionism where the emphasis is moved from demand to supply. Hence the notion of 'supply-side' socialism (Labour Party 1989a: 6) and as Gamble shows (see chapter 5), the perceived need for the state to take action to improve the supply side of the economy.

Labour's Policy Review is a return to revisionism in that it concedes that capitalism needs to be reformed rather than transformed and that markets have a central role in the organization of the economy and the distribution of resources. However, it is a revisionism for a different era which has learnt the lessons of the 1970s. The Labour Party recognizes that it has to be circumspect in its economic promises. Full employment will be difficult to achieve and there are limits to the level of public spending. It recognizes a need for intervention at a different part of the process – supply rather than demand. Nevertheless, intervention is for the same reason: to overcome market failure in order to achieve economic growth for the goal of social justice. As for the revisionists, nationalization and planning are means rather than ends.

The fear of losing a fourth election has made the Labour Party defensive. In order not to offend, Labour has developed a revisionism that recognizes the reality of capitalism but that has little of the vision and radicalism of 1950s' revisionism. It has accepted one half of the revisionist equation – capitalism – but not the second half – radicalism for social justice. Crosland's commitment to equality was very strong (Plant 1981) and he was prepared to propose radical policies like a wealth tax and high and progressive income tax to pay for it. Labour in the 1990s fears the label of being the Party of high taxation. In reconciling itself to the new external circumstances a Labour Government would face, the Party has become almost fatalistic in its economic policy and has failed to consider the means for trying to overcome the constraints of the outside world. Therefore, the Party is much more circumspect in its commitments to social justice and equality than it has been in the past. The Party has eliminated many policies of the left but failed, so far, to develop an alternative radicalism. This can be seen in its view of institutional reform where it is far behind the Liberal Democrats and groups like Charter 88 in pressing for the reform of the State and constitution (see Marquand, chapter 4).

It is clear that the Policy Review has changed some of the

fundamental features of Labour's policy and ideology. Unilateralism has been dropped; detailed planning is no longer an option; and the goal of common ownership of the means of production has been replaced by a belief in wider forms of social ownership and acceptance of the importance of the market. Capitalism is to be reformed not destroyed. In making these changes the Labour Party has not become 'Thatcherite' or even an Owenite social democratic party (see Heffer 1986). It has to some extent returned to the revisionism which dominated Labour through the 1950s and 1960s and to the social democratic traditions that have been important throughout its history (Minkin and Seyd 1977). But this is a modernized circumspect revisionism which acknowledges the failure of Keynesianism and in its acceptance of the social and economic changes has lost the optimism and radicalism of revisionism. This clearly distinguishes Labour from Thatcherism. However, a new problem arises of distinguishing Labour from the post-Thatcherite Conservative Party with its commitment to Europe, the public sector and, apparently, a fairer society.

## CONCLUSION

The Policy Review has seen an important change in Labour Party policy. However, this reform of policy is not the result of the hegemony of Thatcherism, and Labour has not become a 'Thatcherite' party. The reasons for the Policy Review can be located in Labour's past as well as in changes in economic and social circumstances. Labour's leaders have long recognized that the nature of capitalism has changed and that the external constraints a Labour Government will face are very great. They have also been aware of changes in the nature of the electorate and so have attempted to modernize the Party. Usually, these attempts at modernization have either failed or been only partially successful. The importance of Thatcherism is that it has allowed Neil Kinnock the space to transform the party more successfully than any previous leader. Thatcherism was a reaction to a new set of circumstances in Britain and the world and the Policy Review is in some sense Labour's reaction to the same changes.

## ACKNOWLEDGEMENTS

I would like to thank Andrew Gamble and Pat Seyd for comments on earlier drafts of this chapter.

# 3 Labour's renewal strategy

*Patrick Seyd and Paul Whiteley*

> We have now effectively completed the building of the new model party. . . . [T]he product is better, the unity is real, our democracy is healthier, our grassroots more representative and the whole outlook now geared to the realities of government rather than the illusions of opposition.
>
> (Peter Mandelson, Labour Party Director of Communications, reported in *The Guardian*, 16 February, 1990)

The 1980s were regarded by many political observers as the decade in which social democracy collapsed as a major political force in Western Europe. Flaws in Keynesian economics, changes in social structures and the rise of new social demands all combined to undermine social democracy's ability to shape political debate. Britain confirmed this apparent trend by maintaining a right-wing government in office throughout the decade.

The Labour Party's future as a major party of state appeared distinctly uncertain as it lost three general elections in a row and, in 1983, polled its lowest share of votes since 1918. In 1983 it came within 700,000 votes of being pushed into third place in the popular vote. The scale of Labour's loss of vote was staggering. Even in 1931 when the Party was devastated by the collapse of the world's financial markets it did not suffer such a loss. No other West European socialist party suffered such a dramatic vote loss in the 1980s (Merkel 1990). Labour's vote appeared to be haemorrhaging. The future looked bleak indeed. The electoral system would slow the speed of decline but Labour seemed destined to become a marginal parliamentary rump with a vote concentrated into distinct geographic areas of the country. The moment had perhaps arrived when Labour's traditional working-class supporters regarded the Party as archaic and no longer able to meet their needs. The Party seemed to be in the same downward spiral as the French Communist Party. The momentum of decline would gather speed with the defection of MPs and councillors, trade union disaffiliations, and resignations of individual members to the point that the Party would cease to be a major contender for political office.

The election year 1983 was Labour's low point. Long-term demographic changes, inner-city party decay and poor governmental performance all contributed to Labour's decline. In addition, Labour's behaviour after 1979 alienated many of its traditional supporters. The 'forward march of the Labour left' (Seyd 1987) resulted in an electorally unattractive party programme and party leadership, and extensive intra-party discord culminating in the first significant party split since 1932.

Labour fought the 1983 general election with a manifesto which contained policy commitments distinctly unpopular with Labour's traditional supporters (Butler and Kavanagh 1984; Crewe 1983). In addition, the Party was led by Michael Foot – an old-style radical politician appealing to the convinced at rallies of the faithful, but ill-equipped for modern studio-based appeals by reasoned argument to the unconvinced.

In 1983 the Labour Party seemed doomed. The combination of a declining class base and a drop in party identification made Labour's recovery appear impossible. Such a structuralist approach to party behaviour, however, underestimates the scope for political initiative. Parties may indeed fail (Lawson and Merkl 1988) but they also have the ability to revive and recover. They can pursue strategies which may re-establish a viable constituency of support. In the 1980s Labour could have withered as a major party of state but instead it recovered. This is a case of party renewal rather than party failure. How did it occur? How is it that Labour recovered from these undermining influences to become a serious contender for political office again in the 1990s?

The Party's recovery first involved the election of a new party leader and deputy leader, Neil Kinnock and Roy Hattersley, both relatively young (41 and 51 respectively in 1983) and balanced in their left and right traditions: for that reason they were dubbed 'the dream ticket'. However, this dream leadership alone was unlikely to save the Labour Party from destruction: that required a long-term project of policy reformulation and party reorganization. This twin-track approach to regaining power was based upon the leadership's view that for the Party to be electable some of the previous policy commitments had to be abandoned and the power of the party activists had to be reduced. Other contributors to this volume discuss policy reformulation since 1983. This chapter discusses party reorganization and the risks involved in the entire renewal project since, in aiming to regain voter support, the party leadership might have antagonized party activists to such an extent that serious intra-party discontent resurfaced thus making the Party once again electorally unattractive.

## PARTY REORGANIZATION

The forward march of the Labour left in the late 1970s had secured for activists (i.e. those members regularly attending local party meetings) a powerful position within the Party. All parliamentarians had to be reselected by local activists and the party leadership had to be elected by an electoral college in which 30 per cent of the vote was cast by local parties. The traditional dominance of the Party by parliamentarians no longer prevailed (McKenzie 1955). This was a key factor in prompting the Party to split in 1981 with the creation of the Social Democratic Party. The immediate impact of candidate reselection was much exaggerated by opponents of this particular reform; only eight Labour MPs were deselected before the 1983 general election and six before the 1987 general election. Nevertheless, Labour MPs now needed to stick much more closely to the views of their local activists if they were to survive reselection. Thus the parliamentary party's political outlook was much more determined by local activists. The party leadership's first task of reorganization was to reduce the activists' powers. It could not afford just to ignore them, because of their possession of significant constitutional powers. Yet it was electorally inexpedient for the leadership to rely on the block votes of certain trade union leaders to maintain its position at the party conference, because of the trade unions' general unpopularity, even among their own members. Therefore the leadership has been engaged in a strategy of empowering the individual party members on the assumption that they hold more moderate opinions. Implicit in this strategy is acceptance of May's theory of curvilinearity, namely that sub-leaders (i.e. activists) hold distinctly more extreme opinions than either their leaders or individual members (May 1973).

In 1984 the leadership's first attempt to limit activists' powers by introducing the one member/one vote principle for parliamentary selection/reselection was defeated by the party conference. Nevertheless, in 1988 a modified version was introduced when local constituency party electoral colleges were created for the selection/reselection of parliamentary candidates. Under this formula affiliated local trade unions were restricted to a maximum of 40 per cent of the vote and 60 per cent or more of the vote would be allocated to the individual membership, all of whom would be entitled to participate in a ballot. In addition, the party leadership encouraged all local parties to consult their invividual members before casting their votes in the 1988 leadership elections. The party leadership's long-term objective has remained, however, an individual membership party at the local level with only a very limited role for either branch delegates or trade union affiliates, and in 1990 the party conference agreed that parliamentary candidate selection/reselection should be based upon this principle after the next general election. The days of the activist delegate casting votes on behalf of the individual member are over now that the principle of decision-making by the individual member rather than by the delegate has been adopted.

Since 1918 the Party has had both direct (i.e. individual) and indirect (i.e. affiliated) members. Trade unionists have played a key role as affiliated members (6.3 million in 1988). Nevertheless, an overwhelming number play no part in the Party. It is essentially a paper membership which determines the fees that trade unions pay to the Party and the votes they cast at the party conferences. The party leadership believes trade union determination of party policy is electorally counterproductive. Furthermore, it feels that it can induce local parties to recruit greater numbers of individual members by offering as a prize the reduction of trade unions' power and the subsequent increase in constituency parties' power at the party conference. Many trade unions are willing to reduce their relative voting strength at the party conference but they are hostile to the elimination of their indirect role in local party decision-making and any proposals to reduce the role of this affiliated membership may prove extremely difficult to achieve.

An additional objective of the party leadership which has recently emerged is its desire to improve the policy-making procedures by placing less reliance on the annual party conference. The leadership is proposing that a permanent policy forum be established with standing commissions to discuss policy and make recommendations to the party conference. It hopes this reform will improve the quality of policy recommendations by eliminating the present arbitrary process which is squeezed into one week per year, and by widening the representational scope of those participating in the process.

The party leadership is intent on modernizing a party structure that has remained unchanged since 1918. It wishes to encourage an expanded, participative individual membership in a party less dominated by the trade unions. Critics suggest, however, that an increasingly autocratic and unaccountable leadership is imposing its policies, persons and practices on the Party. By reducing the importance of the party conference, by limiting the role of the affiliated trade unions, and by curbing the powers of the activists, they claim that the party leadership is intent on creating a party on the lines of the American model, where leaders dominate and individuals provide money and other means of support and legitimacy, but lack the power to play a significant part in policy-making.

The leadership's strategy of empowering the membership is a leap in the dark, since it has had no clear idea who the members are or what views they hold. Its hunch has been that their opinions are less ideological than the activists but it has only limited evidence for this view.[1] No systematic attempt has ever been made to ascertain the attitudes of the membership.[2] In contrast, the party leadership is aware through a battery of recent public opinion indicators – European Parliament elections, parliamentary by-elections, local elections and opinion polls – that the voters are more favourably inclined towards the 'new model' Party. Now, however, the views of party members and activists can be ascertained as a consequence of the first ever national survey of Labour Party members.[3] Who they are, how active they are in the Party, and what opinions they hold are general questions that we discuss elsewhere (Seyd and Whiteley 1992). Here we examine their opinions regarding Labour's renewal strategy. Has the leadership succeeded in also winning the support of the party membership?

## ATTITUDES REGARDING THE NEW MODEL PARTY

There are ten attitudinal questions in the membership survey which deal with the nature of the Party, such as its electoral strategy and the powers of the leader, the trade unions, the constituency parties and the individual members. A majority of members believe 'the Party should always stand by its principles even if this should lose it an election' and, as we have argued elsewhere, they are committed to the four principled beliefs of public ownership, trade union legitimacy, non-nuclear defence and high public expenditure (Seyd, Whiteley and

Broughton 1991). But members also clearly recognize the need to ensure the Party's policies are electorally attractive and a majority believe the Party 'should adjust its policies to capture the middle ground of politics'. A majority believe that 'the trade union block vote at conference brings the Party into disrepute', that the 'party leader should be elected by a system of one party member one vote' and that 'many people think party activists are extremists'. Finally, a majority reject the view that 'a problem with the Party is that the leader is too powerful'.

On six of these questions dealing with the overall nature and structure of the Party a majority of members have distinct opinions. On the four remaining questions – that 'the trade union movement has too much power over the Party', that 'constituency Labour parties should have the exclusive right to select their own parliamentary candidates', that 'Neil Kinnock will stick to his principles even if this means losing a general election', and that 'the party leadership doesn't pay a lot of attention to the views of ordinary party members' – members are more evenly divided. Table 3.1 details the variations in opinion within the Party on these issues.

On each of these Likert-scaled items responses were scored from one to five and then were structured in such a manner that the higher the overall score the greater the support for the party reforms. We classified respondents as 'modernizers' (i.e. those in favour of the party leadership's electoral strategy and structural changes), 'traditionalists' (i.e. those opposed to the strategy and changes), and 'intermediates'.[4] One in three of the membership are modernizers and one in five are traditionalists.

We might have expected the young to be the modernizers, impatient of the old party traditions and institutions and insistent on new procedures and practices. However, the reverse is the case. The modernizers are more likely to be found among the older party members, whereas the traditionalists are to be found among the very young. The older the party member the less likely s/he is to be a traditionalist. The very young (17–25 years) are almost twice as likely as the retired (66 plus) to be traditionalists.

One of the aims of the leadership in reforming the Party has been to provide greater opportunities for women to reach senior positions. Yet, paradoxically, women members are less likely to be modernizers than males. Women are more likely to adopt an intermediate position of neither strong support for modernization or traditionalism.

It is not surprising to find that among the very active[5] in the Party there are a greater number of traditionalists. It is the activists,

*Table 3.1* The distribution of opinions on the party reform indicators (in percentages)

| Indicator | Strongly agree | Agree | Neither | Disagree | Strongly disagree |
|---|---|---|---|---|---|
| Labour should stick to principles | 25 | 36 | 12 | 21 | 7 |
| Labour should capture middle ground | 19 | 38 | 10 | 22 | 11 |
| Trade unions have too much power in party | 9 | 34 | 15 | 32 | 10 |
| Right of CLPs to select candidates | 26 | 37 | 11 | 22 | 4 |
| Labour leader too powerful | 6 | 9 | 15 | 54 | 17 |
| Conference block vote disreputable | 23 | 49 | 12 | 13 | 4 |
| One person, one vote for leadership | 37 | 44 | 7 | 9 | 3 |
| Kinnock will stick to his principles | 12 | 26 | 16 | 33 | 13 |
| Leader ignores party members' views | 10 | 29 | 17 | 39 | 5 |
| Party activists are extremists | 18 | 57 | 10 | 13 | 2 |

who won increased powers in the Party in the late 1970s and early 1980s, whom Neil Kinnock wishes to restrain in order, he believes, to increase the party's electoral prospects. Almost twice as many of the active compared with the inactive are traditionalists.

Other social differences among the members appear to have little significant impact on party reform attitudes. Class differences between traditionalists and modernizers are not significantly different with the one exception of foremen and technicians (i.e. the blue collar élite) who are more likely to be part of the modernizing wing of the Party. Level of education also makes little difference to opinions on party reform, and it is only among the high earners that there is a greater propensity to support the reforms.

We have written of the party leadership's drive to restructure the Party since 1983; in fact, the reforms have been very closely associated with Kinnock who has provided the personal impetus and leadership

*Table 3.2* Attitudes to party reform by social characteristics and level of activism (in percentages)

|  | Traditionalists | Intermediates | Modernizers |
|---|---|---|---|
| All | 16 | 49 | 35 |
| *Age* |  |  |  |
| 17–25 | 22 | 53 | 25 |
| 26–45 | 20 | 49 | 32 |
| 46–65 | 13 | 48 | 39 |
| 66 plus | 12 | 50 | 38 |
| *Class* |  |  |  |
| Salariat | 16 | 48 | 36 |
| Routine non-manual | 17 | 52 | 31 |
| Petty bourgeoisie | 15 | 48 | 38 |
| Foremen and technicians | 10 | 45 | 45 |
| Working class | 16 | 51 | 33 |
| *Gender* |  |  |  |
| Female | 17 | 54 | 30 |
| Male | 16 | 45 | 39 |
| *Income* |  |  |  |
| Under £10,000 | 16 | 51 | 33 |
| £10,000 to £25,000 | 17 | 48 | 35 |
| £25,000 plus | 15 | 46 | 40 |
| *Graduate* |  |  |  |
| Yes | 18 | 48 | 35 |
| No | 15 | 49 | 36 |
| *Activism* |  |  |  |
| Inactive | 14 | 52 | 34 |
| Occasionally active | 12 | 52 | 36 |
| Fairly active | 17 | 48 | 35 |
| Very active | 23 | 45 | 33 |

to secure the changes. Perhaps, therefore, the strongest criticisms of the party's renewal strategy are reserved for him?

## KINNOCK AS PARTY LEADER

The bulk of the membership are strongly supportive of the party leader and appear well satisfied with his stewardship. Kinnock's personal ranking among members is high; his mean score on the thermometer ranking is 73.[6] It is not as high as that for the Labour Party (a ranking of 84), but this is not surprising since any leader will have his detractors. In addition to this specific ranking question, we asked a wide range of questions regarding Kinnock's qualities as party leader and it reveals considerable warmth of feelings towards him. Over three-quarters of the membership regard him as likeable, caring, capable of being strong and good at getting things done. Less than one in ten regard him as 'not likeable as a person'. The strongest criticism would be the 15 per cent who describe him as 'bad at getting things done'.

Kinnock has his critics but they are few. Those that do criticize him are among his old allies on the party's left. Kinnock's political roots are within the Labour left. He was a persistent left-wing critic of the Labour Governments between 1974 and 1979, and was closely associated at the time with the *Tribune* newspaper and the Tribune group in the Parliamentary Labour Party. In the early 1980s, however, the Labour left fragmented and Kinnock's refusal to vote for Tony Benn in the 1981 deputy leadership election distanced him from the hard left (see Smith, chapter 1). Since becoming party leader in 1983 his actions have distanced him further from his previous left-wing allies.

Kinnock and Benn personify two distinct Labour Parties. The former concerned to adapt party policies in order to win electoral support, to place considerable emphasis upon the party's media image, to distance the Party from the trade unions, and to limit the powers of the party activists; the latter concerned to assert the party's distinct political ideals, even though they may be electorally unpopular, to emphasize the party's links with the trade unions, to spend little effort or resources on polling, advertising, and generally developing a favourable media image, and to reward party activism with extended powers.

Kinnock's support is very strongly related to the members' place on the left–right spectrum within the Party. We asked members to place themselves on a nine-point scale drawn from left to right and have used their position on the political spectrum as one of the distinguishing measures of support for Kinnock and Benn.[7] Members with firm left-wing commitments are thirteen times more likely to regard Kinnock with hostility than those with firm right-wing commitments. Those on the right of the party spectrum are twice as likely to feel very warmly disposed to Kinnock as those on the party left.[8]

In addition, the older the party member the greater their strength of support is for Kinnock. Benn's strongest support is among the generation educated in the 1960s and 1970s, who provided him with a good deal of the support for his bid for power in the Party in the late 1970s.

In contrast with the attitudes of the membership towards the party's overall strategy, class does play a more significant part in determining attitudes towards these two leading personalities. Kinnock's strongest supporters come from among the skilled and unskilled manual workers, while Benn's strongest support is drawn from among the self-employed party members.

Finally, the inactive member cares less for Benn and more for Kinnock, while it is from the very active that Benn draws his most passionate supporters.

*Table 3.3* Attitudes to Kinnock and Benn by social characteristics, level of activism and party viewpoint (in percentages)

|  | Cold | | Cool | | Warm | | Hot | |
|---|---|---|---|---|---|---|---|---|
|  | NK | TB | NK | TB | NK | TB | NK | TB |
| *All* | 4 | 12 | 12 | 25 | 35 | 36 | 50 | 27 |
| *Age* | | | | | | | | |
| 17–25 | 7 | 9 | 13 | 20 | 41 | 45 | 39 | 26 |
| 26–45 | 6 | 8 | 15 | 23 | 39 | 38 | 41 | 31 |
| 46–65 | 3 | 15 | 10 | 27 | 33 | 34 | 55 | 24 |
| 66 plus | 1 | 17 | 7 | 29 | 28 | 30 | 64 | 25 |
| *Class* | | | | | | | | |
| Salariat | 4 | 10 | 14 | 24 | 41 | 38 | 42 | 27 |
| Routine non-manual | 4 | 12 | 11 | 25 | 34 | 34 | 50 | 28 |
| Petty bourgeoisie | 1 | 10 | 13 | 19 | 31 | 39 | 54 | 32 |
| Foremen and technicians | 2 | 15 | 9 | 36 | 24 | 28 | 65 | 21 |
| Working class | 4 | 13 | 9 | 26 | 26 | 33 | 61 | 28 |
| *Gender* | | | | | | | | |
| Female | 4 | 10 | 14 | 25 | 36 | 35 | 46 | 30 |
| Male | 4 | 13 | 10 | 25 | 34 | 36 | 52 | 26 |
| *Income* | | | | | | | | |
| Under £10,000 | 3 | 15 | 10 | 27 | 28 | 31 | 60 | 27 |
| £10,000 to £25,000 | 5 | 10 | 13 | 24 | 37 | 37 | 45 | 29 |
| £25,000 plus | 4 | 10 | 13 | 26 | 43 | 40 | 40 | 25 |
| *Graduate* | | | | | | | | |
| Yes | 6 | 8 | 16 | 23 | 43 | 41 | 35 | 28 |
| No | 3 | 13 | 10 | 26 | 31 | 33 | 55 | 28 |
| *Activism* | | | | | | | | |
| Inactive | 2 | 16 | 12 | 28 | 32 | 35 | 55 | 22 |
| Occasionally active | 3 | 10 | 11 | 26 | 37 | 38 | 49 | 27 |
| Fairly active | 4 | 12 | 13 | 23 | 35 | 37 | 48 | 28 |
| Very active | 6 | 12 | 12 | 25 | 34 | 32 | 49 | 30 |
| *Party viewpoint* | | | | | | | | |
| Left | 13 | 3 | 24 | 7 | 33 | 31 | 30 | 59 |
| Centre left | 3 | 6 | 13 | 21 | 40 | 42 | 45 | 31 |
| Centre | 2 | 17 | 6 | 35 | 29 | 36 | 63 | 12 |
| Centre Right | 1 | 22 | 5 | 40 | 38 | 28 | 57 | 11 |
| Right | 1 | 29 | 7 | 36 | 27 | 26 | 66 | 10 |

These two sets of indicators, one for party strategy in general and the other for party personality, provide us with valuable information about who approves and who disapproves of the 'new model' Labour Party. In general, there is majority support for many of the party reforms and for Kinnock as party leader. Nevertheless, it is clear that the strongest support comes from Labour's traditional constituency – ageing, male, manual workers. Among the younger, highly-educated professionals there is more resistance to the changes.

The party reforms which encourage more local party decision-making to be based upon the principle of one member/one vote are likely to give that traditional constituency of manual workers a greater voice and influence than otherwise would have been the case, although moves to downgrade the importance of the trade union affiliated membership will offset this trend. Thus the party leadership has the support of the traditional voice of Labour in part of its renewal strategy. But just as structural changes in British society have necessitated Labour's adjustment of its electoral strategy to widen its appeal, so also there is the need to rely on a broader social base of support within the Party. The party leadership has to consider carefully how to win greater support among the young and women members for the 'new model' party since these will be an important part of its bedrock into the twenty-first century. That is assuming the party leadership believes a dynamic individual membership is part of the party's future.

The leadership's dilemma is that as far as the day-to-day management of the Party is concerned the trade union affiliated membership is more predictably reliable than the individual, constituency membership. Historically, trade union power at the party conference and in the NEC has sustained the party leadership over many generations (Minkin 1978). However, this reliance on trade union power as a means of party management is now electorally damaging and therefore the party leadership has wanted to reduce it. The problem, which the membership survey reveals, is that members do not hold opinions which fully accord with their leaders. So the leadership is tempted to slow down the process of reducing the trade union role in the Party because trade unions and their leaders are easier to negotiate with and construct deals with than a heterogeneous group of individual members. If there was an initial view among the party leadership that the Party should get rid of its indirect, affiliated membership and create a party of individual members only, this has been modified for reasons of party management and electoral necessity.

Should the leadership bother about its members' views? Perhaps they should be bypassed? Perhaps their role should be that of dutiful admirers willing and able to provide whatever resources the party leadership deems necessary? Some academics have argued that television and advertising play such a dominant part in electioneering nowadays that members have an insignificant role in winning office (Epstein 1967). As money-raisers their importance is limited either as a consequence of corporate donations, in the case of the Labour Party from the trade unions, or by the possibility of state funding in the future. Furthermore, electoral research in the past suggested that local party activities had little impact upon national electoral swings (Butler and Rose 1960). Attempts by the SDP leadership to construct a party in which members played a very subordinate role to the parliamentarians might be attractive to the Labour leadership. It is our contention that party members cannot be ignored as they still play a significant part in electioneering and in political communication.

Katz suggests that members are loyal voters and therefore make up a very important, albeit small, reserve of support (Katz 1990). They provide certain political resources – money, leg-work and political communication – and their roots within society help give the Party a sense of political legitimacy. This last point is reinforced by Scarrow who argues that members act as 'ambassadors to the community' in the sense that they are local opinion carriers and multipliers for the party's point of view (Scarrow 1990).

Nevertheless, they may also be an electoral embarrassment to the party leadership because they hold opinions out of line with the party's potential supporters. They are an unrepresentative group to the extent that they are a very small minority of people – under 10 per cent of the population – interested enough in politics to make a conscious commitment to join a political party (Parry and Moyser 1990). No one in the Labour Party today is quite as uncomplimentary as Sidney Webb in describing local party activists as 'unrepresentative groups of non-entities dominated by fanatics and cranks and extremists', although Austin Mitchell likens them to lepers and refugees (Mitchell 1989). Katz argues that members have become more of a nuisance to party leaders because the task of winning elections has become more difficult with a more volatile electorate, yet members who join for doctrinal reasons may wish to stress political purity at the expense of electoral success.

One particular feature of Labour Party membership in the 1980s was the growth of middle-class members, referred to disparagingly by the political journalist Peter Jenkins in *The Guardian* as the 'lumpen-polytechnic'. Hine argues that this makes party management more difficult because middle-class members possess more participative skills (Hine 1986). In addition, they join the Party for more expressive reasons and are therefore less concerned with electoral success. Furthermore, they are more likely to work in the public sector and will inevitably argue for its expansion at a time when the party leadership may wish to see its contraction.

Earlier in this chapter we noted that party members are committed to four principled beliefs concerning public ownership, trade unions, defence and taxation. Elsewhere we contrast members' and Labour voters' attitudes on these four socialist touchstones and reveal that party members are more militant than party voters (Seyd, Whiteley and Broughton 1991). On the issues of trade unionism and taxation it is a matter of degree, but on public ownership and nuclear disarmament it is a matter of substance. The party leadership does have difficulties in negotiating a trade off between the voter and the member, but evidence from our survey suggests that members share their leaders' desire for political office and as such they are willing to make policy adjustments.

The price of a mass membership party in which individuals are encouraged to play an active role will be differences of opinion expressed in manners not always to the liking of media 'spin-doctors' but the benefits of which will be significant. First, the Party has local opinion carriers to legitimate its viewpoint and local sensors attuned to public opinions. It has to ensure that members are recruited from as wide a spectrum of the population as possible in order to ensure the social representativeness of its communicators. Second, it has a body of people from whom local political élites can be recruited. Third, it has people whose impact on electoral behaviour has been underestimated. Our calculations are that the size of local Labour Party membership has a significant impact upon constituency voting behaviour (Seyd and Whiteley 1992: chapter 8).

## CONCLUSION

At the time of writing the Labour Party has re-established itself as a major party in the eyes of the voters. The funeral epitaphs written for Labour in the mid-1980s were premature. The party's persistence in the face of a major internal split and subsequent electoral catastrophe is striking. Its survival is due, in part, to the electoral system which discriminated against third party challenges in 1983 and 1987. Its recovery is due, in part, to the Social Democratic Party's electoral successes between 1981 and 1987 which forced the Labour Party to recognize the unpopularity of its own policies and, in part, to the political ineptitude of David Owen who, after the 1987 general election, divided the Alliance vote and handed back the political initiative to the Labour Party. But Labour's recovery is due, largely, to the political leadership of Kinnock and his close colleagues in the Shadow Cabinet, NEC and party headquarters.

Rose and Mackie argue the importance of voluntarism rather than determinism in a political party's survival or disappearance (Rose and Mackie 1988). Party leaders can make choices which will determine whether a party survives or not. Kinnock has succeeded in modernizing the Labour Party in such a manner that it now appears more professional in its electioneering than all its rivals and for that he deserves credit. But a cautionary note is also appropriate. The evidence from our survey, confirmed by discussions with party officials, is that the membership is passive rather than active, disengaged rather than engaged.[9] The Labour Party appears to be a 'de-energized' and 'de-activized' organization.[10] This passive membership may well be a consequence of the wide range of political defeats experienced by the left in Britain during the 1980s. It may also reflect the members' desire for political office again and its willingness to do nothing that might be interpreted as damaging that goal. But if Labour is re-elected to office, members may become more demanding.

We have drawn attention to members' principled opinions regarding public ownership, trade union bargaining rights, non-nuclear defence and public expenditure. With regard to public ownership and non-nuclear defence, members' expectations may have been already lowered by the party leadership's political stance; but their expectations may be greater concerning trade union bargaining rights and public expenditure. They may hope for a relaxation of some of the legal restrictions on the trade unions' strike powers and for more government expenditure on the public services. Labour's commitment to a legally imposed minimum wage could turn out to be a test of the relationship between party leadership and membership. The pressures on a Labour Government to drop the commitment, from employers in particular, would be considerable, yet members would expect its introduction as a sign of Labour's resolve to redistribute incomes. An issue such as this one could set the seal on the party's future as a membership organization.

The party's renewal strategy may be successful in regaining office but it may be less appropriate for a governing party. There is a danger that the party leadership in office in the 1990s will assume an acquiescent party membership. If, however, party members try to remind a Labour Government of its principled base then the leadership may ignore the views expressed, as Harold Wilson did in the late 1960s. A party leadership and membership at loggerheads would be disastrous. Social democracy in the 1990s requires electorally relevant policies but also an enthusiastic grassroots. A party of government in conservatively-inclined Britain still requires its ambassadors to the community. Unless Kinnock intends the 'new model' Labour Party to be a European replica of the Democratic Party of the USA the sooner some blood is injected into its veins the better for the future of British social democracy.

## ACKNOWLEDGEMENTS

The authors gratefully acknowledge the financial support of the Economic and Social Research Council and the University of Sheffield Research Fund.

# 4 Half-way to citizenship? The Labour Party and constitutional reform

*David Marquand*

Like all parties of the left, the Labour Party is the child of the society it seeks to change. The consequences have been more paradoxical than is sometimes realized. Democracy came to Britain, not through the overthrow of an *ancien régime* and the establishment of a new one, but, as J.G.A. Pocock puts it, through 'the medieval technique of expanding the king-in-parliament to include new categories of counsellors and representatives' (Pocock 1975). As a result, the British are still, as they always have been, subjects of the Crown, rather than citizens of a state (Dyson 1980). (At least, the English are: whether the same is true of the Scots is a matter for debate.) Sovereignty lies with the Crown-in-Parliament, not with the people, and the sovereignty of the Crown-in-Parliament is absolute and inalienable. The executive consists of ministers of the Crown. They are, of course, accountable to Parliament for the use they make of the powers at their disposal, but the powers themselves are the Crown's, not Parliament's and still less the people's. There is no fundamental law setting out citizenship rights on which the Crown-in-Parliament may not entrench; on some readings of the doctrine of parliamentary sovereignty, there cannot be, since the doctrine implies that no parliament can bind its successors.

To put it at its lowest, these doctrines are hard to square with the egalitarian ethic on which Labour has based its claim to power. Yet it has rarely challenged them or the constitution they have shaped. Its object has been to win power within the existing political system, and to use it to change society in accordance with its ideology and the interests of its constituents. It has shown little sympathy for the proposition that a system permeated with essentially monarchical values might not be compatible with such a project; that its policies might be twisted out of shape, or even aborted, by the mechanisms through which it sought to put them into effect. To put the point another way around, the Party has been concerned with outcomes, not processes; and it has shown scant interest in the possible connections between the two. 'Whig doctrinaires', wrote George Bernard Shaw in 1889, 'accepted the incompetence and corruption of States as permanent inherited State qualities, like the acidity of lemons'. Socialists knew better.

> Make the passing of a sufficient examination an indispensable preliminary to entering the executive; make the executive responsible to the government and the government to the people; and State departments will be provided with all the guarantees for integrity and efficiency that private money-hunting pretends to. Thus the old bugbear of State imbecility did not terrify the Socialist: it only made him a Democrat. But to call himself so simply would have had the effect of classifying him with the ordinary destructive politician who is a Democrat without ulterior views for the sake of formal Democracy – one whose notion of Radicalism is the pulling up of aristocratic institutions by the roots – who is, briefly, a sort of Universal Abolitionist. Consequently, we have the distinctive term Social Democrat, indicating the man or woman who desires through Democracy to gather the whole people into the State so that the State may be trusted with the rent of the country, and finally with the land, the capital and the organisation of the national industry.
>
> (Shaw 1962 [1889])

Grant a democratic suffrage and a professional civil service, in short, and the tested mechanisms of parliamentary election and ministerial responsibility would ensure a State amenable to the popular will and fitted for socialist purposes. Further constitutional arguments, the kinds of arguments that radical 'universal abolitionists' insisted on putting, were frivolous diversions from the serious business of social and economic transformation. *Mutatis mutandis*, that was the predominant view of the Labour movement for the best part of a century. Socialism, after all, asserts the primacy of the social and the economic over the political. For socialists, injustice and exploitation derive from economic relationships, not from political ones. In so far as political rights and political equality are of value, their value is instrumental, not substantive: they may make it possible to redress the balance of the economy in favour of the exploited, and if so they should be cherished, but they are not goods in themselves.

To demand political or constitutional change for its own sake, when it is social and economic change that matter, would be to concentrate on form instead of on substance. In Labour's case, moreover, socialist ideology was buttressed by historical memory. The British trade union movement grew up outside the law. In the nineteenth and early twentieth centuries, it won certain immunities from a common law permeated with individualistic assumptions and hostile to collective action. But these immunities were negative, not positive. Unions could act in ways which would have otherwise have been against the law, but they did not have formal legal rights and the culture of the law was still inimical to them. The result was a curious kind of pragmatism, difficult to describe but impossible to mistake. The workers would win justice through power, not law; the law, and the lawyers who interpreted it, were not to be trusted. Constitution-mongering, and the legalistic wrangling to which it led, was a snare and a delusion.

To be sure, Labour intellectuals sometimes strayed from the path of constitutional orthodoxy. In the early years of this century, the Fabian Society published a series of pamphlets on the 'New Heptarchy', advocating a form of regional government (Hogwood and Keating 1982). For a while before the First World War, the Independent Labour Party favoured proportional representation (Bogdanor 1979). After the war, G.D.H. Cole and the Guild Socialists campaigned for a system of functional representation in place of political representation, while Sidney and Beatrice Webb advocated a 'Social Parliament' to look after the economy, alongside the familiar political parliament (Cole 1920; Webb and Webb 1920). But these were minority concerns at the best of times, and when Labour attained status as a major party, they soon faded away. From the mid-1920s at the latest, Labour was as committed as the Conservatives to the central pillars of Westminster parliamentarianism – cabinet government, based on the twin doctrines of individual and collective ministerial responsibility; a two-party system; first-past-the-post elections; a unitary state; and absolute and inalienable parliamentary sovereignty. Though the second Labour Government flirted unenthusiastically – and to no ultimate avail – with the alternative vote, it did so only under pressure from the Liberals. In the early 1930s, Sir Stafford Cripps suggested that the next Labour Government should take emergency powers to push its legislation through. But his suggestion was indignantly repudiated by the party leadership, and when Labour actually took office in 1945, nothing of the sort was done. The Attlee Government curtailed the delaying powers of the Lords, but apart from that it made no attempt to disturb the constitution it had inherited from its Conservative and Liberal predecessors.

Constitutional orthodoxy was buttressed by an essentially teleological conception of citizenship, formulated most clearly and most famously by the sociologist, T.H. Marshall, and implicit in the thinking of most Labour politicians and intellectuals as well. For Marshall, citizenship had three dimensions – civil, political and social (Marshall 1950). Over the preceding three centuries the struggle for citizenship rights had shifted from the first to the second, and then from the second to the third. Civil citizenship, manifested in equal civil rights, had been established in the eighteenth century. Political citizenship was largely the work of the nineteenth. In the twentieth century the focus had shifted to the struggle for social rights: the real meaning of the post-war welfare state was that the principle of social citizenship was now enshrined in legislation. Though Marshall did not say this, the implication was plain. Social citizenship was the last, culminating stage in an evolutionary process. To re-open questions pertaining to civil or political citizenship when social citizenship had reached the agenda would be a kind of contradiction: it would be to move backwards when history was moving forwards. A similar view pervaded the writings of Anthony Crosland, the high priest of the social democratic revisionism of the 1950s (Crosland 1956). The primordial social democratic ends of greater social and economic equality, Crosland argued, could perfectly well be achieved by and through the existing political system, since that system was already egalitarian. Political rights and political citizenship were secure: because they were secure, democratic socialists could concentrate on social reform and leave the polity to take care of itself.

Yet the Labour Party of the late 1980s and early 1990s has committed itself to a series of constitutional changes, more substantial *in toto* than any carried out by any British Government since the First World War, expressed in and justified by the language of citizenship rights. The left-inclined think tank, the Institute for Public Policy Research, drafted a written constitution for the United Kingdom, as did Tony Benn, the erstwhile leader of the Labour left. The Labour Campaign for Electoral Reform (LCER) campaigned for proportional representation to such effect that, by the summer of 1991, even the party's commitment to the first-past-the-post electoral system could no longer be taken for granted. The objects of this chapter are to tell the story of this shift of assumption and approach, and to speculate about its causes and implications.

## FRAYING ORTHODOXIES

The first thing to notice is that Labour's constitutional orthodoxy has been fraying for some time. As early as the late 1960s, Labour back-benchers were pressing for powerful investigative parliamentary committees, designed, however uncertainly, to strengthen the legislature at the expense of the executive. The Wilson Government of the 1960s tried unsuccessfully to 'reform' the House of Lords and set up a royal commission on the constitution to consider the relationship between central government and the 'several countries, nations and regions of the United Kingdom'. The majority found in favour of elected assemblies in Scotland and Wales, with different degrees of autonomy; a minority report by Lord Crowther-Hunt and Professor Peacock advocated assemblies in Scotland, Wales and five English regions, all with executive powers (Crowther-Hunt and Peacock 1973). During the struggle over entry into the European Community in the early 1970s, the leadership eventually adopted Tony Benn's proposal of a referendum on the issue; in 1975, another Wilson Government proceeded to put its 're-negotiated' membership terms to the first nationwide referendum in British history (King 1977). In 1978, the Callaghan Government – by now in a minority and dependent on Liberal support – included a regional list system in the legislation for elections to the European Parliament, but failed to get it through the House of Commons (Butler and Marquand 1981). Meanwhile, the renewed nationalist upsurge in the 1974 elections had persuaded the Party to abandon its long-standing unionism in favour of devolution for Scotland and Wales, a cause which provoked yet another split and led to the ambiguous devolution referendum result which caused the Callaghan Government to fall (Bogdanor 1979). In a different, though related, sphere, the Party published a discussion document toying with the notion of regional government in England (Labour Party 1977a). In yet another, the left fought hard, though unsuccessfully, to insert a commitment to abolish the House of Lords into the 1979 election manifesto.

Hence, Labour left office in 1979 in a state of constitutional confusion. It proceeded to plunge into a bitter faction fight, in which constitutional questions were once again to the fore. The left of the Party found the explanation for the failures and humiliations of the outgoing Government in a theory of institutional seduction. Labour ministers had been captured by the civil service establishment and the institutions of global capitalism, and had then used the powers which the Westminster model gives to the Government in office to impose their policies on a supine parliamentary party. The remedy was to subject Labour MPs to mandatory reselection, to vest the election of the leader in an electoral college representing the whole party instead of just the parliamentary party, and to give the national executive sole control over the manifesto – thus shifting the balance of party power against the parliamentarians and in favour of the mass party. Only the first two of these proposals were adopted, and the results have so far been modest. In any case, they had to do with the constitution of the Labour Party rather than with the constitution of the country. Yet their implications go wider than might appear at first sight. They were, no doubt, muddled in logic and inspiration, confusing the notion of direct, popular democracy with a notion of party, or caucus, democracy fundamentally at variance with it. But these inconsistencies are not the point. What matters is that, as Samuel Beer noticed, they sprang from a deep-seated, growing and essentially populist dissatisfaction with the norms and assumptions of Westminster parliamentarianism which the party leadership had accepted for more than fifty years (Beer 1981).

As the decade continued, old certainties became even more difficult to sustain. The collapse of the post-war settlement, the rise of the New Right, the radical zeal of the Thatcher Governments and, most of all perhaps, their success in driving their policies through despite having won only a little more than two-fifths of the popular vote, forced intellectuals on the left and centre-left to question many of their assumptions, and not least their political and constitutional ones. In the 1950s, when Marshall proposed it, the teleological, three-stage conception of citizenship described earlier had seemed almost self-evident. Now doubts crept in. It was hard to deny that, by the 1970s, the interventionist, social-citizenship state was losing support: that was one of the reasons why Mrs Thatcher had come to power in the first place. It was impossible to deny that, in some spheres at any rate, the Thatcherite campaign to roll back its frontiers was an astonishing success. The Marshall–Crosland picture of a smooth progression from civil to political to social was called into question. Perhaps the reason why the social-citizenship state had lost support, and why it had been so vulnerable to the Thatcherite counter-revolution, was that the supposed social citizens had come to suspect that they did not control the institutions which acted in their names. Perhaps the reason why they suspected this was that they were right to do so: that social citizenship was not, after all, securely founded in civil and political citizenship and that Shaw's blithe assumption that a democratic suffrage and a professional civil service would, of themselves, secure a social democracy had been altogether too optimistic (Ignatieff 1991). If that were true, one conclusion was that there was more to democracy than Shaw and his *epigones* had imagined; that the struggle for political citizenship, which the post-war generation had assumed to be over, would have to be waged anew; that constitutional change would have to be seen as a pre-condition of social and economic change, rather than as a distraction from them.

A second theme echoed through the left and centre-left debate as well. The central purpose of the New Right project was, of course, to narrow the frontiers of the State and to widen those of the market. But, as Hayek was quick to recognize, a market order cannot flourish in a society permeated with non-market values (Hayek 1979). Since post-war Britain was indeed permeated with such values, it followed that a market order could not be created here without profound changes of attitude and belief. Hence the paradox implied by Andrew Gamble's description of the politics of Thatcherism as a combination of 'the free economy and the strong state' (Gamble 1988). State aggrandizement, the Thatcher Governments came to believe, was a pre-condition of state withdrawal. In order to roll back the frontiers of state intervention and foster an 'enterprise culture', the State had to become more centralized, more aggressive and, in certain respects, more powerful or at least more willing to use the powers it already possessed.

Particularly after their second victory in 1983, the Conservative Government launched an ambitious programme of state-led cultural reconstruction, designed to humble or cripple the intermediate institutions which embodied the social-democratic values of the post-war settlement, and to foster the entrepreneurial values which a market order was assumed to require. This too provoked a painful reassessment on the left. Whether the Thatcher Governments in fact departed from the spirit of Britain's unwritten constitution is a matter for argument. Since the constitution is unwritten, and since there is no authoritative body to decide what its spirit actually is, no one can be certain. What is clear is that many on the left and centre-left believed that its spirit had been violated and that freedoms which the British could previously take for granted had been endangered (Graham and Prosser 1988). It would be wrong to suggest that this experience produced a universal change of heart, but there is no doubt that it led many people on the left to question their previous constitutional indifference and to conclude that uncertain, problematic and fluctuating conventions had to be replaced by explicit and justiciable rights, entrenched in a fundamental law (Hall and Held 1989).

Self-questioning on the left and centre-left, it should be noted, ran parallel with a more muffled debate on the right. Traditionally, British Conservatives have stood for a vigorous civil society, with strong intermediate institutions giving the individual dignity and meaning and, in a characteristic British phrase, protecting the 'liberties of the subject' from state encroachment. The spectacle of a radical New Right Government deliberately using state power to weaken such institutions in order to reconstruct civil society in accordance with an ideology largely derived from individualistic liberalism, made some conservatives uneasy. So did the persistence of a 'social question' manifested in the apparent emergence of an alienated under-class and a corresponding breakdown of traditional social ties and civilizing processes (Dahrendorf 1988); and so, on a deeper level, did the New Right's indifference to what John Gray described as the 'cultural patrimony of individualism' – to the non-individualistic, pre-capitalist moral foundations of the capitalist order it sought to re-create (Gray 1990). In their unease, some reached for the communitarian strands in their own tradition, echoing Douglas Hurd's call for a renewal of the 'English tradition of voluntary service' in an ideal of 'active and responsible citizenship' which, at least by implication, would offer an alternative to neo-liberal individualism as much as to socialist collectivism (Hurd 1988). Another straw in the wind, different in provenance but not so different in effect, was the report of a Commission on Citizenship, presided over by the Speaker of the House of Commons and including representatives of all the UK's political parties, warning that citizenship was 'a cultural achievement, a gift of history, which can be lost or destroyed' and setting out a programme to save it, focused on voluntary service to the community (HMSO 1990).

## LABOUR AND THE REFORM AGENDA

Labour's recent shift of policy and approach must be seen against this background. For practical purposes the story begins after the 1987 election, when the Party suffered its third successive defeat, despite all its efforts to reoccupy the middle ground which it had abandoned at the beginning of the decade. The advent of a third

Thatcher Government, once again backed by only a little more than 40 per cent of the popular vote, but once again able to use all the powers of the central state to instil its values into civil society, gave new urgency to the intellectual reappraisal discussed in the last section: if New Right teaching was not to carry all before it, was it not time for the left and centre-left to counter-attack? In Scotland, where the Conservatives had won only ten seats compared to twenty-two in 1979, it also gave a new fillip to the demand for home rule: why should English votes impose Thatcherite policies on a Scotland which had voted against them? Among ordinary members of the Labour Party it strengthened the appeal of electoral reform: if the strong and authoritative governments – which supporters of first-past-the-post saw as its great virtue – all turned out to be Conservative, was the price worth paying? In the leadership, it led to an anxious search for new directions: if moderate policies and a professional campaign were not enough to turn the Thatcherite tide, what was?

The leadership's answers to the last question can be understood only in the context of the earlier ones. In a sense not true of other policy areas, its search for new constitutional directions, and a new approach to citizenship to correspond with them, had to take place on terrain chosen by others. By now, an implicit reform agenda, based on the assumption that full political citizenship had not been achieved after all, and stressing justiciable rights, open government, the decentralization of power and a proportional electoral system, had taken shape among liberal-minded lawyers like Lord Scarman, in the centre parties, among a range of left and centre-left intellectuals and in some of the media. Like a guest arriving late at a party, and forced either to take part in a conversation which others had started or to stay silent, Labour had to address that agenda if its reforming credentials were to be taken seriously. In so doing, it had to react, not just to pressures from its own party, but to cross-party pressures from beyond its ranks.

The most weighty of these was the upsurge of national feeling north of the Border which manifested itself in the 1988 *Claim of Right for Scotland*, issued by the Campaign for a Scottish Assembly, and the Constitutional Convention which held its first meeting in March 1989. The Scottish Labour Party took part in the Convention along with all the other Scottish parties except the Nationalists and Conservatives, as well as with representatives of the trade unions, the churches, the local authorities and of Gaelic and ethnic communities. But the Convention was not under the control of any of its constituent bodies; its proposals emerged from a process of give-and-take alien to the adversarial traditions of British party politics. In certain crucial respects it went further than the Scottish Labour Party at first wanted to go – proposing that the number of seats in the Scottish Parliament should be 'broadly related' to the number of votes; that there should be an entrenched Scottish Charter of Rights; that Scotland should have strategic economic planning powers in respect of key Scottish industries; and that the structure of UK government should eventually be on federal lines. Yet the Westminster leadership could not have repudiated what its Scottish colleagues had accepted even if it had wanted to; and in November 1990, Roy Hattersley declared that Labour's Scottish policy would be 'firmly based on the framework established by the Convention' (McCreadie 1991). On the Scottish question – a question which the devolution debates of the 1970s had shown to be of critical importance to the governance of the United Kingdom as a whole – Labour's policies were, in short, made for it as much as by it.

The Scottish Convention was only one source of cross-party pressure. Another was Charter 88 – a statement calling for a written constitution – whose authors turned it into a campaigning movement. As its name implied, its publication coincided with the tercentenary of the Glorious Revolution, but it was also intended to recall the Magna Carta and the People's Charter of 1838. It denounced Britain's vulnerability to 'elective dictatorship' and demanded a new constitutional settlement, including all the items in the implicit reform agenda mentioned previously – freedom of information, a bill of rights, proportional representation, an elected second chamber and 'an equitable distribution of power between local, regional and national government'. To the surprise of its authors, it quickly obtained more than 20,000 signatures; and with the help of that signatory base, it developed into a pressure group for constitutional reform and citizenship rights. Unlike the Scottish Convention, the Charter Council was not a representative body. It consisted of individuals, representing nobody but themselves. Also, unlike the Convention, it had no mass base and could therefore be disparaged as a movement of metropolitan intellectuals, out of touch with plain folk. But its influence was out of proportion to its numbers. It struck a chord with opinion formers across the whole spectrum of the left and centre-left; it kept the constitutional issue alive with 'vigils', conferences and articles in the quality press; and, above all, it staked out a clear and comprehensive position against which other proposals could be judged.

External pressures from Charter 88 and the Scots, internal pressure from the LCER, the leadership's belief that it had to strike out in new ways to chime with the spirit of a more individualistic and rights-conscious age, inchoate rank-and-file dissatisfaction with the system and, no doubt, the diffuse public interest in citizenship manifested by Douglas Hurd on the one hand and the Speaker's Commission on the other, all drove the Party towards the reform agenda which Charter 88 and the Scottish Convention had both embraced. But old assumptions – lingering suspicion of 'judge-made law'; the culture of single-party government and adversary politics; and, above all, perhaps, the familiar Marshall–Crosland focus on social rather than political citizenship – pulled it back. The results were predictably diverse. The 1989 Policy Review contained a long series of particular proposals, designed, in the words of the document, 'to put individual rights back into the centre of political debate'. These included a Freedom of Information Act; a Police Act to ensure increased accountability to local communities; the replacement of the Lord Chancellor's Department with a Department of Legal Administration; legislation to guarantee the right to privacy; reform of the immigration laws; Sex and Race Equality Acts to strengthen the existing anti-discrimination legislation; the creation of a Ministry for Women; and repeal of section 28 of the 1988 Local Government Act. Another set of proposals concerned the decentralization of government. Scotland was promised, 'at the earliest possible opportunity', a democratically-elected Assembly with legislative and tax-raising powers. There were also to be elected assemblies in Wales and the English regions. In this way, Roy Hattersley told the party conference, the next Labour Government would 'establish by law the basic rights of a free society' and make sure that Thatcherite incursions on them could 'never happen again' (Labour Party 1989b: 120).

In the Labour movement, however, none of these proposals were contentious. Two other items on the reform agenda – a bill of rights and a proportional electoral system – were a different matter. On both of these, the leadership fought to preserve the *status quo*; on the first, the end result was a compromise, and on the second, a stand-off. At the 1988 party conference – held a month before Charter 88 appeared and before the Scottish Convention had assembled – Hattersley successfully urged for the rejection of a composite calling for the incorporation of the European Convention of Human Rights into British law. That, he declared, amounted to a bill of rights. A bill of rights means that we entrust our liberties not to the elected House of Commons, but to the courts and to the judges. Frankly, I do not trust the courts and the judges to perform that task. Too often – far too often – they take the most restrictive view of freedom, the rights of the rich and powerful to enjoy their wealth at the expense of the rest of society. . . . A bill of rights would . . . act as an obstacle on the road to a more equal society.

(Labour Party 1988b: 124)

In reply to Eric Heffer he added that he had always favoured abolition of the House of Lords and believed that 'a single elected chamber is the best of all safeguards for democracy' (ibid.).

In 1989 there was a change of tune, albeit of a rather subtle kind. The Policy Review first echoed Hattersley's 1988 attack on the notion of a Bill of Rights, though in much weaker terms, and then proposed an alternative. The protection of liberty was no longer to be entrusted to the House of Commons: the House of Commons offered no protection against a government 'with a substantial majority and supine back-benchers'. Instead, the task would be given to an elected second chamber, replacing the House of Lords and reflecting 'the interests and aspirations of the regions and nations of Britain'. This second chamber would be the entrenching mechanism for fundamental rights. It would have the power to delay for the life of a parliament the repeal of legislation 'specifically designated as concerning fundamental rights', thus ensuring that the electorate would be able to decide whether a government which proposed such legislation should remain in office (Labour Party 1989a). As Hattersley put it at the 1989 conference, the rights which Labour wished to enshrine could not be protected by a Bill of Rights, which would have to be interpreted by judges and could be overturned by a one-clause bill.

The only way to protect our freedom is to provide a constitutional change that makes the destruction of our basic rights impossible. For that reason we propose to replace the House of Lords with an elected second chamber with a precise and specific constitutional role.

It will not be a replica of the House of Commons with members dependent on the Prime Minister for promotion. It will not initiate legislation. It will be charged with the protection of liberties and it will possess the power to delay for the full life of a parliament any legislation which reduces personal freedom.

(Labour Party 1989b)

What would happen if the same party had a majority in both chambers, and a 'supine majority' in the second chamber refrained from using its delaying powers – in a way that would embarrass its colleagues in the first – was left unclear.

Before long, the Hattersleian compromise between justiciable rights and parliamentary sovereignty was given a new twist. In June 1991, Hattersley came out for a general declaration or 'loose' Bill of Rights to supplement the specific rights contained in particular Acts of Parliament; this, he implied, would be enforceable in law, though specific legislation on rights could still override it. Despite these changes of front, however, the leadership's approach to the rights issue did not encounter much opposition from its own Party.

On proportional representation it had a rougher ride. At the 1987 conference a resolution calling for an enquiry into the electoral system was easily crushed on a show of hands, after a brief Friday morning debate at the fag-end of the proceedings. By 1989, the reformers were strong enough to mount a vigorous challenge to the leadership, ending in a card vote. The Policy Review ended with a robust peroration in favour of first-past-the-post, on the grounds that talk of a change to the system 'would cause the electorate to question our resolve, our commitment and our self-confidence'. Perhaps in reaction to what many constituency parties must have seen as a provocation, thirty resolutions indicated dissatisfaction with the system; and Roy Hattersley felt it politic to devote nearly half his opening speech to a pre-emptive attack on coalition government, the centre parties, fashionable columnists and the 'reduction of democracy' which pro-portional representation for the House of Commons would entail. 'In a democracy', he declared, 'it is the people who decide who should be Prime Minister during the election campaign. In coalitions the minor parties decide after the election is over . . . I do not say that under PR we would never have a Labour Government again, but I do say that we would never again have a Labour Government that was able to carry out a Labour programme.' The resolution calling for an enquiry was seconded by Gavin Laird of the engineering union and won the votes of around half the constituency delegates. Though the platform carried the day by 4,650,000 to 1,443,000, it was clear that Labour's support for the existing system was more fragile than it had been for nearly sixty years.

The following year, a resolution calling for an enquiry into the system of election for the House of Commons, as well as for the European Parliament and the proposed national and regional assemblies within the United Kingdom, was carried against the platform by 2,766,000 votes to 2,557,000. The enquiry was conducted by a National Executive working party, chaired by the political philosopher, Professor Raymond Plant. Its first report, published in July 1991, made no recommendations, but set out the pros and cons of the various possible systems, against the background of a dispassionate and rigorous discussion of the issues involved. Despite its scrupulous objectivity, however, the Plant report had plainly opened the door to a change of policy. It would be up to the leadership to decide whether or not to walk through it. There were powerful electoral arguments for doing so – a MORI poll in the spring of 1991 showed a two-to-one majority in favour of proportional representation among those with an opinion on the question (MORI/ Rowntree 1991) – but it remained to be seen whether they would carry the day.

In the constitutional field, even more than in other policy areas, the implications of the rather tortuous course which Labour has followed since the 1987 election are hard to assess. The economism which has pervaded its approach to politics for most of this century seems to be losing force; in its ranks, as in the wider society, the late nineteenth-century political radicalism scorned by George Bernard Shaw and the Fabians seems to have experienced an unexpected rebirth. But it is much too soon to tell whether the infant will grow, and if so, how quickly. Labour's partial return to the political radicalism of its great-grandparents is the response of a thrice-defeated party to the disconcerting social and economic radicalism of the triumphant New Right; the leadership's manifest half-heartedness over crucial items in the reform agenda suggests that it might well be abandoned if Labour were to form a majority government itself.

On a deeper level, it is not clear that Labour has abandoned the old Marshall–Crosland conception of citizenship, from which its previous constitutional conservatism sprang. Looked at in isolation, as this chapter has inevitably done, its constitutional proposals imply a remarkable change of heart; in the context of the Policy Review as a whole, they look more like afterthoughts. On the other hand, the MORI poll previously mentioned shows that Labour voters are more radical on these matters than the party leadership (MORI/Rowntree 1991), while, in the battle over electoral reform, pressure for change has come from the bottom-up, not from the top-down. In this field, at any rate, the conventional picture of a right-of-centre leadership anxious to revise old shibboleths and willing to force its revisionism down the throats of a reluctant rank and file is wide of the mark. It is the old, social democratic right of the Party which clings most fiercely to constitutional orthodoxy, the centre and left which are most hospitable to new ideas. All this suggests that a process of conversion has at least begun. No one could pretend that Labour has come out for a new constitutional settlement on Charter 88 or Scottish Convention lines or embraced an ideal of citizenship of the kind that animated the founding fathers of the American Republic or the framers of the French Declaration of the Rights of Man and the Citizen. It is still at least half-embedded in the quite different presuppositions of Westminster parliamentarianism and Westminster sovereignty. Those who look forward to a more fundamental change can console themselves with the thought that a glass that is half-full is also half-empty.

# Part II

# 5 The Labour Party and economic management

*Andrew Gamble*

Changing Labour's policies on the economy became a priority for the Party's leaders after 1983. 'Managing the economy' has steadily increased in importance in modern electoral politics, and politicians seeking office have to project themselves as competent economic managers. Opinion polls throughout the 1980s consistently showed that Labour was perceived as less competent than the Conservatives in this respect. In particular, Labour was not trusted either to keep down taxation or to control inflation.

Labour's poor reputation had several causes, only some of which could be tackled through the mechanism of the Policy Review. Shedding the unpopular policies of the early 1980s was relatively straightforward. But it was much more difficult to dispel the image of Labour as the party of high taxes, accelerating inflation, sterling crises and low growth, which derived from the record of Labour Governments in the 1960s and 1970s. Labour was consistently rated by voters as having the best policies on health, education and other social issues; but voters trusted the Conservatives on the economy and defence, and most electoral research has tended to show that these two issues, particularly the former, were of most significance in influencing voters' choice.

To make the Party electable again Labour leaders have had to find a way to convince voters, sceptical commentators and City analysts that they could manage the economy at least as successfully as the Conservatives, and that a new Labour administration would not instantly plunge the economy into crisis once more. Labour's difficulty was that however bad Conservative management of the economy turned out to be, most voters still instinctively felt that it would be better managed by the Conservatives than by Labour. The Conservatives benefited both ways. When living standards rose the Conservative Government received the credit even if they had no direct responsibility. When living standards fell and the economy plunged into recession, the Conservatives were regarded as the Party most likely to rectify the situation, even when these difficulties had been caused directly by their own policies.

Therefore, one important strand in the thinking behind the Policy Review was to narrow and, if possible, to close the gap between the parties. But there were other factors involved too. As Martin Smith points out in chapter 2, the Policy Review needs to be understood not just in terms of Labour's electoral strategy in response to the party's weak performances in the 1983 and 1987 elections, but also in relation to the party's ideological and policy traditions.

## LABOUR'S ECONOMIC DOCTRINES

Analysing the Policy Review as part of a continuing debate in the Labour Party about its objectives and priorities, rather than simply a response to electoral pressures, helps explain the specific proposals on the economy. During the seventy years in which Labour has been a contender for government it has alternated between two contrasting modes of economic policy. In the first mode, the party leadership has sought to realize the party's socialist objectives within the constraints imposed by the international capitalist economy. In the second mode, it has sought to use the powers of the nation-state to insulate the national economy from those constraints in order to build socialism in Britain. In practice the policies of Labour Governments have often reflected elements of both.

The first mode has been dominant in the economic thinking and policies of three periods of Labour leadership: Ramsay Macdonald and Philip Snowden up to 1931; Hugh Gaitskell, Harold Wilson and James Callaghan in the 1950s and 1960s; and now Neil Kinnock, Roy Hattersley and John Smith in the 1980s and 1990s.

The second mode has been in the ascendancy for shorter periods, but crucially it influenced the programme drawn up by Labour in the 1930s, following the financial crisis of 1931, and the policies of the Attlee Government. It was revived after 1970 and came to dominate policy-making in the party conference and the NEC, although not the leadership (except briefly during Michael Foot's leadership between 1981 and 1983).

The two periods when the national protectionist mode has been strongest have occurred during major recessions in the world economy and following disillusionment and recrimination within the Party over Labour's performance in government. The 1982 programme and the debates around the Alternative Economic Strategy in the 1970s were not some alien explosion of extreme left-wing socialism into British politics, but a restatement of some of Labour's key economic objectives from the 1930s and 1940s, such as full employment, public ownership and redistribution.

The revisionism of the 1950s and 1960s also accepted the goals of full employment and redistribution. What distinguishes thinking about the economy in the two modes is the constraints they recognize in seeking to achieve those objectives. In this sense the importance of the 1989 Policy Review in the development of the Labour Party is that it marks a sharp break with the national protectionism which was the central theme both of the Alternative Economic Strategy and of Labour's 1982 programme, and a return to the mode of thinking about economic policy which characterized the Labour Party under Ramsay Macdonald, Hugh Gaitskell and Harold Wilson.

This tradition does increasingly appear to be Labour's central tradition in economic policy. The revival of national protectionism in the 1970s did not yield a programme on which Labour could win an election and was only very briefly endorsed by the leadership. Although Labour's most successful Government, the Attlee Government, did carry through a national protectionist programme, reverence for its memory hides the extent to which it was the product of a set of very exceptional circumstances – the war economy and the war-time coalition. National protectionism at that time was a practical necessity. Even then the commitment was far from absolute. After 1947 the Government began accepting the case for liberalization. It lost office before the change was complete.

The Attlee Government had an effect on British politics much greater than its relatively brief tenure might suggest. It set Labour politics in a mould from which it is only perhaps now struggling free. In doing so Labour has begun to discover other traditions in its history on which to build. The Policy Review is part of this process.

## THE EUROPEAN DIMENSION

The report on economic policy which is incorporated in the Policy Review is subtitled 'Competing for Prosperity'. Its main themes were already present in the 1987 manifesto, which had jettisoned most of the commitments of the 1982 programme because the leadership regarded them as vote losers. But the Policy Review carries the process further by giving much more detail on the new policies and by supplying a rationale for the change.

'Competing for Prosperity' needs to be read in relation to policy changes detailed elsewhere in the Policy Review – in particular the acceptance of membership of the European Community (see George and Rosamond, chapter 12). This shift is symbolic of the switch away from national protectionism, and signals the readiness of the Labour leadership to develop policies within the constraints imposed by an open economy.

The change from 1983 is stark. The 1983 manifesto simply declared:

the European Economic Community . . . was never designed to suit us, and our experience as a member of it has made it more difficult for us to deal with our economic and industrial problems. . . . The next Labour Government, committed to radical, socialist policies for reviving the British economy, is bound to find continued membership a most serious obstacle to the fulfilment of those policies. In particular the rules of the Treaty of Rome are bound to conflict with our strategy for economic growth and full employment, our proposals on industrial policy and for increasing trade, and our need to restore exchange controls and to regulate direct overseas investment.

(Labour Party 1983a: 33)

By 1987 the commitment to withdraw from the European Community had been abandoned, but the enthusiasm for the Community was still grudging:

Labour's aim is to work constructively with our EEC partners to promote economic expansion and combat unemployment. However, we will stand up for British interests within the European Community and will seek to put an end to the abuses and scandals of the Common Agricultural Policy. We shall, like other member countries, reject EEC interference with our policy for national recovery and renewal.

(Labour Party 1987a: 15)

The perspective of the Policy Review is very different. Europe is perceived as an opportunity rather than as a threat, the essential framework within which a Labour Government's efforts to improve Britain's relative competitiveness will have to be pursued. The Policy Review did express reservations about joining the ERM until certain conditions had been met, but once Britain joined in 1990, these conditions were abandoned. It also ruled out the creation of a new 'superpower' in Europe. But it welcomed the opportunities for cooperation in social and economic policy as the best way of reviving the British economy, rather than viewing the Community as another obstacle in its path. It accepted the single economic market, and urged closer cooperation between member states to achieve coordinated policies on pollution, reflation, social benefits and workers' rights.

Where the 1982 programme had seen the European Community as a fundamental obstacle to the building of socialism in Britain, the Policy Review sees the Community as spearheading the attempt to develop the industrial strength of Europe to meet competition from Japan and the United States.

## MARKETS

The logic of abandoning a national protectionist perspective is followed through in the assessment of markets and the boundaries between the private and the public sector. Labour's commitment to a steady expansion of public ownership had been a key part of its 1930s programme. It had guided the extensive programme of nationalization of the Attlee Government. Directly challenged by Crosland and the revisionists in the 1950s and 1960s, it had then been revived in the various versions of the Alternative Economic Strategy as it developed through the 1970s.

The Policy Review is the most explicit rejection of the policy of expanding public ownership which the Party has ever made. There is no proposal to repeal clause IV of the party constitution, but like Crosland, the Policy Review makes it clear that the question of ownership has become irrelevant to the problems of managing the economy.

Neil Kinnock states in the introduction to the Policy Review that the old debate between the Conservative and Labour Parties on the proper boundaries between the public and private sectors has become outmoded. While natural monopolies should remain in social ownership and control, 'in many areas of economic activity . . . modern technology, modern markets, modern investment systems have dissolved the rigid boundaries'. Kinnock argues that the success of the private sector depends in large part on public investment and involvement, so that 'it is no longer as possible or as necessary as it used to be to draw strict dividing lines between "public" and "private"'. (Labour Party 1989a: 6)

Since the distinction between public and private has become blurred, it makes no sense to propose renationalizing privatized companies or making new proposals for extending public ownership.

Only water and electricity and British Telecom are identified as sectors where a Labour Government would regain direct public control through ownership of a majority of the shares. This policy contrasts sharply with the commitment in 1983 to 'return to public ownership the public assets and rights hived off by the Tories, with compensation of no more than that received when the assets were denationalised' (Labour Party 1983a: 12). At that time the Party pledged itself to re-establish British Aerospace and the British Shipbuilding Corporation as major public enterprises, and to give special support to British Steel. The manifesto also declared that a Labour Government would establish a 'significant public stake in electronics, pharmaceuticals, health equipment, and building materials' and in other sectors as required by the national interest (Labour Party 1983a: 12). The 1982 programme had pledged Labour to establish a state holding in every major industry.

Most of these explicit commitments had gone by the time of the 1987 manifesto. They receive no mention in the Policy Review. Instead of an industrial strategy built around the public sector and its major public enterprises, the Policy Review envisages an industrial strategy in which the State supports the private sector and enables it to do better.

This change requires a much more positive endorsement, of the market and the private sector than the Labour Party has traditionally made. Whatever accommodation Labour Governments made in practice to the market, Labour rhetoric remained hostile. The Labour tradition has tended to equate public enterprise with public service, and private enterprise with private profit. It followed that moving towards socialism required wherever possible the enlargement of the public sector at the expense of the private. This vision was set out in the 1982 programme, which projected a 'steady but decisive transformation in the economy – from one that is unregulated, unaccountable and dominated by the private sector, to one that is subject to planning, characterised by industrial democracy at all levels, and led increasingly by a wide range of socially-owned industries and enterprises' (Labour Party 1982a: 17).

Seeing the private sector and the public sector as equally capable of serving the public has been a major change. Again it was foreshadowed by Crosland. Its practical consequence, as the Policy Review makes plain, is that the delivery of a particular service can be discussed pragmatically in terms of whether public or private provision is best in a particular case, rather than in terms of ideological principle.

From the evidence of the Policy Review, however, Labour has not undergone the kind of conversion to free markets experienced in recent years by the New Zealand Labour Party. Britain still awaits one of its major parties to become fully committed to the free market. The Policy Review is sufficiently influenced by Labour tradition to hedge its approval of markets with a commentary on their deficiencies and on the continuing role for public intervention.

Throughout the Policy Review, and perhaps particularly in Neil Kinnock's introduction, there is a tendency for the 'market' to be contrasted with the State. Kinnock writes, 'Of course, private business can be the most efficient way of producing and distributing many goods and services'. The 'of course' suggests that Kinnock is still testing how far he can go, conscious that many in his party disagree.

Kinnock goes on to argue that the private sector will only be efficient provided that the government regulates commercial behaviour in the interests of the consumer, and restricts monopoly practices in the interests of competition. Beyond this regulatory role, however, there are also other roles which Governments must perform. Left to itself, Kinnock asserts, the 'market' does not do three essential things which a modern economy needs. It does not invest adequately in education and training, science and technology, and research and development; it cannot ensure adequate provision of health, social services and social security; and it cannot protect the environment.

The conclusion of this line of reasoning is a supply-side doctrine for socialism. The economic role of modern government, according to Kinnock, is to 'help make the market system work properly where it can, will and shall – and to replace or strengthen it where it can't, won't or shouldn't' (Labour Party 1989a: 6).

## SUPPLY-SIDE SOCIALISM

Supply-side socialism can be distinguished from national protectionism because its focus is not primarily on how to maintain economic security by insulating the national economy against competition, but on how to make British companies internationally competitive in an open and interdependent world economy. The 1982 programme presented its economic policy as a 'plan for jobs'. All its measures were to be judged primarily by their contribution to bringing down unemployment. By contrast, for the Policy Review, 'the single most important requirement of economic policy is to make Britain internationally competitive'. Labour's changed conception of economic policy focuses attention on how to create an economic context in which wealth creation can flourish.

The Policy Review lists five main ways in which such a context can be created: correcting mistakes in demand management; ending the fixation with the short term; throwing off the 'imperial mentality'; giving a new priority to wealth producers rather than wealth manipulators; and monetary, fiscal and exchange rate policies to promote the competitiveness of British industry. True to the British tradition of adversary politics all of them are presented as reversing Conservative policies rather than building on them.

What the adversarial style of party debate conceals however is that by different routes both parties have come to accept that the problems of the British economy, in particular its persistent failure, except fleetingly in 1986–8, to remain competitive, can only be solved by supply-side measures. Both parties have abandoned their (different) national protectionist traditions and accepted the world market, although both remain prone to bouts of regret for lost national economic sovereignty.

The argument between the parties now centres on what kind of supply-side policy is most appropriate for Britain. The main difference between them results from a different estimation of the importance of manufacturing to future prosperity. The Policy Review regards the 20 per cent decline in Britain's share of the world market for manufactured goods as the fundamental problem that needs to be tackled. It argues that the decline is reflected in the record trade gap, the skills gap, the investment gap and the infrastructure gap. These supply-side deficits have left Britain perilously weak to cope with the challenges of the single economic market, a transformed international economic and political system, and rapid technological, demographic and environmental change (Labour Party 1991a).

### A medium-term industrial strategy

For Labour the competitive weaknesses of the British economy can only be remedied by purposive government action. In place of the Thatcher Government's medium-term financial strategy, Labour proposes a medium-term industrial strategy. The Policy Review insists that this difference in emphasis is a crucial difference between the parties. Echoing an old theme of Harold Wilson, Neil Kinnock declares 'the Conservatives are the party for the City. We are the party for industry and like the Governments of our competitors we will form a Government that helps industry succeed' (Labour Party 1989a: 6).

This theme is picked up throughout the report on 'Competing for Prosperity'. Explicit comparison is made with Japan, where the Government has a developmental as well as a regulatory role:

> The case for a socialist economic policy has always been that the free market, although possessing great strengths which must be utilised, is ultimately incapable of building unaided a strong and modern economy.
>
> (Labour Party 1989a: 10)

Labour's vision of a developmental state as set out in the Policy Review contains several elements, some old and familiar from previous party policy, some novel. In a bid to give institutional weight to its proposal for a medium-term industrial strategy as the lynchpin of the economic policy of a Labour Government, the Policy Review suggests that the Department of Trade and Industry (DTI) would need to be significantly strengthened, and given 'equal if not superior status to the Treasury'. Such a reform has been a long cherished project, although the short-lived experiments with the Ministry of Economic Affairs in 1947, and the Department of Economic Affairs in 1964–9 give few grounds for optimism that the dominance of the Treasury can easily be overcome.

The new DTI would be intended to fulfil the same kind of role as *the Ministry of International Trade and Industry* (MITI) in Japan. It would not try to pick winners, but would seek to 'create the conditions in which winners can come through'. It would need to establish close relations with both employers and unions, and its central aim would be to raise the quantity and quality of investment in British industry. The Policy Review stresses more than once that the DTI would not try to second guess or replace the decisions made by individual market actors or concern itself with detailed operational decision-making, but would instead focus on strategic interventions in key sectors to raise competitiveness.

The need for such a strengthened DTI is to raise the rate of investment. The Policy Review and the later policy document – *Modern Manufacturing Strength* – highlight the extent to which Britain invests much less than its competitors in research and development. The Policy Review sets a target of 2.5 per cent of GDP, against the current figure of 1.8 per cent. A series of measures, involving mandatory and discretionary grants, and tax incentives are proposed to encourage firms to invest more. A major expansion of training to create a 'talent-based economy' is also planned.

The drive for greater investment would also be pursued through the creation of a new public investment institution, a successor to the former National Enterprise Board, to be called the British Technology Enterprise. This new agency would seek out opportunities for investment in new technologies such as biotechnology. The Policy Review stresses that it would not support 'lame ducks'. However, it would apply what are termed 'alternative commercial criteria'. The new agency would accept lower initial rates of return than would be possible in the private sector, as well as a longer pay-back period and higher risks.

One policy that does survive from the 1982 programme is the need for major investment in infrastructure. The medium-term industrial strategy identifies a number of projects which would have strategic importance for the whole economy. Top of the list is the plan for a national fibre optic cable network which would cable every household and business by the end of the century.

The 1982 programme foresaw a major struggle with the City and proposed that at least one of the major clearing banks should be nationalized. The Policy Review is more circumspect. Although it wishes to give priority to the needs of manufacturing it does not seek any direct confrontation with the City. It wishes to moderate the short-term bias of the City's practices, first by changing how takeovers are regulated, making them much more difficult to carry through if they are judged to be against the public interest. Second it proposes a variety of means, such as the British Technology Enterprise and a British Investment Bank, to provide more long-term investment finance to key sectors.

The drive for long-term investment is also a feature of proposals for regional development agencies. These agencies are also a long-standing party commitment, but in the Policy Review their role is placed in the context of the medium-term industrial strategy. Scottish, Welsh and English regional assemblies would acquire greater powers to promote economic development in their regions, interacting as much with Brussels as with Westminster in bidding for funds and coordinating initiatives.

## DEMAND MANAGEMENT

Labour's stress on the need to rebuild manufacturing is intended to provide the Party with a credible programme of supply-side socialism. Demand-side socialism is never far away however and cannot be ignored forever. How would a Labour Government contain the pressures for higher public and private consumption while maintaining full employment? The Policy Review has relatively little to say about it. Naturally it condemns monetarism, which is credited with inflicting enormous damage on the productive capacity of the British economy. Labour's macroeconomic management will not be monetarist, since monetarism is regarded as sacrificing long-term industrial strength for short-term financial success. The problem, as the authors of 'Competing for Prosperity' see it, is that macroeconomic policy in Britain, whether Keynesian or monetarist, has too often been conducted in isolation from industrial objectives.

Labour's policy will be different. But how? The Policy Review declares robustly: 'We shall end the reliance on high interest rates and an uncompetitive currency'. Such a policy is not easily squared with membership of the ERM, which is why no doubt that in the Policy Review Labour was still insisting on certain conditions before entry would be possible. Now that entry has taken place and the leadership has welcomed it, there seems to be no possibility of avoiding high interest rates and an uncompetitive currency, unless a Labour Government is prepared to devalue, which Labour leaders are anxious to deny. The Policy Review states: 'We shall use macroeconomic policy to sustain and encourage the vitally important competitiveness of British industry in international markets', but nowhere is it explained how this is to be done.

The sections on macroeconomic policy are undoubtedly the weakest and least convincing in the Policy Review. The reasons are not hard to seek. Labour wishes to subordinate macroeconomic policy to industrial policy. It wants to make the DTI as important in shaping economic policy as the Treasury. It wants to give priority to the needs of industry ahead of those of the City. Giving expression to these aims means rejecting traditional monetary means to maintain price stability. If Labour is not to resort to deflationary policies to control inflation, what other means will it use?

The Policy Review becomes extremely vague at this point. In the section headed 'inflation' it states that there is no single solution to the problem of inflation, and proposes a variety of policies to tackle inflationary pressure as they arise. A Labour Government would hold down prices in the public sector, keep interest rates low, but it would not attempt to implement a pay policy. The breakdown of previous incomes policies in the 1960s and 1970 has left its mark. The support of trade unions for the Policy Review has not been put at risk by any suggestion that Labour would once again try to use union loyalty to a Labour Government to hold down pay. The most to which Labour is committed is an annual national economic assessment, which would attempt to reach an understanding between the Government, employers and unions as to what 'the economy' could afford in pay increases. The degree of restraint which the unions voluntarily accepted would help determine the level for the statutory minimum wage Labour is pledged to introduce. Beyond that a Labour Government would not take any powers to fix wages or prices.

Rapid inflation would soon destroy any hopes Labour might have of implementing its medium-term industrial strategy. Labour's difficulty is that it needs a medium-term financial strategy as well – one that holds down public and private consumption for long enough to allow a big increase in investment and the reconstruction of a strong manufacturing base. Since it has no plans to control prices directly, the implication is that it will be forced either to abandon its plans for economic reconstruction or to force through a tough financial policy. One of the peculiarities of the history of British economic policy is that although the Conservatives have the reputation as the sound money party, periods of financial austerity have occurred much more regularly under Labour, while the Conservatives have been associated repeatedly with consumption booms that got out of hand (for example, 1955, 1962–4, 1972–4, 1986–8).

Labour does this time, however, have an alibi. It is the ERM. Provided that a Labour Government accepts its discipline, it will be free to develop its supply-side socialism. But its programme will be heavily constrained. The financial strategy will not be subordinated to the industrial, and the Treasury will still dominate. At the margin Labour will be able to direct more resources into industrial investment than would be the case under a Conservative Government. But it may pay a heavy electoral price. The policies of the Conservatives helped to weaken Britain's manufacturing sector during the 1980s, but they also provided spectacular consumer booms, based on credit and imports. Labour appears to be promising to its electorate a long period during which consumption and living standards will be held down to pay for the higher investment needed to rebuild manufacturing. An electorate which in recent years has saved less and less and been encouraged to spend more and more is not likely to be ready for this kind of discipline. It will be hard for Labour to build the kind of long-term electoral coalition that would see the policy through. The Government would be immensely vulnerable to attack by a revived Conservative Party.

Labour's dilemma is easy to define, but hard to resolve. The British political system has not been a conspicuous success at building political support for policies whose pay-off is long term. In the absence of a national emergency, constitutional reform or the overwhelming dominance of one party, why should any political party yoke its fortunes to an economic programme which will not yield its voters short-term benefits?

After the Thatcher decade and the collapse of the Lawson boom the problems of the British economy appear as intractable as ever. The size of the trade deficit in the midst of a sharp recession is one indication. The continuing deficiencies in training, investment and infrastructure are another. The cultural and political shift required to move towards the model of a developmental state looks beyond the reach of one party on its own, especially while the existing electoral rules and adversarial competition between the parties prevails.

## CONCLUSION

The Policy Review is unlikely to achieve all its aspirations. Supply-side socialism may turn out to be a more limited affair than some of its advocates hope. But the change of direction which the Policy Review represents is unlikely to be reversed in government. The commitments which look most vulnerable are the commitments not to increase taxes and not to introduce an incomes policy. Like all parties everywhere Labour proposes to raise public spending but to fund it painlessly out of future growth. Should growth be slower than expected Labour may be forced to choose between raising taxes to fund the extra investment and public consumption to which it is committed, or slashing its programmes, and giving the impression that the Government is dominated by the financial markets. Either course is likely to prove costly electorally.

Labour's only major success in managing the economy and delivering its programme occurred under the Attlee Government. Kinnock needs to secure both electoral victory and a reputation for good government before his rescue of the Labour Party can be judged to have been a success. Many in the Party have accepted the new policies as the price that must be paid to secure a Labour Government. If the Party were to fail in government again old quarrels and divisions might reappear.

If Kinnock succeeds then the Policy Review will be seen as an important milestone in the evolution of Labour's economic thinking. The Party has moved decisively beyond national protectionism, and in some important respects this means beyond Keynesianism as well, since the outlook of Keynesianism was also predominantly in terms of national protection. Labour remains committed to weak forms of corporatism such as the national economic assessment, but has accepted that its policies for full employment, a minimum wage and redistribution will have to be pursued within the constraints of an open economy. The nature of the economic problem as Labour perceives it has been substantially transformed.

# 6 The Labour Party, small businesses and enterprise

*Chris Guiver*

## INTRODUCTION

Changes in the world economy, structural transformation, high levels of unemployment and low growth in the domestic economy now present Labour with diminished economic options. The previous chapter suggests that these factors have greatly affected Labour's room for manoeuvre. This chapter argues that as a consequence, after years of suspicion, Labour is increasingly making small business policy an important part of its plans for economic rejuvenation. It is these economic changes, rather than electoral considerations, or rank and file enthusiasm which have resulted in Labour taking small businesses more seriously.

However, while these 'diminished options' can be described as having 'pushed' Labour towards a small firms policy, this chapter will argue that the wider Labour Party continues to promote a series of agendas that compete to some extent with small firms policies. These 'competing agendas' are Labour's traditional hostility towards capitalist business, higher taxation in order to support the welfare state, a preference for unionized labour and lastly, the new charters for the enhanced protection of workers, consumers and the environment.

## THE SMALL BUSINESS CONTEXT AND THE TORY LEGACY

Small businesses, ranging from micro businesses and the self-employed, to innovative high-tech engineering companies, have expanded greatly in the 1980s. Self-employment 'grew from just above 2 million to more than 3 million' between 1981 and 1988 (Hakim 1989b: 286–7), whilst the total number of enterprises with fewer than twenty employees, 'accounted for 36 per cent of non-Government employment, up from 27 per cent in 1979' (Department of Employment 1991: 3). Small businesses are therefore seen as having potential for job creation.

Throughout the 1980s small business policy was a high profile feature of Thatcherism, and was presented as the vanguard of a new 'enterprise culture' and 'economic miracle'. Small businesses were 'transformed from an economic and social anachronism into a modern "folk hero"' (May and McHugh 1991: 1). Over the last decade the Conservatives spent £2 billion on small business policies (Curran and Downing 1989: 3). Their policies were first, to reduce 'burdens on business' by minimizing taxes and regulations (red tape), and second, to assist with 'finance, information, professional advice, training and premises' (Department of Employment 1991: 14).

Labour's heightened emphasis on small firms policy in the Policy Review might thus appear to be an unimaginative attempt to imitate Thatcherite small firms policy. This chapter rejects such a view. It argues that Labour is highly critical of Thatcherite policies for enterprise and has developed a small firms policy at least partly responsive to its own traditional internal agendas.

Recent evidence of Labour's differences with the Conservative Government's policies towards small businesses has been Labour's criticism of high interest rates and high rates of bankruptcy amongst small businesses during the recession of 1990–1. However, long-term ideological identification means the small business vote is likely to remain Conservative. This again points to Labour's interest in small firms as being economically rather than electorally motivated, although it is possible that emphasizing the flaws in Mrs Thatcher's 'enterprise culture' may push 'floating' voters away from the Conservatives and towards Labour and the Liberal Democrats.

## LABOUR'S INTEREST IN SMALL FIRMS: 1964–1991

Labour's small firms policy has always been a pragmatic top-down policy orginating in the shadow cabinet. Traditionally there has been little interest shown in small firms by Labour Party members. Conference did not have a specific debate on small firms between 1964–91 and Labour backbench attendances at small firms debates in the Commons were so low as to be commented upon during the debates.

Not only does much of the Labour Party lack enthusiasm towards small firms, some sections are quite hostile. Small firms have long been associated amongst the left with 'sweated labour', poor wages and bad conditions. The high degree of non-unionized labour and strong support for the Conservative Party amongst owners of small firms has counted against them, and the left associates them with tax evasion which undermines the welfare state, and poor health and safety conditions which endangers the workforce (Labour Party 1985c).

The strong ideological association of small firms with free market individualism has clearly clashed with Labour's collectivist values, and the small business vote is still considered a virtual write-off. A history of socialist hostility to business materialism and profiteering also explains rank and file antipathy towards small firms (Weiner 1987: 119; Gould 1989: 58). Only Syndicalism, the Co-operative movement and G.D.H. Cole's Guild Socialism of the 1920s gives British socialism any small business pedigree, and these forms of business are collectivist rather than individualist in structure (Foote 1985: 85–116).

Despite this intellectual background, it is possible to trace an increasing interest in small firms from Labour's leadership. This began at the end of the 1960s when Anthony Crosland as president of the Board of Trade, set up the Bolton Report 'to consider the role of small firms in the national economy' (Bolton 1971).

However, the Wilson Government of 1964–70 was primarily concerned with large businesses. The assumption of this Labour Government was that Britain needed to rationalize its industries in order to compete in international markets. The intellectually dominant view at the time was that industries were made efficient by exploiting 'economies of scale'. Small firms were looked upon as left-overs from an earlier form of capitalism and little interest was taken in them until it became apparent that the large firm strategy had its own problems. Labour began to be worried by the inefficiency, lack of flexibility and accountability of these large and powerful firms. A 'small is beautiful' sentiment emerged in the early 1970s (Schumacher 1973), and although it was primarily associated with the Liberals and the small firms lobby of the Conservative Party, the Labour Party was not wholly immune to its charms as interviews with Labour MPs testify.

The 1974–9 Labour Governments began the period with a 'bottom-up' inspired strategy based on the 1973 programme and the February 1974 manifesto. This programme was not favourable towards small businesses. It was primarily concerned with improving trade union rights, extending public ownership and redistributing wealth through higher taxation. However, after 1974 there were signs of a new interest in small firms, with certain sections of the left beginning to take a serious interest in worker cooperatives.

Capitalist small firms were also taken seriously by the leadership of the 1974–79 Governments. Between 1974 and 1977 microeconomic policy on small firms was broadly one of continuity with the Heath Government and was characterized by minor incremental adjustments to a plethora of schemes: expanding advice, encouraging exports and constructing premises. The only significant change in microeconomic policy compared to that of the Heath Government was the creation of employment subsidy schemes to help save jobs in small firms.

In September 1977, Labour's small firms policy dramatically increased in importance. James Callaghan, the Prime Minister, asked the Chancellor of the Duchy of Lancaster, Harold Lever, and Bob Cryer the small firms minister, to examine what more could be done to improve matters for small firms. This led to cuts in taxation for small firms in Denis Healey's October 1977 and April 1978 budgets, cuts in statistical returns and an investigation into small firms' finance which was incorporated into the Wilson Committee on financial institutions (1979). Peter Shore's White Paper, *Policy for the Inner Cities* (1977), also contained a commitment to encourage small firms operating in the inner cities.

The motives behind these policy initiatives were varied. The Liberal leaders claim they were responsible, as easing the burden on small firms was one of the ten demands of the Lib–Lab pact (Steel 1980: 81–4; Marsh 1990: 302). However, it is clear Labour had more fundamental reasons for its interest. Britain's large traditional industries were becoming less competitive in the face of innovative and flexible foreign competition, with the result that many firms were in danger of collapse and had to drastically cut their workforces. In the face of this, small firms became attractive to Labour's leadership. Denis Healey emphasized the role of small firms in job creation, innovation and urban and rural regeneration (*Hansard*, 11 April 1978: 1188). Harold Lever pointed to the need to respond to structural changes in the economy towards smaller and more flexible units. He also pointed out that 'in every other advanced country which is enjoying economic success there has been far more support by government for small firms' (*Hansard*, 17 April 1978: 35–6).

All these themes, the decline of traditional industries, the need for innovation, new jobs and regeneration, together with internationally competitive structural changes towards smaller and more flexible units amounted to a series of diminishing options as to how Britain's industrial policy should be organized. It was no longer clear to Labour's leadership that they could continue along a 'large firm, large union' paradigm. From 1977 onwards the Labour leadership has recognized a pragmatic interest in small firms and the Policy Review documents have taken this a stage further.

Pragmatism because of these diminished options helps to explain why Labour's shift to the left between 1980 and 1983 did not lead to the abandonment of small firms policy. Nevertheless, the 1983 manifesto suggested that small firms policy would have been less centralized, and instead would have been delegated more to local authorities and new regional development agencies (Labour Party 1983a: 25). Labour was also much more enthusiastic about cooperatives and municipal enterprise than previously (Labour Party 1982a: 49; Labour Party 1983a: 12).

At this time Labour was heavily critical of the effects of the Conservative's macroeconomic policies on small firms, and claimed that their own policies of increased public spending, control of imports and lower exchange rates would greatly benefit the small firm (Labour Party 1983b). Labour outlined policies to increase the availability of loans for small firms by extending the loan guarantees scheme and creating a new national investment bank. In addition, exports would be encouraged, public purchasing used to support innovation and the enterprise allowance scheme extended.

Small firms policy did not alter between 1983–7. Kinnock's intention was to alter macroeconomic policy, not micro. The commitment to cooperatives and municipal enterprise was still evident as was the new national investment bank proposal (Labour Party 1985a and b). The 1987 manifesto did not mention small firms directly, although co-operatives were singled out for encouragement (Labour Party 1987a: b). However, part of this enthusiasm for cooperatives was undoubtedly an attempt to demonstrate the leadership's support for social ownership and reconcile the membership to the declining importance of nationalization.

## THE POLICY REVIEW AND SMALL BUSINESS POLICY

It is in the context of a much vaunted 'decade of small business revival' that Labour's Policy Review has developed its own small firms policies. These policies are higher profile and more detailed than in any previous Labour programme. The 1989 Policy Review, *Meet the Challenge, Make the Change*, and the revisions, *Looking to the Future* (1990a) and *Opportunity Britain* (1991b), have a considerable amount to say on small businesses, and the policies seem to increase in importance with each publication. In *Modern Manufacturing Strength*

(Labour 1991a) small businesses are very much integrated into Labour's new supply-side industrial strategy of training, long-term investment, and research and development. Large firms are still considered more important in terms of employment and training, but the thrust of the Policy Review suggests that high-tech small firms are to be the 'dynamic' for long-term industrial regeneration. Labour's objective is to restore Britain's international competitiveness. They argue that this requires the export of high value-added products which would improve the trade deficit, while simultaneously providing well paid, attractive jobs and so supply the wealth to sustain a thriving services sector at home. Labour rejects a low technology, mass production and price undercutting export drive as leading to poor jobs and a 'social dumping ground' economy, which they identify as the Conservative's strategy (Labour Party 1989a: 17).

There are six strands to the policy for small businesses: long-term finance, technology transfer, advice, training, cooperatives and lastly, the promise of a stable economy with 'fair taxes', low inflation and low interest rates. The first two have a clear high-tech bias. Long-term finance would be offered to small firms via two new institutions and three new schemes. British Technology Enterprise and regional development agencies containing investment banks serviced and coordinated by a national investment bank are the institutions, coupled with the investment expansion scheme, the growing business scheme and the new innovations programme.

British Technology Enterprise would be an expanded version of the existing British Technology Group and would take a long-term view with regard to the patenting and licensing of high-tech innovations as well as providing venture capital 'for high-tech projects of national strategic importance' (Labour Party 1989a: 13; Labour Party 1991a: 9).

In contrast, finance from the regional development agencies appears to be packaged as a general opportunity for all small firms to enjoy low interest loans. However, Labour's criteria for small firms support is 'to improve support for growing firms which have already proved they can succeed and now need backing to grow further' (Labour Party 1991b: 10). This would reduce the risk of backing losers, but it does not offer much for the majority of Britain's small firms which typically display stagnant growth (Hakim 1989a: 35–6).

The investment expansion scheme is a corporate tax allowance for investment in new technology, while the growing business scheme offers tax incentives for individuals to invest in growing manufacturing firms and would replace the Conservative's Business Expansion Scheme which Labour argue is too oriented towards property. The New Innovations Programme would involve cash limited funds for small and medium-sized firms to promote research and the marketing of 'ideas from conception to the market place' in 'software, environmental technology and electronic engineering' (Labour Party 1991a: 16). 'Technology transfer' is a further dimension of the high-tech strategy for regeneration. It describes the movement of high-tech ideas and practices between research institutions and small and large firms. Labour is also keen to see large firms give help to smaller firms in developing their products, as well as extending technology transfer to the European network. Technology Trusts are the institutions that Labour would create to arrange these networks (Labour Party 1991a: 17).

Labour's emphasis on high-tech small firms rests on several optimistic premises. They assume that small high-tech firms are good at innovation; that high quality jobs will be created; that in the long term these firms will become large and employ many people and that there is a finance gap for long-term projects.

High-tech small firms are considered to make a significant contribution to innovation, especially in combination with large firms (Rothwell 1986: 137). However, it is not so certain that such firms will create high quality jobs. Some theorists have argued that new technology leads to the de-skilling of the workforce, while others have pointed to a dual labour force with high-tech firms run by a skilled élite and adequately operated by low skilled workers (Goss 1991: 116). It is also not yet evident that these firms will grow significantly enough to make any great impact on unemployment (Storey and Johnson 1986: 42).

Evidence of a long-term finance gap for innovative small firms (DTI 1991: 122) suggests that there could be a role for Labour's British Technology Enterprise and the regional investment banks. However, Labour's plan to back firms that are already growing begs the question as to whether they need the assistance? It might be a better strategy to try and turn around struggling firms. The plans for technology transfer between large and small firms, together with ideas about 'clustering' firms together in mutually supportive networks does have support (Geroski and Knight 1991; Szarka 1990: 10–22), and seems to offer the best prospect for any high-tech solution to Britain's problems. However, given that the increases in the number of small firms and the self-employed in the 1980s was achieved across all sectors apart from retailing and agriculture (Department of Employment 1991: 9), it may prove prudent for Labour to aid small firms across a broader spectrum.

Labour's policy on advice for small firms first appeared in the 1990 document, *Look to the Future* where they announced that the 'core' of their small firms policy would be the creation of a local one-stop business service. The service would give advice on business plans, finance and training – including management training, patenting, licensing, marketing and exporting (Labour Party 1990a: 15). The point of the one-stop business shop is to rationalize the existing system which involves 'dozens of different schemes run by five different government departments' (Labour Party 1991b: 10). This policy seems to be tokenistic and more about bureaucratic order than offering anything innovative. Moreover, the private sector advice agencies and existing local government and TEC sources of advice would probably object to this policy as invading their territory. It is also not clear that small businesses are requesting such a change. The quarterly survey of small business in Britain which surveys business problems has not mentioned advice as a problem (Goss 1991: 44). In light of this, it is interesting that the 1991 Labour documents contain a toned down description of the one-stop shop, no longer saying that it was the 'core' of policy and stating that this service would only 'be set up in every area where there is a demand' (Labour Party 1991b: 10; Labour Party 1991a: 22).

Labour's policies on training also contain an explicit small firms dimension. The Policy Review proposes 'a legal obligation on all employers to train, defined by a duty to spend at least 0.5 per cent of their payroll on training, with the shortfall being paid as a contribution' to their proposed new national training body, Skills UK (Labour Party 1991a: 13). Obviously this would burden the smallest companies struggling to survive. Labour explicitly claims to recognize this problem, but say 'they are anxious to ensure that any exemption from the contribution is as limited as possible' (Labour Party 1991a: 14). Labour suggests that one way out of the difficulty would be for small firms to establish local training consortia with other small firms to provide training that they are unable to provide on their own. This idea is to some extent already being implemented in Japan, Germany and France. However, it remains to be seen whether the traditional individualism of British small firms, strongly reinforced by a decade of Thatcherism, would readily lend itself to a collectivist idea, whatever its merits. There is also reason to doubt whether intrinsically low-skill small firms would benefit from an increased compulsion to train. Does an ice-cream parlour really need to spend 0.5 per cent of its payroll on training? Labour is promoting training as a means to create an upward spiral of skilled, well-paid and internationally competitive workers, but this agenda clashes with the needs of those small firms requiring only minimal skills.

Labour's policy on cooperatives is the only ideologically motivated part of what is otherwise a wholly pragmatic small firms policy. It is also the only part of Labour's small firms policy that is likely to gain any enthusiasm from the party's rank and file. In the 1989 document, cooperatives are grouped with policies to extend democracy in the workplace. It claimed 'our ideal is an economy in which enterprises are owned and managed by their employees,' and went on to advocate the conversion of existing firms into employee share-ownership schemes (ESOPs) or into cooperatives. They also say that they will ease the tax treatment of cooperatives (Labour Party 1989a: 13). The policy is radical in tone and the favouritism in tax treatment given to cooperatives without providing justification can only be described as ideological. Surprisingly though, the later documents lose this radicalism. They are very vague on cooperatives and extending democracy to the workplace, although the commitment to ease the tax treatment of cooperatives remains, even if no details are given. An interview with a Labour Party spokesman elicited the response that 'the political momentum behind cooperatives is not what it was' (11 June 1991).

In addition to specific policies, many of Labour's other policies have implications, good and bad, for small firms. For example, Labour's promise of a stable economy with lower inflation and lower interest rates would clearly benefit all small firms. However, macroeconomic promises are easy to make, but hard to deliver, as the Conservatives discovered when their 'economic miracle' of 1987–8 transformed itself into a recession in 1990–1.

Labour's 'fair tax' policies also have implications for small firms. The plan to raise the top rate of income tax from 40 per cent to 50 per cent when combined with the abolition of the 'ceiling' on national insurance contributions would certainly penalize partnerships and the wealthier ranks of the self-employed. However, the proposal to reduce the bottom band to 20 per cent would aid the more marginal of the self-employed, and plans to improve the access of the self-employed to state social insurance should also help (Labour Party 1989a: 34). Labour does not outline any plans to increase corporate taxation. The only changes are in the area of tax incentives for high-tech firms outlined earlier. However, there may be changes in inheritance taxation, which could penalize the transfer of family firms between the generations (Labour Party 1989a: 34). Small firms in the 'black economy' may also suffer from plans to tighten up on tax dodgers, which is significant in that some small firms start in the 'black economy' and move into the legitimate economy once they have built up a successful business. In total then, high technology firms come off best with the tax incentives aimed at them, while the more prosperous of the self-employed are likely to come off worst. Labour would not see this as a problem, however, because their concern lies in encouraging the growth of firms with potential, rather than with the more numerous stagnant firms.

Labour's plans for an employees' charter, a consumers' charter and tougher environmental regulations have also serious implications for small businesses, in terms of both cost and 'red tape'. The proposed national legal minimum wage to be set at a 'level of 50 per cent of male median earnings which is equivalent to £2.80 per hour in 1989 terms' is perhaps the most serious new burden (Labour Party 1989a: 22). While the larger, more prosperous small firms will probably be already conforming to most of Labour's proposals, the micro-business is unlikely to as they are too marginal to be able to afford decent wages, conditions and high standards of consumer care. Labour's charters are also problematic for small firms that are struggling to compete with large firms. These proposals may place increased constraints on many micro-businesses and so risk forcing marginal companies out of business.

Labour's aim is not to burden small businesses, but to meet the demands of conflicting interests within the Party and the electorate. The employees' charter is to help placate trade unionists in the Party with regard to policy losses in areas of traditional industrial conflict (see Rosamond, chapter 7), while the charters for consumers and the environment are designed to appeal to voters. The problem is that these new charters compete to some extent with the small firms agenda. Moreover, a spokesperson for the Labour Party made it clear that 'we are going to "normalize" our approach towards small business development' (interview, 11 June 1991). What was meant by this was that the favouritism shown to small firms by the Conservatives' generous interpretation of 'red tape' would be gradually removed. Labour's complaint is that some small firms like to call every burden 'red tape' and as a result they:

don't want to pay tax . . . they don't want to pay national insurance, or want health and safety. At the cynical end of the market they don't want to do anything, so in a sense if you took no red tape to its crystal conclusion then you live in a jungle, and we're not having that. . . . You see red tape has a kind of emotive symbolism in the Tory party, and if you're against red tape then you are doing the business, even though for the vast majority of companies, small as well as large, this is not a major consideration.

(interview, 11 June 1991)

Labour's ambiguous relationship with small businesses is likely to create some alienation despite attempts to placate small business interests. For example, the CBI have already made clear its objections to the employees' charter, the training levy and the proposed increases in the top rate of income tax (*CBI News*, June 1991: 11).

## THE POLICY REVIEW AND SMALL BUSINESSES IN PERSPECTIVE

The Policy Review marks a significant departure from previous Labour small firms' programmes. No longer are small firms to be propped up by subsidies to save marginal jobs; rather the aim is now to target specific sectors in order to create a long-term strategy of regeneration. The job creation side of policy remains, but it is now one of jobs tomorrow, rather than today.

Labour needs to tread warily with its own membership on small firms policy. It would not be popular to be seen to like small firms for their own sake, especially when so few of them are fully unionized. This explains why the policies on small firms have not been spelt out at conference. As there is no tradition of ever having debated small business policy at conference, Labour's leadership probably thinks it not worth stirring up ambiguous messages on an issue which could be seized on by Labour's opponents.

Given the lack of conference debate on small businesses, it is peculiar that the small firms policy is afforded such a high profile in the Policy Review documents. The explanation is that Labour could not avoid mentioning small firms when so much of their plans for economic regeneration and the creation of new high quality jobs rest with encouraging small as well as large firms. Moreover, Labour's increased faith in small firms lies with a series of diminishing options on how the economy can be regenerated in the face of the decline of large traditional industries.

Labour's leadership has been fully aware of these diminished options since at least 1977, but the Policy Review marks a qualitative step upwards in the importance of small businesses to Labour's economic policy. The explanation for this lies in Labour taking these diminished options more seriously as a result of new developments that have happened since 1979. First, more than a decade of Thatcherism high on small business rhetoric and policy has forced Labour to take notice of small firms. However, Labour's emphasis on small business policy is not solely an absorption of Thatcherism. Labour has not accepted the Thatcherite notion of the enterprise culture. As one of the Policy Review updates put it, 'the miracle turned out to be a mirage' (Labour Party 1990a: 5), and 'wealth has not "trickled down" to the poor it has steamed up to the rich' (Labour Party 1990a: 35).

Labour further rejects the view that tax cuts create incentives to reinvest, rather they argue tax cuts increase consumption, particularly in luxury goods which tend to be imported and so damage the balance of payments. Labour is opposed to the Conservatives' inclination to call workers' rights and health and safety issues 'red tape', and would seek to repair these rights by 'normalizing' the position of small firms. Furthermore, Labour's rhetoric suggests that they are trying to emulate successful competitor economies like Japan, Germany and France, rather than merely patch up what they see as the inadequacies of Thatcherism and John Major's economic policies.

Second, Labour's new enthusiasm for Europe and the prospect of increased competition from the creation of the single market in 1992 has reinforced the message that strong economies in Europe have significant small firms sectors. Third, Labour's shift away from nationalization and the 'planning agreements' of the 1970s has left a policy void which had to be filled with new policy. Small business policy with market socialism and the new charters is part of this new policy.

Fourth, and most importantly, is the rise of new theories about structural changes in the economy. It has become increasingly apparent during the 1980s that, alongside the growth of huge multinationals, there has occurred a fragmentation of industry. This has taken the form of a revival of small firms, and the deliberate fragmentation of large firms into smaller units (Shutt and Whittington 1984). The reasons for this fragmentation are based on technological and consumer changes. First, technology has made it possible to organize industries more efficiently into smaller units. Second, at least in developed countries, consumers have moved away from standardized mass produced goods. This has created new opportunities in specialist and personalized niche markets, which tend to be most efficiently supplied by smaller units of production. Theorists have grouped these changes under the term 'post-fordism'.

Labour's reaction to these changes has been both pessimistic and optimistic. The pessimism is based around the idea that these changes in the economy have led to the creation of a dual economy of well-paid and trade union-protected full-time jobs in large firms, and an increasing number of poorly paid temporary and part-time jobs in other sectors (Labour Party 1989a: 21). There is a belief that the shift towards smaller workplaces threatens to weaken the trade union movement (Gould 1989: 79) which tends to be stronger in large anonymous organizations than in smaller more personalized firms. Moreover, the absence of trade union activity in many small firms does not necessarily indicate harmony and good working conditions (Curran and Stanworth 1981: 14–25; Goss 1991: 69–91).

Labour has also developed an optimistic interpretation of these structural changes, believing that they offer an opportunity for greater 'flexibility' which 'can mean better services and more efficient industries. It also must mean more choice for people about when they work, how long they work and when they retire' (Labour Party 1989a: 21). This kind of optimism has a certain resonance with those who advocate 'flexible specialization' and 'post-fordism' as a way forward for modern society (Piore and Sabel 1984; Hall and Jacques 1989).

## CONCLUSION

Labour's small firms programme in the Policy Review is in totality a pragmatic response to the same diminishing economic options that faced the 1974–9 Labour Governments. However, developments in the 1980s have led to Labour adopting a heightened interest in developing small firms policy as an integral part of its long-term strategy for economic regeneration, although this chapter has argued that this small firms policy is perhaps too strongly biased towards high-tech small firms.

Labour's increased interest in small firms is evidence against the superficial view of some commentators that the Policy Review is 'little more than a silver anniversary re-print of the 1964 manifesto' (Wilton 1990: 14; *The Economist*, 1 June 1991: 32). As this chapter has shown, Harold Wilson's 1964 programme was very much based on a large firm strategy. Thus, although there are similarities between the two programmes on training, high-tech industry, scientific research and a belief in the mixed economy, the switch to a combined large and small firm strategy is a significant change.

Labour's current small firms policy has a considerable degree of continuity with the policies of the 1970s. Indeed, at the micro level of policy (with the exception of Labour's subsidies at the end of the 1970s), there has been a considerable degree of continuity of small business policy ever since the Heath Government enacted most of the recommendations of the Bolton Report of 1971. The 1980s were different quantitatively rather than qualitatively. Both parties have agreed since 1977 that taxes and red tape should be kept at a minimum for small firms. The difference between the two parties lies in the interpretation of where that minimum should sensibly lie. Of course, the other main difference between Thatcherite small firms policy and that of the Labour Party lies in their rhetorical representation. The Labour Party wishes to incorporate small firms policy into a long-term strategy to regenerate the economy along more egalitarian lines. In contrast, the Conservatives respond to small businesses as an 'insider' pressure group (except where macroeconomic objectives conflict), while at the same time trying to promote a 'rough and tumble' individualistic and entrepreneurial society.

# 7 The Labour Party, trade unions and industrial relations

*Ben Rosamond*

## INTRODUCTION

The formulation and implementation of policy in the areas of employment law, industrial relations and trade union affairs have for a long time provided the Labour Party with some of its most acute dilemmas. From the late 1960s onwards industrial relations had been vulnerable terrain for the Party, not only because of legislative failure and the inability of the leadership to construct an enduring alliance with the trade union movement, but also thanks to the political capital that Labour's relations with the unions offered to the party's opponents. From the outset the credibility of industrial relations policy was always going to be an index of the success of the Policy Review as a whole, and, therefore, of the Labour leadership's aims to present itself as a viable alternative to the Conservatives.

Indeed two long-run factors would appear to have been influential in the composition of the Policy Review. First, the role of trade unions in the Party meant that they were more than 'recipients' of Labour Party policy. The party structure and the mathematics of its policy-making process ensured that affiliated trade unions had a significant say in policy approval. Consequently in its re-evaluation of industrial relations policy, the Labour leadership had to be concerned with both the reception of the new policy on the 'shop floor' and its potential effects upon the delicate fabric of the party coalition. Second, the close relationship between the Party and the unions was seen in some quarters as an electoral impediment. Opinion polls have shown frequently that the majority view trade unions as worthwhile components of a democratic society and Gallup's sample of August 1990 suggested that only 30 per cent regarded unions as too powerful. However, the same poll revealed that 50 per cent agreed with the statement that 'The trade unions have too much say in the affairs of the Labour Party' (Gallup 1990).

In addition, a number of other factors had to be considered. These included general developments in the world of work such as trends towards flexibilization, the 'feminization' of the workforce, the increasing incidence of low pay and the growing number of part-time workers. Second, a new industrial relations strategy would have to be reconciled with Labour's developing economic policy. Third, a nascent industrial relations policy could not be divorced from parallel developments within the European Community. Finally, the significant intervention of the Thatcher Governments into the areas of trade union and employment law could not be ignored.

## BEFORE THE POLICY REVIEW

The 1970s and early 1980s provided vivid illustrations of the operation of the twin constraints of union–party relations and electoral opinion. Much of the 1970s was devoted to the reconstruction of relations between the Labour Party and the TUC, following the Wilson Government's attempt to inaugurate wholesale reform of the British industrial relations system in 1969 by introducing a system of legal rights. The White Paper, *In Place of Strife*, was defeated by a combination of internal party resistance and trade union hostility to specific provisions which sought to regulate unofficial strikes and introduce balloting before industrial action could take place. The internal schisms caused by *In Place of Strife* had long-run repercussions. Indeed it has been suggested that the groups which opposed the White Paper formed the basis of the coalition of Labour left which became increasingly dominant within the Party throughout the 1970s (Seyd 1987: 21).

A further long-run implication was that the Labour leadership did not promise wholesale reform of the industrial relations system until the genesis of the Policy Review some nineteen years later. The party élite, while aware of the need for reform in this area, also understood the overwhelming extent to which some unions would jeopardize union–party relations in defence of free collective bargaining. The major project of the 1970s, therefore, was the construction of a viable working relationship between the Party and the unions which became known as the social contract (see Taylor 1987: 6–83). The achievement of consensus was facilitated by the opposition of both the Party and the TUC to the Heath Government's Industrial Relations Bill of 1971 and in the same year the TUC–Labour Party liaison committee was formed. The social contract came to signify an arrangement where the union movement would gain influence over public policy and sympathetic legislation in return for wage restraint under the Labour Government of 1974–9. While the wave of public sector strikes which became associated with the 'Winter of Discontent' (1978–9) reflected the tensions between the Labour Government attempting to deal with rising inflation in a receding economy and the unions struggling to retain wage increases through collective bargaining, Labour's opponents successfully attributed the problems to the links between the Party and the unions.

There was no questioning of the union–party link as the tide of debate within the Labour movement shifted leftwards in the wake of electoral defeat in 1979. Variations of the Alternative Economic Strategy (AES) appeared within the trade union movement as well as the Party and the 1983 election manifesto promised to repeal the Conservative's employment laws and initiate systems of industrial democracy within firms. This enabled workers to have a say in the running of industry and complemented the system of national planning in which trade unions were to play a significant part (Labour Party 1983a: 9–10). However, the beginnings of the Policy Review agenda were apparent by the time of the 1987 election. The party's election manifesto said virtually nothing about partnership with the unions and offered a modest package of 'rights and responsibilities' which would 'foster good industrial relations and democratic participation in industry and trade unions' (Labour Party 1987a: 13).

## THE POLICY REVIEW AND INDUSTRIAL RELATIONS: THE DIMENSIONS OF AGENDA CHANGE

In the course of the Policy Review the Labour leadership made a conscious attempt to move away from the connotation of industrial relations as the domain of industrial conflict, towards a wholly new agenda which emphasized individual and collective rights and the concept of 'social partnership'. This was certainly the message contained in the published Policy Review documents (Labour Party 1989a, 1990), and it is worth examining the evolution of this approach to demonstrate some of the intra-party dynamics at work.

In the early stages of the Policy Review process it was the 'people at work' group which proved arguably the most problematic from the viewpoint of the leadership. It had apparently been agreed from the outset that the group's task would be to shift the debate on industrial relations onto a terrain more favourable to the Party. In practical terms this implied a need to stop talking about industrial relations in terms of strikes, picket lines, secondary action and trade union militancy and shift the debate in the direction of the rights of people in the workplace, the importance of vocational training, equal opportunities and the eradication of low pay. However, the early Policy Review debates were concerned more with the extent to which the Thatcherite interventions into industrial relations and trade union law should be repudiated. Something of an internal struggle developed within the Party. A group surrounding Neil Kinnock and the TUC leadership displayed a willingness to repeal some of the more obviously iniquitous elements of the Thatcherite repertoire, but refused to make wholesale policy commitments at that stage. The 'people at work' group, which was headed by the shadow employment spokesman, Michael Meacher, considered that a much more thoroughgoing set of policy proposals was required. To complicate matters for the leadership, the Meacher group favoured the extensive repeal of most of the Thatcherite reforms (Hughes and Wintour 1990: 143–52).

The resulting policy document was accepted at the 1988 Labour Party conference and the same assembly rejected a motion calling for the complete eradication of the Thatcherite laws from the statute book, albeit not without some ambiguity (Labour Party 1988b: 80–90).[1] 'People at work' was clearly a compromise document which had been hastily constructed. Even sympathetic observers found it deficient. For example, Philip Bassett favoured an injection of the notion of individually-based employee relations. Otherwise, he argued, Labour's employment policies would seem irrelevant to the workforce, which could have damaging electoral consequences: 'it will mean Labour going into the next election . . . still presenting its political opponents with the opportunity to make maximum electoral gain out of the charge that the union tail is still wagging the Labour dog' (Bassett 1988: 1–2).

Although these remained genuine problems, it was also clear at this stage that key players within the trade union leadership were attempting to secure a convergence of trade union and party policy. The Transport and General Workers (TGWU) and the GMB welcomed the review's proposals for a charter of basic legally enforceable rights at the 1988 party conference. It appeared that some of the largest unions still put a high premium on the election of a Labour Government and would perhaps remain silent regarding their desire to see the repeal of the Conservative legislation.

The remainder of the Policy Review process might be seen as an elaboration and clarification of the dimensions of this new agenda. The 1989 document, *Meet the Challenge, Make the Change*, offered its industrial relations proposals as part of a framework for economic efficiency: 'Economic success depends on good working relationships and partnership in industry' (Labour Party 1989a: 17). Labour's proposals were not to be construed as favours for its union constituency or indeed as mere expressions of the tenets of social justice, but rather as crucial prerequisites for the efficient operation of the British economy. The report placed great emphasis on an effective and properly funded training policy which would be the province of not only employers, but also government, the unions and the individual. Rights at work would be clarified in a charter for employees which would include such essentials as basic contracts of employment, equal opportunities, a minimum wage, health and safety regulation, protection against unfair dismissal and workplace representation (Labour Party 1989a: 18–26). These proposals were accepted by the 1989 conference. Nevertheless, commentators focused on the ambiguities which the policy document displayed in the areas of the settlement of industrial disputes and the precise definition of secondary industrial action (e.g. *Financial Times*, 5 October 1989).

Similar scrutiny awaited the employment law proposals contained in *Looking to the Future* (Labour Party 1990a) which was drafted under the auspices of Meacher's replacement, Tony Blair. Developing the ideas of *Meet the Challenge Make the Change*, the document placed heavy emphasis on the importance of investment in education and training, and stressed the importance of an economy founded on partnership. The employees' charter was compared to the European Commission's social charter, which would be signed by a Labour Government the moment it took office. In addition, there were proposals for an industrial court which would have competence to adjudicate in industrial disputes. Properly conducted ballots prior to industrial action were seen as a prerequisite for fair legal treatment. The right to be represented by a trade union was stressed and the legal right to union recognition was regarded as essential. Sympathy action would be permissible in circumstances where there was a shared direct interest of an occupational or professional nature. Finally, secondary picketing would be allowed where a second employer was directly assisting a first employer in the frustration of a legitimate industrial dispute (Labour Party 1990a: 11–13, 32–5).

These proposals cleared the crucial hurdle at the 1990 TUC conference and were passed rather more comfortably at that year's Labour Party conference. Blair was keen to show that the Party was at last addressing long-neglected themes in British industrial relations. However, Michael Howard, the Conservative Employment Secretary described the proposals as 'a charter for easier strikes, more frequent strikes and more damaging strikes'. Labour, he argued, was advocating a return to the 1970s and it was fraudulent of the unions to claim that they actually supported some of the changes installed by the Thatcher Government. Arthur Scargill and Ron Todd would 'laugh all the way to the picket line' (*The Guardian*, 4 September 1990). Labour's opponents obviously felt more comfortable when interrogating the Policy Review in terms of the old agenda. Particular attention was paid to the precise definition of secondary industrial action, the role and operation of the industrial court and the procedures by which union recognition would be achieved (e.g. *Financial Times*, 2 July 1990; *The Times*, 4 September 1990).

The concept of partnership surfaced again in the 1991 document, *Opportunity Britain*. Unions were given status as social partners in the formulation of the proposed national economic assessment (Labour Party 1991b: 12). Partnership was a key concept in the Policy Review process. The same could be said of the idea of individual rights which sat at the centre of the substantive policy proposals. The emphasis on individual rights, according to Tony Blair, should not be interpreted as a retreat from the important notion of the collective. The individual and the collective should be seen as complementary concepts and not mutually exclusive categories. The collective was a means by which individual rights could be advanced and protected, but all individuals had rights against any form of collective – company, State or union (interview with the author, 7 February 1991).

**BEYOND THATCHERISM?**

The Policy Review's concern with individual rights forms the starting point of a comparison with Thatcherism, which always claimed to act in the interests of the individual worker against the oppressive collectivism of the trade union. This view was derived from the ideas of neo-liberals such as Hayek who saw trade unions as monopolies which interfere with the free workings of the market, inducing imprudent government intervention and coercing individual workers (Hayek 1960: 265; 1978: 66–77). The substantial intervention by the Thatcher Governments in the field of trade union law was justified in terms of the liberation of the market and the freeing of the individual worker from the coercive grip of trade unions (Mitchell 1987: 33–5). An impressive body of literature has built up on the relationship between Thatcherism and trade unionism (e.g. Coates 1989; Coates and Topham 1986; Longstreth 1988; MacInnes 1987; Milward and Stevens 1986; Mitchell 1987). While a scholarly consensus appears to suggest that the Thatcherite claim to have changed the nature of British industrial relations was essentially hyperbole, most analysts would concede that the sheer scale of the Conservative's legislative agenda combined with the confrontational discourse employed had repercussions for the political arena as a whole and the Labour Party in particular.

It would be mistaken to regard the Conservative's legislative record on trade union law as the only manifestation of Thatcherite intervention in industrial relations. Colin Crouch (1986, 1989) has suggested that the relationship between Thatcherism and trade unions can be described in terms of the following classification: actions seeking to weaken the position of workers and unions *vis-à-vis* employers; actions reducing the institutional regulation of conflict, thereby exposing industrial relations to the free market; actions diminishing the legitimacy of trade unions as partners in national public life; and legal measures aiming to increase the power of union members or workers in relation to trade unions (see also Longstreth 1988).

This type of classification allows the inclusion of the broad macro-economic thrust of early Thatcherism, which rejected the view that there was a role for the State in the preservation of full employment and pursued a policy of pay restraint in the public sector which amounted to an imposed and non-negotiable incomes policy (Thompson 1986: 134). It also obviously covers the five Acts of Parliament which dealt with trade unions and industrial relations by narrowing the lawfulness of secondary action, altering the definitions of trade disputes, undermining trade union immunities and legislating against the closed shop. Compulsory secret ballots were introduced for internal union elections, the legitimation of strike action and the maintenance of political funds to the Labour Party. A further element lay with Thatcherism's distaste for corporatism which was demonstrated by the marked decline in minister – union contacts and the downgrading or abolition of several tripartite institutions.

It is important to place the Labour proposals in the context of Thatcherism even though some commentators have emphasized that the Policy Review reflected a long-run evolution in party thinking (Shaw 1990; Smith, chapter 2). The Labour leadership was also keen to stress that the Policy Review should be seen as a response to developments in the real world and not a capitulation to elements of Thatcherism. Nevertheless, a body of opinion within the labour movement did suggest that Labour's new industrial relations policies amounted to a sort of 'crypto-Thatcherism', since significant parts of the Thatcherite reforms had been retained and the policy took as its starting point the rights of individual workers. For example, the Policy Review accepted the use of secret ballots in union elections and strike votes, the retention in some circumstances of the sequestration of union funds, the view that the closed shop is unacceptable and the limitation of both secondary and mass picketing. Therefore, it was argued that the party's policy-makers had come to accept the weakening of the trade union movement in several key areas and, as some pointed out, the new policy did not even comply with the codes of the International Labour Organisation (ILO).

The emphasis on individual rights certainly suggested that the party leadership would not accept the dominance of the collective over the individual. Although the stress on the individual worker hinted at 'liberal' preconceptions, the emphasis on social partnership between employer, unions and the State and the recognition of trade unions as a valuable component in the regeneration of the British economy militated against a wholesale neo-liberal interpretation. Thatcherism sought to shift the legal balance in industrial relations firmly in the direction of employers, whilst pulling the State out of this sphere. The Labour leadership claimed to be interested in the establishment of a fair and balanced system of industrial relations law which would operate in the light of a government taking responsibility for the conditions of economic success (Labour Party 1990a: 6) and an economy founded on partnership.

The concept of partnership had appeared in the 1983 Labour election manifesto, but in a rather different guise. Labour's plans for the socialist regeneration of Britain 'can be carried through if a Labour government commands the support of the other great democratic institutions in the land . . . Labour is the only party which desires and can secure the working partnership between the government and the trade unions essential to national recovery' (Labour Party 1983a: 5). Unions were to be involved in the construction of a national economic assessment which would plan the growth of national output and determine the allocation of resources and the distribution of income. They were allocated a definite and central place within the policy-making process. The Policy Review fell short of such wholesale 'corporatism', but nevertheless revived the idea of an annual economic assessment in which unions (as well as employers) would have a key role. However, the concept of partnership contained in the Policy Review did not denote the links between the Labour Party and the unions but rather the unity of purpose between the State and the social partners (unions and employers). Therefore, while it would be incorrect to describe the Policy Review as corporatist, there are grounds for suggesting that it aimed to reverse the Thatcherite policies of withdrawing from the institutional regulation of industrial conflict and attacking the legitimacy of trade union participation in public life. The major difference was that union involvement in national policy decisions was to be limited to discussions about Britain's economic circumstances, feasible policy options and the coordination of collective bargaining (Labour Party 1991b: 12).

## THE EUROPEAN DIMENSION

Thatcherism acted as an important contextual factor in the Labour leadership's reconsideration of its industrial relations agenda. The same could be said for the growing influence on British politics of developments in the European Community.

Of particular importance was the debate which evolved in response to the European Commission's '1992' package where the Labour Party and the trade unions became increasingly identified with the struggle for a social dimension to compensate for the liberalization of the European market (see Rosamond 1990). From the point of view of industrial relations the debate came to surround the issues raised by a number of Commission proposals, most notably those involving the reactivation of the *Vredeling* directive on employee rights to information and consultation, the European Company Statutes which would require (for companies choosing to operate as European concerns) the implementation of some form of employee participation and finally the social charter (see Teague 1989). In Britain the debate took on added significance because of the Thatcher Government's hostility to measures which would either interfere with the free market of '1992' or pose a threat to British national sovereignty.

Labour's embrace of the social charter was swift and a policy document supporting its provisions appeared soon after the Strasbourg summit of December 1989 (Labour Party 1989c). This document aimed to demonstrate the proximity of Labour's policies to those of the Commission and show the extent to which the Thatcher Government was out of step with the other member states. The great advantage of the charter was that it dealt with issues such as the improvement of living and working conditions, employment rights, vocational training, equal opportunities and health and safety. These were issues with which the Party could deal comfortably; the social charter was not preoccupied with British definitions of industrial relations or the intricacies of trade union law. It gave the Labour leadership an ideal opportunity both to show how its 'rights agenda' matched the European industrial relations agenda and to criticize the intransigence of the Conservatives without becoming embroiled in the old 'conflict agenda'. It allowed the exploitation of an area of obvious Conservative weakness (the EC) to advance Labour's case for its new industrial relations agenda.

## THE REACTION OF THE UNIONS

For all the advantages afforded by the European dimension, it was still likely that the party leadership's proposals would be imperilled unless they gained the support of the trade unions. The mathematics of the Labour Party conference gave the affiliated unions a potentially important role in policy approval, if not necessarily in policy formulation. More importantly, the willingness of the unions to work within the parameters set by the revised policy would partly determine the efficacy of the new agenda. Industrial relations issues cut across the classic divide between the industrial and political wings of the labour movement and in some circumstances – for example, *In Place of Strife* – have led not only to problems in Labour–union relations but also to 'policy failure' (on the relationship, see Harrison 1960; Minkin 1980; Simpson 1973; Taylor 1987).

Perhaps the most crucial test of Labour's proposals occurred at the 1990 TUC conference which endorsed a General Council statement in support of the Policy Review on industrial relations and passed a composite motion, sponsored by the National Communications Union, which reiterated the party leadership's line. However, an opposition coalesced around a dissenting motion moved by the (unaffiliated) local government union, NALGO. The NALGO motion claimed to support the broad thrust of the new Labour position, but revealed that forces within the union movement were uneasy with the use of ballots, the Policy Review's tight definition of secondary action and its ambiguity on the whole question of trade union immunities. This second group was joined by unions such as the National Union of Mineworkers (NUM) which remained committed to the abolition of all Thatcherite industrial relations legislation. Some unions, notably the TGWU and the Society of

Graphical and Allied Trades (SOGAT), found themselves in a highly ambiguous position through declaring support for both composite motions on the grounds that they supported Labour's proposals, but with reservations in particular areas (see *The Guardian*, 4 September 1990).

The Labour leadership could claim that the unions as a whole had accepted the basic premise of the Policy Review: that there should be a legally enforceable charter of workers' rights. Indeed, the number of unions which remained tied to the old agenda and the abolition of the Thatcherite laws had clearly diminished since 1988. The concept of workers' rights had become increasingly appealing to many in the trade union movement and this was a transition aided by the campaigns of the TUC and several of the unions in support of the social charter. Even those unions, such as NALGO, which displayed some scepticism about the charter none the less looked at the means by which it could be improved (e.g. NALGO 1990). In other words the debate within the trade union movement had moved away from the 'conflict agenda' towards the 'rights agenda'.

In spite of the apparent consensus, specific and problematic issues continued to divide the trade union movement. All unions claimed to support Labour's proposals for a statutory minimum wage, but by the summer of 1991 it was apparent that some unions, especially those representing the skilled workforce, had serious reservations about the prudence of its immediate implementation (Baxter 1991; *The Guardian*, 12 June 1991). In addition, some unions had become suspicious of the increasing influence of the GMB in Labour's policy-making circles. The proximity of Labour's notion of a national economic assessment to the GMB's preference for the compression of the annual pay round into a period of three months did not go unnoticed. This led some union leaders to suspect a hidden agenda of a return to an incomes policy (Baxter 1991: 23). The TGWU was committed to the party policy of a fair and balanced system of industrial relations law, but remained adamant that this should replace all anti-trade union legislation (*The Guardian*, 25 June 1991).

The substantial block of unions with specific reservations over details of the new Labour proposals should not be ignored, and it would be imprudent to overstate the degree to which a consensus on Labour's proposals had come to exist within the trade union movement. The waning of union opposition to the Policy Review may have indicated a convergence of union and party priorities, but also demonstrated the value attached by the majority of the unions to the achievement of a majority Labour Government.

## CONCLUSIONS

The Labour Party emerged from the Policy Review process with a set of policies designed to meet the realities of industrial relations in the 1990s and carefully constructed to assuage both trade union and electoral opinion. The main preoccupation of the leadership was to shift the debate on industrial relations onto a more favourable terrain for the Party. This meant moving away from the connotation of industrial relations as industrial conflict, towards the construction of an agenda based on positive rights and social partnership. This was incorporated into Labour's overall economic strategy which made the link between social justice and economic efficiency. The acquisition of the necessary political support, although not fully achieved, was certainly facilitated by the emergence of the EC's social charter and the repercussions which that had for domestic politics.

A number of potential problems still remained though. First, it is difficult to predict the extent to which the delicate intra-party consensus could be maintained, especially if a Labour Government found itself operating in a situation where the discipline of the Exchange Rate Mechanism proved an insufficient curb on inflation. The resort to an incomes policy would certainly damage the goodwill of the unions. There is no guarantee that the proposed national economic assessment might not evolve into a forum for wage restraint since it was seen as 'a crucial means of informing the participants in the collective bargaining process' (Labour Party 1991b: 12). Second, as a succession of commentators have noted, Thatcherism was unable to erode long-established British industrial relations practices. A Labour Government, although armed with a legal framework and a hands-on approach, might find its aim of creating a new culture of partnership in British industry an extremely difficult project to accomplish. Finally, the party leadership paid little attention to the formulation and implementation of industrial relations policy at the EC level. It assumed that a majority Labour Government would enact and improve on the provisions of the social charter. Consequently, there was very little criticism of the redrafting of the social charter which removed provision for a minimum wage and implied that the articles of the charter could be implemented in accordance with national practices. In other words, the party leadership made no attempt to struggle for compulsory implementation of the charter regardless of the nature of national governments. The Labour Party used the social charter adroitly to alter the industrial relations debate at the domestic level. But its leaders seemed reluctant to concede that industrial relations policy could be implemented by an agency which was not based at Westminster.

## ACKNOWLEDGEMENTS

This chapter is based on a paper originally presented to the annual conference of the Political Studies Association at the University of Lancaster in April 1991. A number of helpful comments were made, for which I am grateful. I would also like to thank Gallup for permission to quote from the *Gallup Political Index*.

# 8 The Labour Party and energy policy

*Simon Bromley*

In order to grasp the significance of the recent changes in Labour Party thinking on energy policy it is necessary to appreciate something of the context in which post-war energy policy has been formulated and how this has now radically altered. For it is only when the new policy proposals are viewed from this broader perspective that it is possible to offer an assessment of both their overall cogency and their prospects of successful implementation. Furthermore, without some understanding of the wider energy environment in which policy has been formulated, whether in or out of office, the nature of energy policy formation in the Labour Party is difficult to judge. Accordingly, the following is divided into four parts. To begin with, I briefly outline some of the salient trends in post-war energy use and the principal policy developments up until 1979. Next, I consider some of the most significant transformations of energy markets and policies that have taken place since 1979 and which have formed the background against which the Labour Party has tried to fashion a coherent response. Following this, I examine the development of a more explicit energy strategy by the Labour Party in response to the changing nature of the energy environment, contrasting the thinking of *Labour's Programme 1982* with the results of the Policy Review process. Finally, I assess the prospects for the new policy agenda in the light of the major issues which are likely to face any Government in the 1990s.

## POST-WAR ENERGY POLICY

After the Second World War, all the economies of Western Europe were strongly dependent on coal. In what was later to become the bloc of European Community states, for example, the share of coal in total primary energy requirement (TPER) was 75 per cent in 1950. However, during the post-war boom, there was a general and rapid shift away from coal. Oil and gas captured most of the industrial, railroad, commercial and residential fuel markets and thereby surpassed coal as energy sources in much of the Western world. Coal use was increasingly confined to electric power generation and coking coal was used for iron and steel – the former market expanded rapidly until the recessions of the early 1980s, while the latter was stagnant for much of the period and then declined rapidly in North America and Western Europe. The net result was that the share of coal in TPER for the EC states fell to 20 per cent in 1971. On the other hand, the share of oil in TPER rose from 10 per cent in 1950 to 60 per cent in 1971, and most of this oil was sourced from the Middle East and North Africa.

Now, whilst the United Kingdom experienced a similar pattern of change to that seen in the rest of Western Europe, its overall development was marked by a number of particularities. In the first instance, the dominance achieved by coal in the UK economy was quite exceptional – still providing 90 per cent of all energy needs in 1947. The general threat posed to coal by petroleum, therefore, was doubly exaggerated in the UK case by the most important difference from continental Europe: the discovery of large reserves of natural gas and oil in the North Sea. In addition, the UK was strongly positioned within the international oil industry by virtue of the activities of British Petroleum and Royal-Dutch/Shell. As a result, the relative and absolute decline of coal was paced by two major changes:

> first came the dramatic penetration of the energy market by cheap Middle East oil in the fifties and then, just when it seemed that the coal industry would experience rebirth in the aftermath of the 1973 oil price explosion, cheap natural gas from the North Sea flooded the market. The arrival of these two waves of competition corresponds to the major phases of contraction in the industrial market (hit by oil) and the gas and domestic markets (hit by natural gas).
>
> (Wright 1986: 3)

Still, it is important to see that neither in the West European case, nor in that of the UK, were these developments the result of the operation of free markets in energy production and distribution. Throughout the post-war period all Governments in the advanced capitalist countries have intervened directly and extensively in both their domestic energy 'markets' and those of others (Bromley 1991; Samuels 1987). Most obviously, the cheap oil of the post-war boom was underwritten by the political and military role of the leading Western states, above all the United States, in the Middle East. Second, the large, vertically-integrated majors effected a degree of cross-subsidization of fuel oil (which competed against coal) by petrol (which had no direct competitors) in their European markets. Finally, the fiscal incentives adopted by European Governments reinforced oil company policy by keeping taxes high on petrol and low on fuel oil. At the same time, public investment in coal was held back.

Against this background, UK energy policy until 1974 was basically one of nationalization followed by a purely pragmatic regulation, with little variation according to political party. Indeed until the 1960s, energy policy received little official attention. Both the *Simon Report* (1946) and the *Ridley Report* (1952) argued against a strategic plan for the energy sector as a whole, recommending instead competition between fuels to encourage efficiency in what were in many cases otherwise, effective monopolies. Inter-industry competition, set within a general framework of public ownership and the financial requirement to break-even, was reckoned to be the best route to an efficient use of fuel. But such competition only became a reality in the late 1950s when the technology to use oil for electricity generation became available. It was speeded up in the 1960s and early 1970s by the public/private sector led exploitation of North Sea gas and the private sector led exploitation of North Sea oil. In addition, there was continuous support from the mid-1950s through to the late 1970s for a series of nuclear power programmes. The discovery of North Sea gas, in combination with the launching of the ambitious advanced, gas-cooled reactor programme, simply meant that the central concern of government energy policy would be how to run-down the coal industry. Between 1957–71 around 400 of 700 pits were closed with the loss of 400,000 jobs from a total of 700,000 – falling demand and technological progress were equally responsible for this (Burns *et al.* 1985). As a result, coal's share of TPER fell steadily from 90 per cent in 1947 to 50 per cent by 1969, and to 33 per cent in 1974.

Social democratic attempts to plan energy production – as in the proposals for a National Hydrocarbons Corporation in the mid-1960s, or in the White Papers associated with the National Plan, *Fuel Policy* (1965) and *Fuel Policy* (1967) – failed even to get off the ground. It is certainly true that some forecasting was adopted, and energy policy was more closely integrated with concerns about the balance of payments. But overall, Labour followed the liberal, non-interventionist policies set by the Conservatives, whilst taking a slightly tougher stance on the distributive question of how to tax monopoly profits by using the British Gas Corporation's monopsonist position. The failure to consolidate a more interventionist, coordinated approach to the formulation of energy policy meant that control over key decisions pertaining to the rate of exploitation of North Sea reserves increasingly passed to a private sector that was dominated by the 'seven sisters' (the seven largest oil companies).

Then in 1973–4 came the first of the so-called 'oil shocks', with the price of oil rising roughly eightfold between 1973 and 1979. Competitive changes in the international oil industry, adverse developments in the strategic position of the United States and a greater degree of market control by OPEC had demonstrated the macroeconomic and energy dilemmas associated with high levels of import dependence for oil. The common response among the Governments of the advanced capitalist states was to attempt to reduce their reliance on oil imports. In particular, they sought to increase the role of coal and nuclear power in electricity generation, to expand the role of natural gas in other markets, to increase the production of oil (and gas and coal) outside the OPEC sources, and to encourage the conservation of energy in domestic and industrial markets.

The Labour Governments of 1974–9 tried to cope with this new situation in a number of ways. In the first place, it pushed for a rapid expansion of North Sea oil exploration and production, aiming for self-sufficiency and net exports. Notwithstanding the establishment of the British National Oil Corporation (BNOC), and its equity participation in a range of North Sea developments, the dominance of private (predominantly, US) capital was further consolidated by the rapid pace of development. In fact, the left's agenda for full public control to be accomplished through BNOC and the renegotiation of existing licensing contracts was essentially defeated (Cameron 1983). Rather, rents and revenues from the North Sea were geared to the priorities of stabilization policy, coming under normal Treasury control, and were thereby denied to the putative strategy of industrial modernization that was proposed by the left. Second, the Government adopted the *Plan for Coal* (1974), finding capital expenditure for the expansion of deep-mined coal and the introduction of new mining technology. Together with the settlement of the miners' pay claim, this had the effect of insulating the NUM from the industrial struggles of the period. In the case of nuclear power, Tony Benn managed a stalling operation in the build-up of a new round of the programme. But the PWR lobby in private engineering and construction companies, as well as in the nuclear industry and the CEGB, went substantially unchallenged, despite growing evidence of its uneconomic character (Cannell and Chudleigh 1983; Sweet 1983).

Overall, Labour's maximalist policy was supply-determined and paid no attention to where the demand for all this fuel might be found – to describe *Plan for Coal* as a back-of-an-envelope calculation is too polite. The attempt to appease the range of producer interests, from the majors in the North Sea through the workers in nuclear power stations, to underground miners, simply stored up problems for coal in the future. This was especially true given that the reduced rates of growth after the early 1970s meant that the rate of growth of demand for electricity would fall, thereby counteracting the advantage coal derived from the increases in the price of oil. Once again, the opportunity for a strategic review of the energy industries was foregone and no long-term planning mechanisms were set in place. Instead, the position remained one of (regulated) competition between the nationalized utilities and a general requirement to break-even in the public sector.

## ENERGY POLICY SINCE 1979: CONTINUITY AND CHANGE

From 1979 onwards, some strands of energy policy broadly followed the parameters set by the Labour Party. In the crucial area of the North Sea, for example, the activities of private companies remained unhindered. Indeed, favourable changes to the tax regime encouraged further development, thus expanding the sector's contributions to the balance of payments and state revenues (Devereux and Morris 1983). This time, however, the resources thus derived were geared to macroeconomic management of a deflationary cast, driving up the exchange rate, financing capital outflows and inflicting severe damage on domestic productive capital (Hall and Atkinson 1983).

Elsewhere, there were a number of significant new departures. To begin with, there have been a range of initiatives designed to open and liberalize the energy markets (Porter *et al.* 1986: chapter 5). Liberalization has been facilitated by a general tightening of the external financing limits of the nationalized industries which, together with the maintenance of the restrictions on competing with, and raising capital from the private sector, have resulted in the imposition of restructuring packages to meet these new financial disciplines. A more open market has been encouraged by the removal of past constraints on the internationalization of energy supply as price considerations have been privileged over those of security of supply and the balance of payments. This new focus on market-based disciplines was also introduced into the heart of the energy supply nexus through the 'joint understanding' negotiated between the CEGB and the NCB, allowing the CEGB to use 'world market' prices to pass productivity increases in the mines into the balance sheets of the electricity generators (Gibbon and Bromley 1990). The chances of reversing this shift to the market have been further limited by the devolution of decision-making to private capital as a consequence of a spate of privatizations – e.g. BNOC/Britoil, the BGC and the CEGB. Significantly, it is only in the case of nuclear power that the Government has been prepared to countenance an ideological retreat: for as the turn to the market increasingly exposed the 'Alice in Wonderland' economics of nuclear power to public scrutiny, so the Government has moved to safeguard a nuclear future by re-regulating this domain. Finally, a range of institutional changes – the abolition of the corporatist Energy Commission, a significant shift to using the Monopolies and Mergers Commission to enforce market-based discipline in the public sector, most clearly in the case of coal, and the consequent downgrading of the role of the Department of Energy in formulating overall energy policy – have further reduced the capacity of the State to regulate these newly liberalized and open energy markets. (The present Conservative Government has made it clear that it is sympathetic to the calls from such international energy corporations as BP and the think tanks of the right – from the Institute of Economic Affairs in particular – for the abolition of the Department of Energy and the transfer of its residual functions to the decidedly liberal Department of Trade and Industry.)

The composite legacy of these developments, then, has been the privatization of most of the energy supply industries in the UK, a significant reassertion of the role of market forces in the determination of future decisions in the sector, and a growing internationalization of the sources of supply. More specifically, the major unresolved questions concern the future of the electricity supply industries – the coal industry, nuclear power and the role of alternatives and renewables – and the forms of regulation which will apply to an increasingly international and European (rather than national) set of energy markets.

## FROM *LABOUR'S PROGRAMME 1982* TO THE POLICY REVIEW

*Labour's Programme 1982*, which was to form the basis for its electoral promises in 1983, restated the importance of the objectives the Party had defined in the 1970s and the need for a considerable extension of state-directed planning to achieve these ends. At this juncture, Labour's policy agenda was still explicitly based on a demand for corporatist concertation in the process of policy formulation; the need for a state-led definition of, and planning for, national objectives; and the importance of direct regulation of the market for successful policy implementation. Thus the *Programme* stated that:

> An immediate task would be to re-establish the Energy Commission, composed of representatives from the TUC, CBI, the Department of Energy and consumer bodies. The Energy Conservation Agency [to be established] would also be represented on the Commission. A primary duty of the Energy Commission would be to advise the Secretary of State in its drawing up of an energy plan to be presented ultimately for discussion by parliament. The plan would ensure that the interests of all energy producers and consumers are fully accounted for. Meanwhile, the Department of Energy would prepare an annual energy budget or statement, which reports on the progress of the energy plan and gives a clear indication of how resources are allocated to the various energy sectors. The Secretary of State for Energy would be responsible for the contents of the energy plan and annual statement and present both to parliament for full discussion.
>
> (Labour Party 1982a: 60)

Within this framework, the Labour Party made a number of specific proposals with regard to the principles that should guide energy pricing and the conservation of resources. Whilst prices should increase sufficiently to fund new investment, a comprehensive set of allowances would have to be introduced in order to guarantee equity and abolish fuel poverty. Conservation would be promoted by an ambitious programme of public investment, directed towards the domestic, industrial and commercial sectors, which would simultaneously contribute to job creation. In regard to the major sources of energy, once again considerable emphasis was put on the expansion of the coal industry: the Party proposed a sustained increase of coal output, a return to an emphasis on physical planning rather than financial indicators, a new concern to develop clean-coal and more fuel-efficient technologies, and an end to the rigged competition with foreign producers that were the beneficiaries of state subsidy. For gas and oil the policy centred on two related objectives: first, the introduction of stricter depletion controls in order to extend the time-scale of UK self-sufficiency; and second, an expansion of the role of the public sector in the North Sea. The latter was to be accomplished by a reversal of the privatization of the BGC and the restoration of the powers of BNOC. In addition, the *Programme* reaffirmed the party's 'commitment that BP should be brought fully into public ownership, and that, in line with our commitment to bring North Sea oil into public ownership, BP and BNOC together should be responsible for all future exploration and development' (ibid.: 63). In the case of nuclear power, the PWR programme being promoted by the Conservative Government was opposed; a commitment was made that all future nuclear development would occur in the public sector; and the work of the prototype fast breeder reactor at Dounreay was supported. For future electricity generation, Labour proposed that to help support the coal industry 'a great deal of new plant should be coal-fired', and 'that plant built for oil use should, where practical, be converted to coal' (ibid.: 64). The *Programme* also argued the need for the development of combined heat and power schemes to provide cheap urban heating and to maintain employment. Finally, in what looked like something of an afterthought, there was a brief mention of the role of renewables: a promise to increase funds on research and development 'as fast as is practicable' (ibid.: 65).

As is evident from this brief review, *Labour's Programme 1982* carried forward most of the previous emphases of the left and those trade unions which represented workers in the power industries, advancing the case both for a reversal of moves towards the market made by the Conservatives and for some new extensions of the role of the state – for example, the promise to develop a national energy plan and the proposal to take BP fully into public ownership. In other respects also the *Programme* represented continuity with the past: most notably, Labour policy focused almost exclusively on the problem of supply without making any attempt to discuss questions of the type or quantity of demand that the future might bring. Finally, despite the ritual obeisance paid to Labour's internationalism, the whole set of proposals considered as a strategy was strongly nationalistic. Conservation of 'national' resources, promotion of UK commercial and industrial interests, obdurate refusal to recognize the UK's growing integration into international energy markets, and the promise to leave the EC – all of these were in tune with that protectionist gamble of a social democracy on the defensive which characterized the rest of the party's economic agenda.

As with the previous and similar proposals from the trade unions and the Labour left, a number of questions could be asked. How could energy planning be taken seriously if there was no reckoning of projected demand? Furthermore, given that proposals from the left for more public ownership and more planning in the energy sector had been defeated twice before – in the period of the abortive National Plan and during 1974–5 – what reasons were there to suggest that these promises would not suffer a similar fate? Indeed, would not the moves towards the market and a greater international openness, which had been systematically promoted since 1979, simply make Labour's task still more difficult? Though never really challenged on these questions, in large part because of the relatively low electoral salience of energy-related questions, the Labour Party clearly did not have any convincing answers.

In what ways, then, do the proposals that have issued from the Policy Review process differ from this agenda? Let us begin by outlining the current state of Labour Party thinking. To start with the general framework, *Meet the Challenge, Make the Change* argues that 'the ideology of the "free market" is nowhere more misguided than in energy policy' and that the two considerations which should govern long-term policy are 'the interests of the consumer and the environment'. (Labour Party 1989a: 16) In *Looking to the Future* the Party maintains that because of the scale of investment in the energy sector, together with the typically long lead-times that are involved, the 'government must be involved in strategic decision-making' (Labour Party 1990a: 16). The role of the Government in this process is to secure the interests of energy consumers, the country as a whole and the health and safety of those who work in the sector, as well as that of the general public. In addition, security, supply and the balance of payments are to be accorded priority. In order to secure this framework for strategic decision-making, Labour now proposes a thorough institutional overhaul of energy policy formulation. The Party will establish an Energy Efficiency Agency (EEA) and an agency for the development of renewable forms of energy, and both of these bodies will be required to provide parliament with annual reports. Within the Department of Energy there will be a diversion of R&D resources from nuclear power towards renewables. Labour will create an Environmental Protection Agency with 'teeth and resources', and there will be an upgrading of the environmental protection functions of the Department of the Environment. Further, as part of the introduction of a Freedom of Information Act, Labour will establish registers of environmental information which will be available in online electronic form to outsiders.

Substantively, as outlined in Labour's major statement on the environment, *An Earthly Chance*, the Party is committed to a number of changes in the current direction of UK energy policy. First, and most generally, Labour wants to encourage the conservation of energy use rather than the simple expansion of supply. This will be bolstered by the second major area of proposed changes, the organization of the electricity supply industries. Here Labour recognizes the need for the introduction of least cost planning. This is an arrangement whereby utilities must consider whether expected demand can be satisfied more economically by investing in the consumer's energy efficiency rather than in new generating capacity. To promote this, and to gain strategic leverage in the electricity industries, Labour plans to bring the National Grid company under public control, giving it the responsibility for security of supply, the promotion of alternative energy sources and the development of energy efficiency. A third change that would also contribute to energy conservation will be the imposition of specified investment targets on the gas and electricity utilities for insulation, conversion and efficiency measures. Two further proposals will also contribute to this overall approach: the EEA is to be given the brief of promoting a national efficiency programme; and a new Consumer Protection Commission will take over the duties of the energy regulators, placing more emphasis on environmental and conser-vation issues by developing a pricing structure which encourages these ends.

Other areas where the Labour Party is committed to specific proposals include the future of coal, the use of natural gas, the question of nuclear power and the development of alternative energy sources. Labour is committed to a continued major role for coal in electricity generation, the reversal of the currently rising trend in coal imports, and the conjunction of CHP schemes and clean coal technologies (fluidized bed combustion and retrofitting flue gas de-sulphurization) to improve the thermal efficiency of generation and to reduce global warming. Reinforcing this defence of coal is the Party's scepticism regarding gas. The Labour Party is opposed to what it calls the 'dash for gas' in the form of combined-cycle, gas-fired power stations, arguing that gas is a premium fuel which should not be allowed to further undercut the market for coal. *An Earthly Chance* also argues the need for a gas-gathering system in the North Sea to prevent the wasteful flaring of some 5 per cent of UK gas production every year. In the case of nuclear power, the Labour Party has thus far refused to give a commitment to abandon Sizewell B and has endorsed, subject to a review, the Thermal Oxide Reprocessing

Plant at Sellafield (due on stream at the end of 1992). However, the Party is committed not to invest in further nuclear capacity, nor will it continue with proposals currently in the planning process. As a result of these actions, Labour predicts that nuclear power will be all but redundant in the UK by 2000. In general, the Party believes that the economics of nuclear power, in combination with the still unresolved safety and environmental problems, render it publicly unacceptable. As to the alternatives, the Party is proposing to encourage the use of biomass by the local building of CHP schemes using landfill gas (methane) or the incineration of domestic waste. In addition to the general shift of resources to renewables noted above, the Labour Party is specifically committed to the reactivation of work on the potential for wave power, a full consideration of the prospects for tidal power, and the further development of wind power.

As is clear from this summary, the Labour Party's current proposals represent a clear departure from the past, producer-interest dominated agenda. This can be seen most clearly in the new importance accorded to environmental questions in general, and to the problems of energy conservation and fuel efficiency in particular. Also evident, and of equal importance, is the switch from a focus on direct public ownership and planning to a concern with the appropriate forms of market regulation and the means of influencing strategic decision-making. Notwithstanding the continued commitment to coal, the overall thrust of Labour policy now gives a much higher priority to conservation on the demand side (always an afterthought in the past) and to exploring new, renewable or alternative sources of supply. Proposals for the public ownership of North Sea resources have been unceremoniously abandoned. In part these changes reflect the new environmental agenda which all political parties have had to adapt to. They also reflect changes in the thinking of the TUC, where it is recognized that 'an acceptable balance between energy and environmental objectives has now become a main pillar in the application of sustainable development' (TUC 1990: 78). Equally, the TUC shares the Labour Party's hostility to the free-market approach of the Conservative Party, arguing the need for 'a new strategy encompassing direct regulations, enforceable targets and standards, subsidies and incentives' (ibid.: 78). More generally, however, the transformation in Labour Party thinking on energy policy is of a piece with the more general shift to the market embraced throughout the Policy Review. For whilst Labour claim that the market needs to be regulated in the interests of social justice and economic efficiency, and hence proposes a veritable plethora of new agencies and commissions to effect this, it has to a considerable extent accepted the neo-liberal critique of those institutions and mechanisms which sought to override or even supplant market decision-making.

As elaborated so far, the main applications of market-based forms of regulation can be seen in the proposal to introduce least cost planning for energy supplies and in the commitment that the Consumer Protection Commission will encourage environmental concerns by developing an appropriate pricing structure. The aim in each case is to rig the calculations of agents in the market so that both the adoption of best practice techniques (for example, selling energy efficiency, rather than more energy, to consumers) and the alignment of private and social costs (as in the case of the externalities of pollution) are achieved through normal market activity. This presumes that the best practice is known and that social costs can be identified, measured and evaluated. If this is to amount to more than a series of *ad hoc* responses to particular problems, then there will have to be significant degree of overall coordination and planning. Thus far, the Labour Party has not given any specific information about how this would be done or what its particular priorities would be (say between coal use and the reduction of carbon dioxide emissions). But given that the information base required in any such planning could only be developed in close association with the main producer interests, and given also that policy implementation would depend on their cooperation, it is difficult to see how the planning process itself can escape their influence. If Labour Party policy is to work here, then genuine independence and authority would have to be granted to the EEA and the Consumer Protection Commission.

## AN EARTHLY CHANCE?

In the field of energy policy, this acceptance of the market takes the form of an apparent innocence concerning the real workings of national and international energy markets. Without going into detail, it is necessary to sketch in some of the more important of recent developments by way of providing a backdrop against which to measure Labour's prospects of successful policy implementation. Beginning with coal, during the 1980s there was a rapid expansion in the international trade of steam coal for power stations and this has been dominated by opencast mining controlled by mining and energy multinationals (Rutledge and Wright 1985). Given the falling demand in industrial and power-generating markets, this new production resulted in low prices throughout the 1980s. This meant, for example, that in 1989 (after four years of successful restructuring in British Coal) delivery prices to the UK were roughly one-third cheaper than UK-produced coal, and in 1990 they were still one-quarter cheaper. The use of these coal prices to beat down the price that British Coal could get from the CEGB, together with the changed financial position of the nationalized industries and rising unemployment, provided the context for the recent developments in the coal industry. Yet the coal that is traded internationally, and thus the import prices which the CEGB use, represents about 4 per cent of world coal production and originates from a few dedicated mines and subsidized dumping. By this mechanism, deep-mined reserves in the UK are sterilized for potentially short-term, cheap imports.

Indeed, the international market in coal has been developing alongside the closure of European deep-mined coal. Both the EC and Japan have expanded their imports from the international market. This trend is set to continue. Given the continuing desire of the advanced Western states to reduce their dependence on Middle East oil, the EC is planning to increase the role of electricity generated by coal (although environmental questions abound as carbon dioxide and acid rain gases present a continuing problem). The new electricity generators in Britain are keen to increase the role of cheap coal and (especially) heavy fuel oil imports in place of BC's deep-mined production. This is leading the latter to close pits, expand super-pits and increase opencast mining.

The growing integration and deregulation of the European (and indeed global) gas industry also poses clear challenges to coal's market. One forecast has suggested that if EC restrictions are removed, and if the North Sea markets are liberalized and Soviet exports increase as planned, then up to 20 per cent of Western Europe's electricity could be generated from gas by 2020 (cf. 3 per cent in 1991). Taken together, then, coal imports and natural gas might yet pose a formidable problem for British Coal and the UK's energy self-sufficiency (current contracts with BC expire in 1993). Both National Power and PowerGen have plans to close old coal-fired plants and build small, combined gas cycle turbine plants (to this end they have joined consortia which bid for North Sea licences); to increase cheap coal imports (this is especially true for PowerGen which has four out of five of its large coal stations near suitable port facilities); and, especially in the case of National Power, to invest in overseas facilities (e.g. coal production or electricity generation). British Coal and other European producers, as well as concerned MEPs, have proposed that the Commission establish a minimum floor price for coal in the EC in order to prevent dumping. (The Commission's own estimate of the sustainable price for coal imports is about one-third higher than current world prices.)

In opposition the Labour Party has been consistently critical of these developments and its MEPs have taken up these questions at an EC level. However, in order to realize its present commitments, a future Labour Government would have to be prepared to effectively ban further coal imports and the building of new, gas-fired power stations. This would involve a significant diminution of the commercial freedom granted to the generating industry when privatized. And if the Commission does not find in favour of BC, then it might also bring the Government into direct conflict with the EC. A sense of the current direction of market trends such as these is all but absent from the Policy Review documents – though not from those of the TUC. In fact, the Party's continued commitment to deep-mined coal production, whilst satisfying obvious producer interests as well as those of long-term energy planning, generally runs counter to its (regulated) market approach. For as we have seen, in this area at least the current logic of the market is operating in the opposite direction.

Significant hurdles remain in the case of nuclear power. After early government encouragement, the nuclear power programme was halted by the privatization of the CEGB; the nuclear component was removed from the sale and allocated to Nuclear Electric and Scottish Nuclear; the Dounreay experimental reactor is to be phased out (1994–7); but the THORP facility at Sellafield and Sizewell B are to go ahead, and consent was given for the Hinckley C station. The maintenance of Nuclear Electric, Scottish Nuclear and THORP in the public sector, in combination with the result of the Hinckley C inquiry, has left the future of the industry indeterminate. The whole question is due for review in 1994. The forces favouring an expansion and relaunch of nuclear power in the mid-1990s are far from beaten. Nuclear Electric has identified a number of possibilities. The short-term option is to use the Sizewell design for a new plant at Hinckley Point; a medium-term possibility is to use the latest French or Japanese designs, as yet unlicensed in the UK; and in the long term, it is suggested that 'inherently safe' reactors could be imported – as yet none exist. In addition, Nuclear Electric argues for a nuclear levy in the form of an environmental credit (because it is suggested that it produces little carbon dioxide, although it produces much more than any non-fossil alternative) as well as a nuclear subsidy since it allegedly maintains security of supply.

In sum, throughout the 1990s governments will face continuing pressures to run-down the coal industry, substituting gas and coal imports for domestic production, and to renew the expansion of nuclear power. On the one hand, the closure of coal capacity will increase the UK's dependence on energy imports and the drain on the balance of payments. On some estimates, UK production of coal could fall by 50 per cent or more by the next decade. (The shift from planning the sector in relation to the economy as a whole, to a consideration of price alone has, of course, meant that the social costs of closing coal capacity, including the shadow price of foreign exchange, go uncalculated.) On the other hand, the previous ability of uneconomic nuclear power to persist in the public sector, and Labour's failure to halt this nonsense, does not give grounds for optimism. Many of the key decisions here will be taken either by the private capital which now dominates the sector or by the EC – Labour has not made it at all clear how it can realistically impose its priorities on these sites of decision-making. At one level, this is entirely realistic – a Labour government could not so impose its priorities. Indeed, whilst the Policy Review documents made some passing references to the EC in the context of energy policy formulation, there is precious little sense that decisions at an EC-level will become increasingly important for the regulation of UK energy markets. In this regard, at least, the TUC position is more clear-sighted than that of the Labour Party, as it notes with concern the 'one-sided emphasis on deregulation and open competition' in current EC policy (TUC 1990: 213).

There is, finally, another relevant area of concern that was not broached in the Policy Review proposals. We have seen that in both current thinking, as well as in the past, the Labour Party has singularly failed to analyse what mechanisms might secure its policy objectives in the face of opposition from the private sector or recalcitrance in the (European) state system. But one of the things that *would* be worth learning from the Conservatives is the art of strategic thinking in the political domain. Perhaps the critics of Labourism are correct: the Party, as presently fashioned, is just not constituted for such activity. But is it really too much to expect that the Labour Party think more carefully about how it could create constituencies of interest and power, outside of the electoral field, which would support its objectives over the medium to long term. To argue this, is, to be sure, to question one of the key but unstated assumptions of the Policy Review process, that policy changes and new ideas are the key to political revival; but sets of policies only begin to become political strategy when, amongst other things, they constitute and organize bases of political and economic support that cannot be readily undermined. To this end, probably the most useful thing that a future Labour Government *could* do would be to genuinely empower regional/local government, community groups and trade unions to develop small-scale, decentralized, alternative and renewable sources of energy supply and projects of conservation. Not only is this desirable in itself, but it might begin both to raise the salience of such decisions in people's lives and to create independent networks of organizations committed to a saner energy strategy. In the long run, it is only the creation of such networks and alternative political and economic constituencies which could impose social priorities over those of the market and an increasingly distant and bureaucratic process of decision-making in the EC. Conservative strategy empowers its shock-troops through the imposition of market forms; the Labour Party and the trade unions need something to counter this. Sadly, by neglecting the question of how to empower collectivities outside of the formal political process, the new agenda of the Policy Review has been premised on denying the relevance of such considerations. Without further campaigning and strategic planning at this level, however, none of Labour's many worthwhile proposals stand much chance of long-term success – the market and, for the present at least, the EC are moving in the other direction.

# 9 The 'greening' of Labour

*Neil Carter*

The environment is now on the political agenda to stay. There can be no political last word on the environment, but I believe that Labour's latest contribution will not only be good for the cause of environmental protection and enhancement, but will give us important political advantages over our opponents.
> (Bryan Gould, Shadow Secretary of State for the Environment, 22 October 1990)

In October 1990 twelve members of the Shadow Cabinet were present for the launch of Labour's 37-page environment document, *An Earthly Chance* which received a positive reception from leading green pressure groups including the Green Alliance, Friends of the Earth and Greenpeace (*The Independent*, 16 October 1990). Yet, as recently as 1986, despite ritualistic references to the issue in manifestos and policy documents, Labour could not seriously claim to possess an 'environment policy'. This chapter charts the emergence of an environment policy in the Labour Party over the last decade. These developments are set in the broad context of the politicization of environment policy in Britain and accompanying changes within the Party. The extent of the substantive policy change is assessed and compared to that of the Conservative Government. It concludes by anticipating some of the implementation problems that might face a future Labour Government.[1]

## A PARTY OF ECONOMIC GROWTH: PRE-1985

Labour Governments have a respectable record of introducing regulatory legislation on many traditional environmental issues, including the formation of the Nature Conservancy Council, various Town and Country Planning Acts and the protection of access rights for ramblers. But, in general, what we would now know as environment policy were fragmented elements never brought together coherently. The whole issue was low on the policy agenda. For example, despite producing a rudimentary environment statement in 1978, there was still only a single page devoted to 'our environment' in the 1979 manifesto, with broad, unspecific promises to conserve resources, control pollution, recycle waste and eliminate lead from petrol. There were plans to improve energy conservation and keep freight traffic off the roads, but the Party remained firmly committed to the development of the nuclear power industry. Similarly, the 1983 manifesto contained a slightly longer, though still uncoordinated, 'shopping list' of policies, others that have only recently come under the rubric of the 'environment' (such as the provision of cheap public transport and the promotion of worker cooperatives), but still no coherent environmental strategy (Pepper 1986: 132–3).

There were individuals and groups lobbying the Party on specific issues. For example, in the late 1960s, middle-class socialist conservationists campaigned against damage to the countryside, but such groups were always marginal to the mainstream labour movement. More influential was the Socialist and Environment Resource Association (SERA), formed in 1973, born out of the publicity surrounding the United Nations Environment Conference in Stockholm and the *Limits of Growth* study (Meadows *et al.* 1972). Established 'to identify the social and economic problems affecting the environment and to formulate socialist policies to deal with them', SERA sought to deflect trade union fears about environmentalism by demonstrating its job creation potential through active involvement in the Lucas Aerospace shop stewards' plan for socially useful products (See Barratt-Brown *et al.* 1976). Other pressure groups achieved some isolated successes. For example, in 1981 a coalition of groups pressed for a Labour filibuster during the Commons committee stage of the Wildlife and Countryside Bill. This filibuster forced government concessions on several issues including the creation of marine nature reserves and the safeguarding of sites of special scientific interest (Lowe and Goyder 1983: 70). Hence, Labour's interest in the environment was sporadic and uncoordinated, and, as such, simply reflected wider public indifference.

However, environmental policy also posed some ideological and strategic dilemmas for Labour (dilemmas that, as will be shown, still exist). Despite Robin Cook's assertion that 'there are strong areas of congruence between socialist and ecological theorists in their rejection of the capitalist organization of production' (Cook 1984), Labour's

commitment to economic expansion through the effective management of capitalism made the Party unsympathetic to the burgeoning
debate about green issues (Ryle 1988). Crosland (1971) articulated
this antipathy in his vitriolic counterblast against the environmental
movement for its hostility to growth and indifference to the economic
needs of ordinary people. For example, he condemned middle-class
environmentalists for wanting 'to kick the ladder down behind them'
(Crosland 1971: 5) by focusing on threats to rural peace, wildlife
and beauty spots, while ignoring urban decay. Although conceding
the need for 'strict social control over the environment' (ibid.: 1),
Crosland argued that such intervention could be funded only by the
fruits of rapid economic growth. Moreover, he defined the problem
primarily in terms of the urban environment: the need for inner-city
redevelopment and town planning. This deep suspicion of environmentalism as being irrelevant to the needs of the working classes was
(and still is) shared by many Labour MPs and activists. For example:

> many of the Greater London Council's radical and imaginative
> green policies were greeted with derision by Militant supporters
> in Liverpool, on the grounds that providing bicycle lanes, inves-
> tigating alternative energy sources . . . was a diversion from the
> all-important socialist class struggle.
>
> (Porritt and Winner 1988: 64)

This antipathy transcended the left–right spectrum. Serious discussion of environmental issues was noticeably absent during the early-
1980s when the Party was racked by internecine conflict: for example,
it was barely mentioned in contemporary books debating the future of
the Labour Party (e.g. Curran 1984; Hodgson 1981; Kaufman 1983;
Lansman and Meale 1983; *inter alia*). The brief ascendancy of the
'hard left' committed the Party at the 1983 election to proposing a
massive increase in public expenditure, extensive state intervention
and the pursuit of rapid and sustained economic growth as a means
of creating millions of jobs. This Alternative Economic Strategy gave
scant regard to the environmental impact of such expansion.

Some trade unions have also obstructed the development of
environmental policy on specific issues. Primarily concerned with
short-term considerations of job protection and wages, unions expect
Labour to be committed to economic policies based on growth. More
specifically, trade unions representing some manufacturing workers
objected to environmental proposals that directly threatened the
livelihood of their members. This led to the Party either ignoring
these issues or producing contradictory policy statements. Shortly

before publishing its *Statement on the Environment* in 1986 (see p. 122), a document on *Labour and the Motor Industry* promised a huge increase in car production that was clearly designed to please the big general unions (Anderson and Cooper, in Ryle 1988: 33).

Energy policy posed particular problems for Labour. Trade unions representing workers in nuclear power stations battled against proposals that the Party should reject the use of nuclear energy. At a local level, union members near Trawsfynydd power station were issued with a list of shops they should boycott for displaying notices about an anti-nuclear demonstration. As one shop steward stated: 'People must realize that all anti-nuclear lobbying is endangering employment' (Ryle 1988: 33). This dilemma was neatly illustrated by the fact that Jack Cunningham – supporter of the nuclear power industry (the Sellafield nuclear power station was located in his parliamentary constituency) – was Labour's environment spokesperson. The National Union of Mineworkers (NUM) also resisted criticisms that coal-fired power stations were responsible for acid rain damage (Pepper 1986). Indeed, the 'enlightened' opposition of the NUM to nuclear power was clearly the exception that proves the rule; for here was a union patently acting in its own interests rather than out of concern for the environment.

Powerful forces therefore impeded the progress of the environment lobby within the Party. Overt opposition involved direct lobbying by MPs or trade unions on specific issues; less overt, but probably just as effective, was the overwhelming scepticism and apathy towards environmental issues. The growing number of environmentalists found this 'deadweight of reactionary tradition' immensely frustrating: one party worker reflected that 'those of us trying to get ahead of the wave of concern about environmental issues kept running up against people saying "why are you making waves? This isn't an issue. Why are you making such a fuss about it?"'. Thus, most often, environmental issues did not even make it on to the agenda for serious discussion.

Yet, despite these constraints, by 1988 the leading green activists, Porritt and Winner, conceded that 'considering just how far back they started, the Labour Party moved further and faster than any of its rivals . . . [its] stance on green issues had changed dramatically' (1988: 63).

## MEETING THE CHALLENGE: 1985–1991

During this period the Labour Party 'discovered' the environment as a political issue, laying out its policies in three main documents:

the *Statement on the Environment* in August 1986; the section on 'A Better Quality of Life' in the final report of the Policy Review *Meet the Challenge, Make the Change* in 1989; and *An Earthly Chance* in October 1990. This dramatic turnaround was provoked primarily by the growing public concern about the environment from the mid-1980s. A disparate set of developments, ranging from the wider dissemination of scientific knowledge about damage to the planet to more parochial fears regarding salmonella in eggs, stimulated this interest. Opinion polls in mid-1990, at the peak of interest in the issue, reported that some 30 per cent of people regarded the environment as the most important problem facing Britain.

A further indicator was the huge increase in membership of green pressure groups (*The Independent*, 17 January 1991). Indeed, in Britain, unlike many of her European neighbours, the politicization of the environment has been shaped by pressure groups rather than by the activity of a green political party. Until the late 1970s moderate environmental groups were effectively incorporated into the process of departmental policy-making, while radical groups were excluded (Lowe and Goyder 1983). However, the adverse economic and political climate of the early 1980s reduced the access and influence of pressure groups and hence the potential for environmental reformism (Flynn and Lowe 1991). The first nine years of the Thatcher administration were also characterized by a policy of 'deregulation by stealth' (Ward and Samways 1992) involving significant cuts in regulatory expenditure and careful selection of 'less regulation-minded appointees', rather than major legislative rollbacks. These developments prompted pressure groups to adopt a more populist campaigning style; a shift encouraged by the growing influence of broader environmental groups like Greenpeace and Friends of the Earth. Thus, a primary factor in the party politicization of the environment has been the need to respond to this open, indirect pressure group lobbying and to the public and media interest it has aroused (Flynn and Lowe 1991).

The transformation in public consciousness of environmentalism opened up new issue areas so that, to its embarrassment, Labour found itself without a policy in several important areas. Discontented murmuring about the party's outdated stance on the environment grew louder after the defeat of the 'hard left' and the ascendancy of a soft-left/centre coalition under Neil Kinnock. Although Kinnock himself was no 'environmentalist', these changes encouraged criticism of a number of party shibboleths, such as the commitment to undifferentiated economic growth (though a sympathetic hearing was still uncertain). For example, Robin Cook (1984) wrote a trenchant critique of the Alternative Economic Strategy for pursuing economic growth at the expense of the environment. The number of resolutions on environmental issues at the annual conference rose sharply after 1984 (Pepper 1986). Several Labour-controlled local authorities introduced practical environmental initiatives; indeed, Porritt and Winner observed that 'the most radical green policies yet seen in British mainstream politics were carried through by the GLC between 1981 and 1986' (1988: 64). It is probable that this gradual shift in attitude within the Party was helped by the emergence of a younger generation that had lived through the 1960s, had been active in local councils and, consequently, were more sympathetic to decentralist, green strands of thought. Put differently, more members regarded green issues as *their* issues, not those of an eccentric, rather detached wing of the Party. However, it was the Chernobyl disaster in 1986 that acted as the catalyst for a broader internal debate on green issues in general, and energy policy in particular. Not least, it actually persuaded the Shadow Cabinet rapidly to rethink its policy (Anderson 1991).

As the momentum for change increased, a Joint Policy Committee was established to review environmental policy. It consisted of representatives from the NEC, the PLP, trade unions and various 'outsiders' from councils, universities, SERA and, significantly, other leading pressure groups such as Wildlife Link, Greenpeace and Friends of the Earth.[2] Ironically, Jack Cunningham, the environment spokesperson, was regarded by environmentalists as a major obstacle. Cunningham's position of responsibility in a future Labour Government obviously meant that he needed to be convinced that proposals were practical and could be sold to voters; but his support for the nuclear power industry and his links with workers in the chemical industry also made him personally unsympathetic to many suggestions from environmentalists. To some extent this was balanced by the influence of local government representatives who could draw on, for example, the experience of the various successful and popular GLC initiatives.

Many battles were fought; significant compromises were made; but this dynamic committee, by all accounts ably chaired by union leader Tom Sawyer, eventually secured the support of trade unions and the party leadership. The result was the party's first comprehensive environment policy, sufficiently radical and wide-ranging for Porritt and Winner, no friends of the Labour Party, to concede that this committee had produced one of the party's 'most intensive and constructive policy reviews ever' (1988: 63).

The statement introduced policy in a number of new areas and brought together several existing policies. Notably, it proposed the establishment of a Ministry of Environmental Protection and two regulatory agencies, an Environmental Protection Service and a Wildlife and Countryside Service: in short, an entirely new regulatory framework for enforcing tougher controls on air and water pollution. There would be new powers for democratic planning of inner-city regeneration based on a zoning policy. The countryside policy aimed to extend planning controls into agriculture as well as forestry and countryside policy, and planned a shift in financial support away from agricultural production towards good environmental management and job creation. Environmental concerns would be built into the production process. The rhetoric also stressed the job creation potential of environmental industries; a theme given substance in 1987 when David Clark, Labour's first environment spokeperson, produced a document outlining how the pollution control and environmental protection industries would receive £10 billion over ten years to create 200,000 jobs.

Energy policy was omitted from the statement at the last minute because of internal party conflicts and was eventually published in a separate statement on *Civil Nuclear Power*. Yet, dramatically, following Chernobyl and active lobbying by SERA, the 1986 party conference committed itself to phasing out existing Magnox nuclear reactors, scrapping Sizewell and building no new nuclear power stations.

Although the Labour Party has never been instrumental in shaping the green debate in Britain, the 1986 statement allowed it, for a short time, to anticipate the debate among mainstream political parties. Despite this head start, the environment remained low on the party's political agenda. The 1986 statement was given very little publicity and was poorly distributed; it was available only in an unappealing collection of conference statements. The environment was virtually ignored in the 1987 general election manifesto and only one, largely unreported, press conference was devoted to the issue during the campaign. Obviously, after the infamous 1983 manifesto with its plethora of uncosted promises, the party leadership was anxious to produce a more credible manifesto containing few unattainable promises. Many items were excluded; the environment among them. The argument that it could be a symbolic, electorally-attractive issue was ignored, partly because no one in the party leadership fought for its inclusion but, more significantly, because private party opinion polling indicated the low salience of green issues.

After the publication of the 1986 statement there seems to have been a period of self-satisfaction within the party leadership, apparently content that the committee had produced a far-reaching document. This was illustrated by the retention of Jack Cunningham in post after the 1987 election: a choice regarded by environmentalists as strange for a party wishing to boast its green credentials. Moreover, despite the appointment of a spokesperson for environmental affairs, the departmental agenda was dominated by the poll tax. The Policy Review made little difference. As it was intended to examine specific areas and remove unpopular pledges rather than totally to rewrite all policies, it is perhaps unsurprising that the original list of Policy Review groups excluded the environment (Hughes and Wintour 1990: 42). Admittedly, within a year the environment was included in Neil Kinnock's speech to the annual party conference – a sign of the growing importance of an issue which, under the title *The Physical and Social Environment*, did eventually form one of the seven review groups. However, *Meet the Challenge, Make the Change* offered little more than the 1986 statement. The rhetoric showed the influence of the Brundtland Report (1987) by espousing the four principles of a 'presumption against pollution', the 'precautionary principle', 'freedom of environmental information' and 'the polluter pays'. Contemporary concerns about the poor quality of food and water were reflected in the inclusion of new commitments to set up a Food Standards Agency and to introduce a Clean Water Act. The only radical change was a transport policy promising the construction of new high-speed rail links, the introduction of passenger charters to help maintain standards and the use of tax incentives to improve vehicle efficiency. While the 1986 statement was, at the time, widely regarded as adventurous, events had moved on and, by 1989, the Party had been caught up by its political rivals.

However, during 1989 two developments pushed the environment temporarily towards the top of the political agenda and shook Labour out of its self-induced complacency. Perhaps most remarkable was the Pauline conversion of Mrs Thatcher, dating from her speech to the Royal Society in September 1988 in which she warned of the growing global environmental crisis. This declaration generated widespread interest; as one party worker remarked, 'It made the cynics sit up. If she was worried about green issues then perhaps there was something in all this after all.' Yet, given the Conservative record, it appeared that Mrs Thatcher had offered a hostage to fortune. For example, by privatizing the water industry the Government had unintentionally provided an excellent opportunity for pressure groups and opposition parties to make political capital out of the deteriorating condition of Britain's water, sewers, beaches and rivers. The Government's reputation was damaged further by a series of food scares culminating in the resignation of Edwina Currie, a junior health minister.

But it was the remarkable performance of the Green Party in the European elections that really shook the mainstream parties out of their complacency. Suddenly it appeared that green issues were a salient electoral issue. Every party scrambled onto the bandwagon by reviewing and updating their environment policies; politicians vied with each other to forward the 'green' claims of their party. The environmental White Paper, *This Common Inheritance*, published in September 1990, despite doing little more than updating and bringing together a number of existing policies – even *The Times* declared it was 'Not Green Enough' (Rose 1991: 323) – sustained this political interest and obliged Labour to respond with *An Earthly Chance*. Crucially, just as in the aftermath of Chernobyl, the party leadership was now demanding action.

*An Earthly Chance* outlined a far more comprehensive and substantial programme. Its radical content benefited from the replacement of Cunningham by Gould in 1988. As a senior pressure group worker put it: 'Gould is genuinely interested in the environment; since he took over a whole logjam has broken away'. His sympathy is enhanced by a deep suspicion of the centralizing tendencies within the labour movement and his lack of ties with the entrenched opponents of green issues (although his constituency does contain Ford's Dagenham factory).

Trade union opposition also become less of a constraint in this period; again, influenced by broader public concern. Unions are, understandably, most interested in those environmental issues that directly affect the well-being of their members, such as health and safety at work. There are signs, however, that union leaders are adopting a wider perspective involving the protection of the rights of their members as citizens, not simply as employees. Hence the motion at the 1986 party conference to scrap nuclear power was carried with the support of several of the biggest unions. Individual unions have also, on occasion, taken decisions that threaten the livelihoods of their own members, such as the campaign by the National Union of Seamen to stop the British Government dumping nuclear waste at sea (Pepper 1986). Subsequently, the TUC called for a 'Charter for the Environment' (TUC 1989), set up an environment action group to research and develop policies, and published a submission to the white paper couched in language notably sympathetic to environmental concerns (TUC 1990). It is probably significant that these changes occurred at a time when the power of manufacturing and energy industry unions within the labour movement was declining relative to white-collar and service sector unions who generally have less to lose by stricter environmental regulation.

Thus it is important to set the development of Labour Party policy in the context of changing public knowledge about the environment. The party's interest in green issues has grown more or less in line with that of society at large; the biggest advances in policy coincided with periods of heightened public concern about the environment. Labour has therefore responded to a broad politicization of the environment rather than to a Thatcherite agenda.

## MAKING THE CHANGE?

There is no doubt that the Labour Party has transformed its environment policy over the last twelve years. The 1986 statement was its first comprehensive environment policy and, at the time, was widely regarded as a radical programme. It was in many respects a compendium of policies that various pressure groups had been campaigning for over a long period. The document's main weakness was its poor integration into Labour's broad programme. Thus the proposal to set up a new Ministry of Environmental Protection with the responsibility 'to ensure that environmental concerns are reflected in all the areas of policy of the next Labour Government' (1986b: 13), was not backed up by an enforcement structure. Policy areas remained compartmentalized; in particular, the economic policy documents made no attempt to address the environmental impact of growth. For example, the 1987 party document, *Industrial Strength for Britain* was primarily concerned with raising production and economic growth and made no reference to the commitments made in the environment statement (Ryle 1988).

*An Earthly Chance* was built on similar philosophical principles to those of the 1986 statement and *Meet the Challenge, Make the Change*. However, in addition to containing several new policies and greater detail on existing proposals, it differed from the earlier documents in three key respects.

It recognized that environmental issues require a new way of thinking that transcends traditional policy areas by outlining a comprehensive programme intended to integrate environmental considerations into all policies. At the centre of the programme was the concept of sustainable development which 'requires a reappraisal of economic policy and its objectives' (1990b: 9), an acceptance of the idea of 'quality growth' (as opposed to the simple size of growth) and the need to change consumption patterns. The earlier proposal for a separate Ministry of Environmental Protection was dropped. It was argued that a separate ministry could be marginalized, whereas the operation of an environmental appraisal system supervised by a Minister for Environmental Protection within the DoE would have a greater influence over other departments. However, there may also have been some reluctance within the leadership to downgrade the leading Cabinet post at the DoE by 'hiving-off' green issues.

The second difference it contained was a sophisticated analysis of the various 'tools for sustainable development', which provides a framework for the complementary use of regulatory and market mechanisms. There would be an active role for the State both in policing environmental protection and in stimulating an 'environmentally helpful infrastructure' by investing in and consuming new products. An Environmental Protection Executive would incorporate the National Rivers Authority and Her Majesty's Inspectorate of Pollution to form a strong regulatory structure empowered to impose tougher penalties on wrongdoers. In addition, in contrast to earlier statements, there was an explicit acceptance of market mechanisms:

> Labour is prepared to rely not just on the traditional instruments of intervention, through prohibition and regulation, but will also use the market – through the price mechanism and fiscal measures – wherever they can be put to good use.
>
> (Labour Party 1990b: 6)

This was obviously influenced by the success of the Conservative Government's tax incentive on lead-free petrol, but the Policy Review was also important in creating a climate where the use of market mechanisms was acceptable (and, in his previous post, Gould had instigated the inclusion of market mechanisms in the economic policy review). Consequently, taxes would be used to encourage the use of catalytic converters, smaller car engines and recyclable goods (although a carbon tax was rejected as being regressive, recessionary and, one suspects, electorally unpopular).

The third contrast lies in the changed rhetoric which suggested a growing belief within the Party that a serious commitment to environmental policy meant that the Party had to cast off the image of being dominated by trade unions:

> [we] must overcome our traditional image as a 'producing' party, apparently giving priority to jobs and pay packets rather than to environmental concerns. We have to recognise that some of the decisions will be unwelcome – at least in the short term – to some of our closest supporters.
>
> (ibid.: 6)

Whether this was simply the bravado of opposition remains untested.

Only on nuclear energy policy was *An Earthly Chance* less radical than the 1986 statement. The commitment to commission no new nuclear power stations remained, but there was no promise to close the half-built Sizewell B power station, and the nearly-completed Thorp reprocessing plant would be retained. The official explanation for this climbdown was that the leadership feared the existence of secret trade agreements that would be costly to break. There might also have been the feeling that, once built, the power station may as well be used; a view no doubt put forcefully by the relevant trade unions.

*An Earthly Chance*, despite sharing many of the assumptions and strategies underpinning *This Common Inheritance*, outlined a more radical programme than the white paper; a conclusion shared by leading environmental pressure groups. A detailed comparison of the two documents is not possible here, but some of the main differences can be highlighted.

The fundamental distinction between the two approaches was the greater willingness of Labour to use regulatory mechanisms to intervene in the operation of the market. Labour planned more and better-funded agencies possessing greater monitoring and enforcement powers. Regulation remained the basis of Labour policy; the use of taxes and duties were essentially supplementary to this framework. Although both the major parties were committed to improving the coordination of environmental policy right across government, Labour's plan for an environment unit within each department appraising all programmes, supervised by an inter-ministerial committee, appeared more far-reaching. Labour had a radically different transport policy involving an expenditure shift in favour of public transport, and away from roads to railways. It would seek to change the priorities of the energy industry through least-cost planning by creating a built-in interest to conserve energy. Within Europe, Labour wanted to extend majority voting within the Council of Ministers on environmental matters, an EC environmental agency to monitor compliance with environmental law, and a European charter giving all community citizens basic rights to a clean and safe environment (Bryan Gould, press release, 22 January 1991). Labour would widen public access to the countryside and use green premiums to encourage less intensive agriculture. Lastly, the emission of greenhouse gases would be cut by 2000; five years earlier than the existing government target. So, Labour therefore has a more radical programme than the Conservatives, but would it be able and willing to implement this policy if it came to power?

## LABOUR IN POWER?

It seems likely that there will continue to be considerable external pressure on governments during the 1990s to be more active in protecting the environment; in particular, the European Community will be an increasingly potent enforcer of greater regulation. However, a future Labour Government would undoubtedly face a number of administrative and political constraints on its environment policy, of which four stand out.

First, despite changing attitudes, the support of all unions and constituencies is not assured; many sectional differences of opinion remain. Indeed, *An Earthly Chance* bore the scars of behind-the-scenes wrangling over the issues of the treatment of nuclear waste and energy policy. For example, the emphasis on developing clean-burn coal power stations and the fudging of the nuclear power issue undoubtedly reflected the interests of the NUM and power workers respectively. Moreover, in opposition, constituency parties and unions may acquiesce to ideas like the planned regulation of the chemical industry, but once those policies actually threaten jobs in local communities and of union members, then the response might be quite different. Nor is it hard to envisage the labour movement and the CBI joining forces during a recession to demand rapid, undifferentiated, growth.

Second, in addition to these political costs the financial cost of implementing several of Labour's proposals, including the development of clean-burn power stations, may prove prohibitive. However, to some extent this could be balanced by the cheapness of certain high-profile proposals, such as setting up the regulatory framework, which could prove electorally attractive (and maybe distract attention from some of the less pleasant features of Labour's austere economic programme?).

Third, it is still true that 'with few exceptions, Labour talks about the environment only when it is talking about the environment' (Anderson 1991: 38). The party's environment policy may be integrated on paper, but it is uncertain whether this would be the case in practice. For although a 'quality of life' committee already coordinates action across departments, there has been considerable variation in the response of shadow ministers. The transport, overseas aid and energy teams have all adopted a broad environmental approach. Most significantly, since 1990 Chris Smith of the Labour Treasury team has produced a 'green budget' pointing out the environmental impact of the government budget and suggesting alternative fiscal policies (*The Independent*, 14 March 1991). However, not all departments have shown similar enthusiasm. Once in power a Labour environment minister would probably face the same interdepartmental constraints that diluted or removed most of the radical measures planned for in *This Common Inheritence* (Rose 1991).

Last, given the various political and financial costs, and the interdepartmental nature of environment policy it is likely that little could be achieved without the enthusiastic and active support of the leadership. It has been the genuine enthusiasm displayed by many leading members of the Labour Party that, perhaps more than specific policy differences, has distinguished it from the Conservatives. Yet Neil Kinnock is an unconvincing convert. Although he had created the post of 'Minister for Environmental Protection', by the summer of 1991 he had still to make a keynote speech on the environment and had rarely raised the issue at parliamentary question time. Even during the 'no confidence' debate in November 1990 he made only a passing reference to 'the standard of transport' and a brief criticism of the Government's failure to support 'the extension of majority voting [in the Council of Ministers] to secure greater protection for the environment' (*Hansard*, 22 November 1990: 440–5).

The cynical observer might say that the leadership will only be committed if the issue remains electorally salient. Yet this had declined by early 1991. Media coverage plummeted after the huge publicity accompanying the publication of *This Common Inheritance* in the summer of 1990. Green issues were mentioned less frequently in MPs' mailbags. Opinion polls reported that less than five per cent of voters regarded the environment as one of the most important issues facing Britain. It may be that the environment is a mid-term issue, made peripheral at general elections by the dominance of traditional economic concerns.

## CONCLUSION

Environment policy seems to represent an exception to other policy arenas covered in this book. Labour first developed a comprehensive policy in 1985 and it entered the 1990s with a policy qualitatively different and more radical than 1979, 1983 or 1987. The primary motivating force behind this transformation was the growing public, media and pressure group interest which prompted the broader party politicization of green issues, initially in 1985–6 and later in 1989. This broad interest was reflected in the rise of environmentalists and environmentalism within the Party and parts of the trade union movement, which helped remove or weaken many of the previous constraints on change. The environment was not central to the Policy Review, but became important for other reasons. Nevertheless changes that occurred within the Party as a result of the Policy Review did contribute indirectly to the emergence of a more radical environment policy. However, despite possessing a coherent, radical programme, unless the party leadership fully embraces environmentalism a future Labour Government would struggle to overcome the political constraints on the implementation of its environment policy.

# 10 The Labour Party and the welfare state

*Pete Alcock*

## THE POLITICAL LEGACY

Despite the images of radical reform sometimes associated with the Labour Government of the 1940s which introduced most of the institutional framework of the post-war British welfare state, Labour's policy on welfare throughout the three decades following the war was very much contained within the 'Butskellite' consensus on the role and the scope of what Therborn (1984) has called 'welfare state capitalism' (Raban 1986). Fundamental to this consensus was the belief that expanded provision for welfare could be paid for by the fruits of capitalist economic growth, and that as long as growth continued then hard choices over the priorities within public spending or between public spending and private income and wealth could effectively be avoided (Klein 1980).

This was an approach which began to be challenged during the Wilson administration of the 1960s when pressure to contain expenditure led to the curtailment of welfare spending plans and an increasing emphasis upon selective targeting or 'positive discrimination' in welfare services. It was also an approach which, despite improvements in overall levels of welfare provision, had done little to reduce inequalities within post-war British society (Royal Commission 1980) – a failure which was sharply criticized by Fabian commentators following the departure of the Wilson Government (Townsend and Bosanquet 1972).

When growth gave way to recession in the 1970s, however, the Keynesian welfare state, as many critics called it, faced new and seemingly irresistable pressures. Economic pressure was most graphically exemplified by the International Monetary Fund which, as a condition of international financial support for the British Government, demanded controls on public expenditure growth. This was compounded by political pressure which was a direct consequence of the policy of financing welfare expansion indirectly out of economic growth without any challenge to the primary distribution of resources within society. The effect of this was to extend the fiscal burden of public expenditure lower and lower down the income scale. Arguably, this was a burden which could be borne, at least politically, as long as overall levels of income were rising; but, once incomes began to stagnate or decline in the recession, further expenditure on welfare, financed by increased taxation, began to pose a threat to the political stability of the welfare state regime.

This 'overload' thesis of a political, as well as an economic crisis in welfare expenditure was advanced amongst others by Bacon and Eltis (1976), and as a thesis was largely accepted by the Labour Government of the late 1970s. The conclusion which flowed from it was that future political, as well as economic, stability depended upon curtailing, or at least restraining, growth in welfare expenditure.

The consequences of this diagnosis of the crisis of the late 1970s are well known. Labour, under Callaghan, did reign back public expenditure growth. However, in order to do this without contributing too harshly to deprivation amongst the poorest, Labour was forced to maintain and even extend the reliance upon selectivity and means-testing within welfare provision. This accentuated the drift away from universal welfare provision which had begun in the 1960s, and it appeared to confirm the view that Labour in government was only able to deliver universal welfare services when these could be financed directly or indirectly out of capitalist economic growth.

As in the 1960s, this meant that Labour was unable to secure any sustained moves towards greater equality, and this again received trenchant criticism from the Fabian Society (Bosanquet 1980). In the 1970s, however, continued inequality was compounded by the sacrifice of welfare expenditure, leading Bosanquet (1980: 39) to comment that, 'The government seemed to have no belief in public services'. If the retreats on welfare and inequality were not a major factor in the loss of the election in 1979, it is likely that they cost Labour as much support as their courageous economic realism had won them.

Moreover Labour's economic realism in the 1970s created a political and economic legacy, which the Conservative Governments of the 1980s under Thatcher were able to exploit, and which Labour in opposition found difficult to shake off. Of course, the Thatcher Governments of the 1980s were quite open about their lack of belief in both the viability and the desirability of public services and their commitment to ensuring that economic priorities determined social policy planning. Commenting on 'The New Politics of Welfare', McCarthy

(1990) argued that the 1979 election constituted a 'watershed' in welfare politics, after which government support for state welfare was effectively abandoned.

Most commentators argue that the changes introduced by the Thatcher Governments were neither as sudden nor as revolutionary as this (e.g. Hills 1990; Johnson 1991). There is no doubt that they did lead to significant cuts in state welfare services and significant increases in the extent of poverty and inequality (Townsend 1991). However, the cuts made were far from fatal; and indeed in health and education, for instance, expenditure continued to grow. Also, despite growing inequalities, surveys of public attitudes towards welfare throughout the 1980s revealed continued and growing support for spending on the major public institutions of the welfare state and for increases in taxation to reduce inequalities (Taylor Gooby 1985, 1991).

By and large Labour recognized this continued support and sought to capitalize on the apparent weakness in Thatcherism that this represented by maintaining a commitment to improve and extend public welfare as part of their programmes and manifestos during the decade. This was a logical continuation of previous attempts to associate Labour whilst in opposition with the promise of positive welfare reform. As we shall discuss later, however, it failed to address the legacy of Labour's past failure to protect public welfare adequately during government, and thus it provided ammunition which its opponents could use to conjure up images of disillusionment and distrust.

## LABOUR'S WELFARE POLICY

Throughout most of the 1980s, therefore, Labour's policy on welfare showed little change from the policies, though not necessarily the practice, of the 1960s and the 1970s. Although in other areas the Party experienced a swing to the left in the early 1980s and later a swing back to the right, it is hard to detect any such ebb and flow on welfare issues. Indeed, although there were some important shifts in welfare policy, the changes which were made were more the product of pressures and changes external to the Party than of debates within it. Of particular relevance are the reforms to existing welfare services made by the Thatcher Governments and the criticisms from the non-aligned left of the past failings of state welfare.

In *Labour's Programme 1982* and their 1983 manifesto the Party concentrated on promises to repeal those Conservative policies seen as attacks on public welfare, notably the then controversial 'right to buy' for council tenants, and to increase expenditure and improve services in areas such as health and housing. There were also commitments to introduce piecemeal improvements in a range of social security benefits such as pensions, child benefit, death grants and invalidity pensions. These contrasted rather sharply with other vague promises of review and reform; for instance, the suggestion of a thorough review of National Insurance and the reference to a greater emphasis on prevention within health and personal social services.

The detailed policy promises also had obvious public expenditure implications; and yet, apart from the guarded admission in the manifesto that 'some taxes *will* have to be increased' [emphasis in text], not much was said about the relationship between social policy planning and broader economic priorities. Despite the extent of changes promised, social reforms were also largely contained within the existing institutional framework of state welfare and lacked any clear central themes, apart from opposition to Thatcherite anti-statism.

There was thus little to suggest that the problems of inequalities which had not been tackled in the past would be given any higher priority now. Also the failure to challenge some of the problems of bureaucracy and paternalism within existing welfare institutions, which had been a focus for Thatcherite anti-statism and for left-wing criticisms of state welfare, also suggested that the best Labour could offer on welfare reform was 'more of the same'. Faced with this, memories of the 1970s may have suggested to many that, if economic pressures could not be challenged or resisted, then once in government more could quickly come, in practice, to mean less.

Labour's 1983 manifesto was rather cruelly dubbed the 'longest suicide note in political history'. In contrast, therefore, the 1987 manifesto was much briefer and more general, and in keeping with the general character of the campaign, the commitments on welfare were stronger on rhetoric and weaker on promises. However, despite the generality of the rhetoric, there were some significant changes in policy which had resulted from some reconsideration of the impact of eight years of Thatcherite reforms and the legacy for a future Labour Government. The promise to repeal the 'right to buy' was dropped and replaced with a promise of 'real choice in housing'; and, after years of campaigning within the trade union and labour movements against the growing problem of low pay in the British economy, a commitment to introduce a statutory minimum wage was included. Once again a number of specific commitments on benefit improvement were listed: pension increases of £5 a week (£8 for a couple), child benefit rises of £3 a week, the introduction of a new disability income scheme and the extension of supplementary benefit for the long-term unemployed.

The 1987 manifesto also included more specific proposals for paying for priority programmes. These were primarily a 2 pence increase in income taxation and a £3 billion extension of public sector borrowing. There was also a summary of the five-year programme which was based upon the development of manufacturing industry to generate jobs and create the wealth necessary to expand public welfare services. There is no doubt that Labour's performance in 1987 was more credible than that in 1983, but it was still unsuccessful. It suggested to many that whatever social attitude surveys may suggest, Labour's policy promises were still not sufficiently appealing when set against the Government's record of apparent economic success.

Therefore, the establishment of the Policy Review following the 1987 election defeat represented an opportunity to rethink and restructure welfare policy to take account of changed circumstances, and to re-examine the relationship between welfare policy and economic planning. The review groups were deliberately established with agendas such as 'economic equality' and 'consumers and the community' which cut across previous institutional and departmental boundaries. This focus, together with the public process of review, threw open the debate on policy prescriptions to contributions from sympathetic, but critical, voices within the movement.

The reviews did not in practice do much to stimulate grassroots input into the policy debate and consultation conferences planned to facilitate this were cancelled. But the review groups actively sought the advice and assistance of experts in social policy, many drawn from the Fabian circles who had been so critical of previous Labour administrations. These experts were keen to use this new found influence to introduce onto Labour's policy agenda a range of new initiatives.

The first two policy documents ran to forty-eight and eighty-eight densely packed pages respectively (Labour Party 1988c and 1989a). They included a wide range of initiatives on service delivery which had not previously been features of party programmes; for instance, the establishment of public quality commissions, social audits and customer contracts for welfare services. They implied a significant shift towards improved accountability in public welfare, greater participation in the delivery of welfare services, and improved promotion of the individual benefits of state welfare, for instance, preventative health care. The documents also included proposals for broader restructuring of tax, wage and benefit policies to create 'pathways out of poverty'. These included moves towards more comprehensive and progressive taxation policies, potentially radical reform of social insurance entitlement, and, once again, the promise of a statutory minimum wage.

The Policy Review documents thus contained a wealth of new ideas on welfare policy when compared to the narrow-minded shopping list of 1983 and the broad, but vague, gestures of 1987. They also implied a response to Thatcherism which involved more than simply a reversal of Conservative welfare reforms. However, as Plant (1988a) commented, they fell short of providing any link between the different issues to produce clear themes which could translate into a programme for reform which could readily be publicized.

The more detailed review documents were thus followed in 1990 by a shorter summary document, entitled *Looking to the Future* (Labour Party 1990a), outlining the major priorities identified for a future Labour Government. However, even this briefer summary was not intended as a statement of manifesto commitments. Despite the new ideas generated by the review process, the party leadership remained convinced that commitments to welfare reform, and in particular welfare spending, must be considered in the context of economic circumstances. Thus on many of the new initiatives for improving public welfare services there was silence from the Labour leadership in the period leading up to the 1992 election, and clear promises were only made on items which had been officially costed, within existing economic constraints, by the Treasury team.

These commitments included, once again, promises to increase pensions (as in 1987 by £5 a week, £8 for couples), child benefit and disability benefits – to be paid for by removing the ceiling on National Insurance contributions and reintroducing higher rates of income tax for the higher paid. They also included a commitment to direct the £20 billion which it was claimed would flow from growth in the economy, into welfare expenditure rather than tax cuts, as the Conservative Government was promising.

These seem to be meagre returns from the wide-ranging Policy Review process and, as later discussed, may presage a continuation of the cautious refusal of Labour to challenge the subordination of welfare reform to economic policy priorities. However, they do not directly repudiate the tenor of rethinking and reform which characterized the overall approach towards welfare policy within the review process. To a significant extent therefore, the review proposals represented the culmination of a gradual development of the scope of Labour's policies for welfare whilst in opposition.

In part the immunity of welfare policy from the swings in Labour politics in the 1980s was the product of a shared belief that welfare policy meant primarily support for the institutions of state welfare, and that this was a popular policy within the country at large (if not perhaps a sufficiently important one) and a non-contentious policy between left and right within the movement itself. When Labour was in government, welfare issues were often seen as specialist areas to be left to the secretaries of state and their advisers; in opposition, when the need to administer welfare was hypothetical, such specialism attracted mainly tolerant disinterest when other, apparently more important issues were pressing.

More seriously, however, the lack of contention over welfare policy may have been disconcerting evidence of a lack of understanding of the issues involved, or of their broader political and economic significance. The failure of the 1964–70 and 1974–9 Labour Governments to protect welfare expenditure and reduce economic inequalities were significant departures from manifesto commitments, with significant social, and probably political, consequences, as the Fabian Society criticisms demonstrated. They were the product, of course, of Labour's attachment to the Keynesian (Butskellite) model of welfare which had predicated social expenditure upon continued economic growth. When economic growth was no longer able to sustain continued welfare expansion, then expenditure was curtailed and universal welfare sacrificed for selective measures to ameliorate the worst consequences of continued inequality.

This was an acceptance of a monetarist rationale for restraining welfare expenditure in order to foster economic growth, which was seized on by the Conservatives in the 1980s as evidence of effective support for their, further-reaching, claim that economic policy needs must be the sole determinant of public expenditure planning – because it was the health (or in this case, ill-health) of the economy which was first duty of any responsible government.

Despite the potential support for welfare throughout the 1980s, Labour was faced with the Conservative Government's claim that this could not provide an effective basis for support for Labour, because in practice both they and the Conservatives recognized the primary importance of economic policy. Given also Labour's contradictory promises to return to expansionist public welfare, the Conservatives claimed that only they could be trusted to maintain expenditure discipline and deliver economic success. As recession gave way to (apparent) economic success in the late 1980s, this economic rationale acquired a political momentum which was sufficient to displace even significant public support for welfare expenditure. So it seemed that a sufficiently large section of voters, when faced with an apparent choice between welfare expenditure and economic discipline, were inclined to put their fears for their pockets before the hopes in their heads or their hearts. This was a rational reaction to the apparent cross-party consensus on welfare policy, rather than any ideological drift towards Thatcherite economic individualism – or as one critic put it 'voters prefer Labour's social policies but Tory economic policies; when choosing how to vote a majority regard the latter as more salient' (Gough *et al.* 1989: 247).

Thus, there is evidence that Labour failed to recognize the continued influence of the legacy of welfare policies of the 1970s on their political credibility throughout the 1980s; and, as we shall discuss in the next section, this is a legacy which may continue to haunt them if they return to office in the 1990s. However, there were other pressures too which developed outside of the narrow confines of internal Labour politics during the 1980s. These pressures, despite the caution of the leadership's recent limited promises on welfare, are unlikely to be excluded for long from the agenda of any Labour Government in the 1990s which maintains a commitment to the development of state welfare.

## THE NEW AGENDA FOR WELFARE

In large part the new agenda for welfare in the 1990s has been set by the Thatcherite reforms of the 1980s. The Thatcher Governments were openly contemptuous of the Butskellite consensus on welfare and were strongly influenced by neo-liberal views on the deleterious consequences of over-extensive state services. This was translated in popular rhetoric into a series of attacks on the bureaucracy, paternalism and inefficiency of state welfare services and the open encouragement of private market alternatives to the State, which could offer greater freedom of choice and control over delivery to consumers.

It was as consumers, rather than as clients, that Thatcherism portrayed the individual recipients of welfare services. This was a deliberate attempt to undermine the collective focus of state services and the notion of shared needs and interests which had always informed this, and to substitute in its place a market-oriented conception of individual freedom through contract. It was a conception that in the late 1980s and early 1990s was introduced into state services too, via the creation of 'internal markets' in some welfare services, such as health and social services; and, after the replacement of Thatcher by John Major as Prime Minister, by the development of the idea of a 'Citizens' Charter' which would give individual compensation for failures in the delivery of state services.

Despite the obvious shortcomings of the individual model of welfare needs and the inefficiencies and inequities associated with market-based delivery of social services, the emphasis upon choice, accountability and control within welfare in the 1980s did tap a rich vein of dissatisfaction with, and even alienation from, many of the public services of the post-war welfare state. The problems of paternalism and bureaucracy were real enough, and were part of the real experiences of the users of state welfare; for instance, council tenants treated as irresponsible and temporary occupants of their own homes. Thus, the right to buy their council tenancy was popular with many tenants, even though it could not in practice be a solution for the majority.

The Thatcherite solution to the paternalism of state welfare – opting out into the private market, or bringing the market into the State – could not of course provide decent, or accountable, welfare services for all. The continued evidence of support for public welfare services demonstrated that many presumably recognized and accepted this. But accountability and control over welfare services did become part of the expectations of many people who needed little encouragement to recognize that they have interests as individual users of services as well as the collective beneficiaries of universalism and greater social justice. Any future development of public services must now recognize and plan for such accountability and control. It will not be feasible simply to contrast the advantages of the State to the disadvantages of the market, for people have been encouraged to recognize that the advantages and disadvantages run the other way too. If future state welfare does not incorporate some of the apparent advantages of the market, past disillusionment may quickly be rekindled.

The development of alternatives to state welfare in the 1980s also leaves another legacy for any incoming Labour Government – a mixture of state, private and other forms welfare delivery established within the country. The 'mixed economy of welfare', as commentators refer to this combination of state and non-state in service delivery, is not of course merely a legacy of Thatcherism. Private, voluntary and informal welfare services have coexisted alongside the state sector throughout the history of the post-war welfare state. For instance, Beveridge anticipated that additional private insurance would be used to supplement state social security payments, and in health and social services informal care in the community (or family) has been the basis around which state and voluntary support has largely been built.

What commentators have argued more recently, however, is that this welfare pluralism must be identified and planned as part of any future development of welfare by government, because in practice future welfare services will be situated within, and will develop from, the mixed economy which currently exists (Judge 1988; Johnson 1990). For some this is largely a pragmatic response; Klein and O'Higgins (1985) refer to it as 'purposeful opportunism'. Whereas for others there are positive advantages to be gained from diversification in the delivery of services (Hadley and Hatch 1981). All supporters of welfare pluralism, however, point to the need for coordination between the different sectors, and this will require a future Labour administration to broaden its concerns beyond the future of state welfare services alone.

Further pressure upon a future government to broaden their view of welfare planning will also come from more radical critics of the past limitations of state welfare, whose voice is found mainly in new social movements which have developed outside of the established labour movement. Such critics include feminists, black activists and others who have argued that existing state welfare services have been based upon limited (white, male) models of need which have effectively excluded or marginalized large sections of the population (Williams 1989). They also include environmental activists, for instance in the growing green movement, who have argued that state welfare services predicated upon further capitalist economic growth cannot be sustained without unacceptable ecological costs; and that as a consequence such 'consumerist conceptions of citizenship' (Ferris 1985) should be replaced with small-scale, localized self-determination in welfare planning.

From a more general analysis of the implications of such radical, non-aligned political activism Keane (1988) has argued that what is implicitly involved is the development of new forms of democratic structures and a displacement of much political struggle over welfare away from the central state into the broader terrain of civil society. This would involve a restructuring or replacement of the existing institutions of British democracy; this is not something which the existing (rather inchoate and loosely organized) movements could press directly onto Labour's immediate agenda for welfare reform. However, the importance of such non-aligned political organizations in Britain has grown significantly in recent years, and in most other advanced capitalist and Eastern Bloc countries; and a prospective Labour administration will ignore such voices at their peril. Indeed the promises already made in the 1987 manifesto for the appointment of a Minister for Women suggest some recognition by the Party of the need to introduce the voice of marginalized constituencies into the decision-making process. It is unlikely that this will be, or will be seen to be, sufficient response to the changed agendas presented by the new social movements in the 1990s.

Finally, and perhaps in the short run most importantly, there has been change and development throughout the 1980s and early 1990s in debates on welfare services and welfare reform amongst social policy circles close to the labour movement itself. Fabian Society critics had strongly challenged both the 1960s and 1970s Labour Governments on their records on welfare policy. In the early 1980s the Fabian Society produced a new book, *The Future of the Welfare State* (Glennester 1983), which opened with the claim that many commentators shared 'the belief that all is not well in the welfare state as we know it – and not just because of Mrs Thatcher's cuts'. Contributors to the book went on to argue the need for structural changes within welfare provision to respond to issues such as anti-discrimination, decentralization and citizenship within welfare services as a necessary addition to any more general commitments to the expansion of provision. Underlying much of the recent thinking on welfare in Fabian and left-wing circles has been a growing concern with the delivery welfare services. For some, rethinking has gone further and challenged the whole basis of the relationship between social policy and economic policy planning.

As discussed in chapter 4, citizenship is a widely used, and unfortunately a widely misused, concept which has been taken up by the right as well as by the left in the early 1990s (Barry 1990; Andrews 1991). However, particularly in the work of Plant (1988b), it poses an important challenge to many of the existing institutional structures and practices of state welfare, and amongst new thinkers on the Fabian left it is being used as a vehicle for introducing into welfare planning a focus on individual enforcement of rights to welfare and user participation in local planning of the delivery of welfare services (Sheffield Group 1989). Underlying this is a concern to ensure that any future expansion of public welfare does not simply expand professional control over it. As Plant puts it, 'More resources for welfare without empowerment of consumers within it will not meet the mood of the times' (1988b: 13).

Concerns over the relationship between social and economic policy planning amongst the new Fabians are partly linked to the new focus on citizenship and rights, but they stem in large part from a more traditional disillusionment with the limitations of welfare spending set by capitalist economic growth in the post-war Keynesian welfare state. In particular concerns focus on the stagnation and decline in welfare expansion which occurred under the Labour Governments of the 1960s and 1970s, leading to the conclusion that, rather than social policy following on from economic growth (or not), social policy and economic policy can, and should, be planned together (Walker 1984). If this line were pursued, they argue, it would lead to a rather different, and more extensive, role for government in determining the goals of economic development as well as those of social policy (Gough and Doyal 1991).

This restructuring of economic and social priorities has consequences well beyond the arena of welfare services alone – indeed it is really part of a broader strategy for the restructuring of the capitalist economy within British society. We will return shortly to the wider consequences of this for a future Labour Government but it is worth noting here that within this broad brush are some important specific social and economic policy changes, which have already been widely debated within the labour movement, such as the introduction of a statutory minimum wage. The minimum wage was a policy commitment in the 1987 election manifesto and it was repeated in the 1989–90 Policy Review. It is primarily identified as a means of challenging poverty in employment without recourse to extensive means-tested support for low wages; but, as the Low Pay Unit (1988) and Bayliss (1991) discuss, implementing it will require a future government to engage in a level of intervention in economic development previously avoided by post-war administrations.

As discussed previously, some new Fabian thinking had begun to inform the processes of Labour Party policy development through the involvement of experts in the Policy Review. But this influence was rather incoherent in its overall effect and has not been carried through into clear manifesto commitments in the period leading up to the 1992 election. Thus far, therefore, the influence of recent new left thinking on Labour could perhaps be described as embryonic at best. Against this has to be set the continuing problems and contradictions in the overall commitment to improving or extending state welfare which stemmed from the legacy of the narrow commitment to the Keynesian welfare state revealed by previous Labour administrations. Despite some of the advances made on welfare policy within the Party in the 1980s therefore, and its escape from some of the wilder swings to left and right within the Party, a future Labour Government faces a number of crucially important issues underlying policy commitments which still remain to be resolved. Past evidence unfortunately suggests that if these had not been resolved in opposition, then they will not be resolved in government either.

## THE PROBLEMS FACING LABOUR

The most important issue facing a future Labour Government in the early 1990s is the same issue which faced previous administrations in the past and which dogged Labour's electoral performances throughout the 1980s: the balance between economic growth and social spending, and underlying this, the relationship between economic and social policy planning. As already discussed, it is far from clear that, despite thirteen years in opposition to a radical Conservative Government, and a process of policy review within the Party, Labour has divorced itself from the post-war consensus on the economic basis of the Keynesian welfare state. Indeed the cautious view of the dependence of social policy upon economic policy priorities which remains at the heart of decision-making within the Party seems to be confirmed by the limited promises on welfare made in the early 1990s following the Policy Review, and the concern to link these to what were claimed to be justifiable predictions about the prospects for future economic growth.

Of course the immediate concern here was to counteract potential attacks by the Conservative Government on any 'unaffordable' promises made by Labour, and to demonstrate, in an apparent recognition of the economic rigours of office, a readiness for government. But the defensive reaction implied within this strategy also suggested a continued acceptance of the economic, as well as the political, validity of potential government attacks. Also it demonstrated the increasing dominance of the Treasury team, and their concern with the short-term costs of all manifesto commitments over the broader processes of policy development within the Party.

The linking of welfare expansion, beyond immediate pensions and child benefit reforms, to the £20 billion generated by realizable economic growth is thus posed as an alternative to Conservative plans for tax cuts. This Labour alternative it is hoped, and expected, will appeal to an electorate who appear to have demonstrated, in attitude surveys and opinion polls, their support for the expansion of state welfare. This appears as a sensible, even a laudable, claim; but it does not resolve the questions of what to do if growth is not achieved, or, once the £20 billion has been accounted for, how further welfare needs will be met.

As stressed, the Conservative Governments of the 1980s were able successfully to exploit Labour's apparent acceptance of the pre-eminence of economic over social policy planning. Perhaps ironically, it may be that the Government's own economic failings eventually lead to Labour returning to power in the 1990s. But, if the continued acceptance of this relationship between economic and social policy is not challenged, then the room for Labour to meet welfare promises, or pursue new and different initiatives in state welfare policy, will almost certainly be fatally constrained.

Further evidence of the continued failure to address the problem of economic and social policy planning and the consequent relegation of welfare planning to the limited dividends of economic growth, is the continued confusion in policy debate in the Party over the role of universal versus selective provision within welfare services. In the past the drift towards selectivity has appeared as an inevitable consequence of the acceptance of limited resources for welfare services and the resultant abandonment of commitments to reduce inequality through service expansion in favour of protection for the poorest through targeting. Any future commitment to reducing inequality, especially if this would involve the redirection of resources to expand universal services and raise standards, is a direct challenge to the containment of welfare expansion within the constraints of economic growth.

There are consequently serious problems facing Labour in attempting to reverse the increased inequalities which they will inherit from the Conservatives. Given the drift from universalism towards selectivity which developed throughout the 1960s and 1970s, before the Thatcherite policies of the 1980s, much of the political basis for support for increased universal state spending in order to redistribute via a strategy of equality had already been effectively undermined. Labour's failure to address these problems in the past thus continues to create pressure against any challenge to them in the future.

As a result the Policy Review documents are confused and non-committal on aspects of universal welfare policies to reduce inequalities; for instance, on the reform of social insurance to replace means-tested benefits for those outside the labour market. Although the commitment to raise the universal child benefit levels is an important part of the early priority commitments of a new Labour Government, the promise is only to restore the benefit to 1987 levels which will secure only a very limited redistribution of resources to tackle the growing inequalities between families and childless households.

By contrast, the failure of Labour to take up at an ideological level the issues of universalism and redistribution is exaggerated by the open debate which the Thatcher Governments of the 1980s fostered on the desirability of targeting welfare spending and accentuating inequality in order to stimulate investment and economic growth through the expectation of reward. The opportunity was created for a challenge to the Thatcherite appeal of targeting and individual wealth creation to be made and counterposed by a different model of economic development based around an egalitarian ideology and the use of government intervention to steer resources towards collective benefits for all rather than individual riches for some.

What Labour seemed to have pursued instead, however, has been an attempt to reassert the Keynesian model of gradual amelioration through the fruits of sponsored, but not directed, growth within existing economic frameworks. The evidence from the past is that the precarious ideological and political support for this is contingent upon its economic viability and that this is something which may largely be out of the Government's hands. As stated before, it is now clear that inequalities were extended during the 1980s under the Conservative Government (Townsend 1991); what is less clear is whether Labour would be either willing, or able, to reduce them again in the 1990s.

The second major issue which will confront a future Labour Government in developing its welfare policies is the wide-ranging debate on delivery of services, accountability, rights and citizenship which has been conducted with increasing fervour within and outside the Party throughout the last decade. As said earlier, some of the proposals in the Policy Review documents suggest that these are issues which are forcing their way onto the policy agenda for a future government; but, if their potential importance is to be recognized and realized, much more attention will need to be given to the implications of this for the structure, and the control, of state and non-state welfare services.

John Major's Citizens' Charter suggests that this is an issue which has already been identified by the Conservative Government in the 1990s. If this is followed through, even in part, it is likely to herald the beginning of a different relationship between public sector service providers and their users. In the light of the potential threats within this for public sector managers and workers, there may be a tendency within the labour movement to seek to defend existing institutions and practices and thus to aim to restore them in the future. To quote again Plant's earlier phrase, 'this will not meet the mood of the times' (Plant 1988b: 13).

One of the few positive legacies of Thatcherite welfare policy will be the interest it has focused upon the issue of the delivery of services. This is an issue which, as discussed, has been taken up by left-wing critics both within and outside the labour movement. Labour has rightly denounced the market as the solution to the problems identified in the delivery of welfare services through the State, and Major's individualistic and pecuniary model of the citizen's rights to compensation for public service failures offers little hope of real improvement here.

However, solutions to these problems must nevertheless be found, and this will involve a review and a restructuring of the institutions of public welfare, of management structures and working practices within them, of the extent of democratic control and user participation in service development, and of the relationships between the State and the private, voluntary and informal sectors. Professional jealousies and trade union protectionism will inevitably come under scrutiny and challenge in such a review.

Labour will need to recognize, and indeed champion, the case for such challenges. But this will require a broader and more critical approach to the structure as well as the size of state welfare than has so far been revealed in political debate and policy planning. It will also require a departure from the centralist style of Westminster and Whitehall-based decision-making which has characterized past Labour, as well as Conservative Governments; and a departure from the heavy reliance upon professionals and advisers who could easily come to dominate the proposed quangos and commissions.

The third issue facing a Labour Government, and perhaps ultimately the one which any future British Government would find itself least able to avoid, is the challenge (or the opportunity) of Europe. Already the next British Government is scheduled to inherit the consequences of the single European market after 1992. This will have far-reaching economic and social consequences for every aspect of policy planning. It is also likely to be accompanied by pressures from within the EC for greater harmonization in the social policy field and more concerted cross-national planning for both economic and social development.

The EC generally, and most European countries themselves, already have much more developed interrelations between economic and social policy planning than Britain has experienced in recent years – some would say this largely explains their relative economic success. The consequences of these interrelationships after 1992 are likely to exert ever greater pressure for similar approaches to be adopted in Britain, as European unity extends from free trade to currency union, planning agreements, development funding and guaranteed community welfare rights.

In 1989 Britain was the only member state who refused to endorse the 'Community Charter of Fundamental Social Rights of Workers', despite the dropping, at Mitterrand's request to placate the Thatcher Government, of the commitment to introduce a minimum wage throughout Europe. Given Labour's new-found recognition of the potential for cooperation with our partners in Europe, a future Labour Government presumably would not, and should not, adopt such isolationism. However, the real importance of developments such as the charter is that they demonstrate the potential for achieving much greater social and economic policy reform within Britain through European cooperation.

Of course, it is far from clear that the EC is sufficiently united both politically and socially to be able to deliver on many of the potential social policy promises which have emerged on occasions from Brussels and Strasburg. Nevertheless the example of a European minimum wage would be a significant spur to poverty prevention and income planning within Britain, and would have far reaching consequences for investment planning and business support by a British Government. In the longer term it may also be the trigger for greater economic cooperation and support across national boundaries within the Community more generally.

A Labour Government at the forefront of such social and economic planning within Europe would be evidence of a significant departure from the narrow nationalism of the 1980s; but it would also require a greater acceptance by potential ministers and prime ministers of the need for cooperation within Europe over a range of major policy issues, which have previously been the province primarily of national governments. Labour's publicity statements refer to the need for Britain to be 'strong in Europe'. This is an ambiguous phrase which could be interpreted to mean something akin to Thatcherite petty nationalism. Unless it is proven to mean 'strong on Europe', Labour will not be placing itself and Britain in a position both to benefit from and to exercise control over the inevitable moves towards greater continental harmonization in the 1990s.

## CONCLUSION

The issues facing a future Labour Government over welfare policy thus include both old problems and new ones. The most immediate concern remains the fear that the continued commitment to an old model of welfare reform dictated by the success of the Government in securing economic growth, is evidence of a failure to recognize the need for new thinking on the joint planning of economic and social policy; and it is likely to lead in practice to restrictions on the scope for reform if, or when, economic targets are not met. If this is the case then all the advances in policy debate which have been made throughout the Thatcher years and in particular in the Policy Review could well be left to stagnate or decay; and selectivity in welfare could continue to exercise the divisive influence which flourished under both Labour and Conservative administrations in the previous two decades.

In addition to this, however, must be placed the fear that many of the advances in the welfare debate have been welcomed by Labour only in part, and without full recognition of their structural, and political, implications for welfare services within the State, and outside it. Even if Labour is able to deliver on some of its commitments to expand welfare provision, this will not meet the new expectations of the 1990s unless it includes significant elements of a restructured accountability in service delivery, which thus far is only beginning to penetrate the policy debate within the Party.

Finally there will be the challenge of Europe. Few informed commentators now doubt that the relationship between the British Government and the British State, and the European Community and its other member states will have changed dramatically by the end of the next decade. This change will be felt in welfare policy as much as, if not more than, in other areas. Labour must recognize that this will require a new model of cooperation and joint planning across the range of state services if Britain is not merely to be a reluctant and late recruit to future harmonization.

# 11 The Labour Party and women: Policies and practices

*Valerie Atkinson and Joanna Spear*

Although Labour Governments in the 1970s had passed several important pieces of legislation designed to grant women equality in the workplace, it was not until the swing to the left in 1981–2 that the Party began to address itself seriously to the needs of women. As discussed in the next section, the 1982 programme was exceptional in its analysis of the problems women faced. The solutions it suggested have remained central tenets of the party's policies towards women, although there has been a distinct change of emphasis in the way that policies are presented.

The cycle of development of policies towards women does not follow that pattern discussed elsewhere in this volume. Although women were involved at all stages in the Policy Review process, there was no review group specifically to look at this area. Moreover, there has been no significant reorientation of policy in the post-review period, again in contrast to many other policy areas. In this sense then, policies towards women are similar to policies on the environment in having remained independent of the Policy Review process.

In the next section we examine the attitude towards women and the development of what is now the flagship of policy: the Ministry for Women. In the following section we examine the Labour Party's internal reforms designed to encourage greater participation by women and their advancement within the party structure. This is particularly important as the Party has to be seen to be practising what it preaches.

It is important to understand the context within which the Labour Party was operating in the 1980s as it developed its policies towards women. The era is often described as post-feminist. Evidence cited to support this includes the fact that for eleven years Margaret Thatcher served as Prime Minister. As Neustatter noted 'The popular line these days is that women have had their battle, got what they want and are happy being post-feminist company executives' (Neustatter, 1991). This is a label that the authors reject as it implies that women have enjoyed the full fruits of feminism and have now moved on. This is mistaken on many counts; particularly important is that although middle-class women may be achieving more in society (and John Major by his Opportunity 2000 initiative admits that even this is not enough as women are significantly under-represented at the top echelons of business, the civil service, etc.) the position of many other women has been undermined by the Thatcher years. Successive Conservative Governments' actions have had fundamental effects on the National Health Service, social security, education, housing, public transport, etc. (Donnison 1991; Travis 1991). The prime users of all these services are women and, as they have been undermined, this has had detrimental effects on the lives of women. As Alcock noted in the previous chapter, the cutting away of services and greater reliance on the community means in effect women taking over. The Thatcher years also saw an emphasis on the family and family values, which was an ideological attempt to push women back to home and hearth. Overall then, it is our contention that the term post-feminism is misleading and unhelpful. The real message of the 1980s was that 'the struggle continues'.

## POLICIES TOWARDS WOMEN AND THE MINISTRY FOR WOMEN

At the end of more than a decade of Conservative government, the Labour Party has in place a Shadow Minister for Women, and on 25 March 1991 it was reaffirmed that, if the Party were to come to power at the next general election, a cabinet minister for women would be appointed. The campaign, by women, to effect this innovation has been underway through most of the 1980s, and the creation of a Ministry for Women was announced as part of the party's campaign agenda launched in April 1987 in anticipation of that year's general election.

Reaction to the announcement was, inevitably, mixed. 'Should there be a Ministry for Women?' asked Margot Norman in the *Daily Telegraph*. 'Labour's aims', she added, are pretty unexceptional [and] also pretty vague' (Norman, *Daily Telegraph*, 7 April 1987). Along with Angela Neustatter in *The Guardian*, she suggests that cynics may have seen the sudden launch of a women's campaign as a piece of calculated engineering.

Women had, however, been – by their own efforts – on the Labour Party policy agenda for some considerable time prior to the 1987 election campaign. Jo Richardson, the MP who has been designated Shadow Minister for Women and has been the driving force behind the introduction of women's issues into mainstream party policy, was at the time of the announcement reported as being 'markedly irritated at the idea that anyone should suggest that Labour targeting women [was] a bit of a flash-in-the-pan expediency' (Neustatter 7 April 1987).

It is important to note, nevertheless, the unmistakable fact that a tension lies between the wide-ranging aspirations of Jo Richardson and her associates in their drive to improve women's lives by party political means, and the electoral ambitions of a male-dominated political party. In examining the development of the Labour Party's commitment to women's issues, some of these tensions will become evident.

## EARLY INITIATIVES

The publication *Labour's Programme 1982* included a section on women and women's rights. 'Our aim', it declared, 'is to create a very different society in which women are no longer oppressed'. Attention was focused on the effects of Conservative policy both on women in the workplace and in the home, with emphasis being laid on the consequences of government spending cuts. Areas that were highlighted included rising unemployment in the service sector; the low-pay, low-status nature of the majority of those jobs still accessible to women; discrimination in tax and social security structures; and disappearing community services such as school meals, nurseries and day centres for elderly and handicapped people.

In order to ameliorate the damage caused by Conservative policies, the Labour Party committed itself to a number of strategies to be undertaken when they came to power. These included: a major expansion of child-care facilities and support services; a comprehensive positive action programme to help women to train and apply for better paid, more skilled jobs; and the introduction of a statutory minimum wage. A Labour Government would, it claimed, 'build on the foundation of the Sex Discrimination, Equal Pay and Employment Protection Acts to achieve much greater equality for women in employment' (Labour Party 1982a).

The 1982 programme was remarkable for its inclusion of a broad analysis of some of the causes of the 'female condition'. It recognized that many women are 'forced into economic dependency on men, subject to considerable stress and deprived of the opportunity to exploit their full potential' and furthermore that:

[t]his dependency is reinforced by the narrow stereotyped roles assigned to women by society. They are venerated as wives and mothers and exploited as sex objects. They are rarely recognised as 'successful' and when they are, they are dismissed as exceptions – a man's mind in a women's body.

This observation reflected a recognition that women are subjected to superficial, misleading representation in the mass media and advertising, that this 'constant and insidious conditioning has a powerful impact' and that the Party should 'seek to introduce a code of practice to control sexism and the way the mass media and advertisers portray women'. During the next nine years, this powerful language was noticeably toned down. Indeed, the incisive analysis of the 1982 text disappeared, as comparisons with later statements will reveal.

However, earlier in 1983 the Labour Party manifesto, *The New Hope for Britain*, had included a section entitled 'A Better Deal for Women' in which many of the proposed strategies of its 1982 publication were echoed (Labour Party 1983a). These included the commitment to amend the Equal Pay Act and to strengthen the Sex Discrimination Act and the role of the Equal Opportunities Commission. The establishment of an integrated system of child care was still given strong backing, including a statutory duty on local authorities to provide nursery education for all pre-school children 'whose parents wish it'. This final phrase could be seen as a retreat from the stridency of the 1982 programme and a recognition that there were different views *among women* over the care of children.

By 1983, however, some of the emphasis had changed: the setting up of a comprehensive positive action programme had become a commitment to expand current positive action programmes, with no mention of a requirement for the civil service, government contractors, local authorities, employers and education bodies to implement such programmes (as had previously been stated). Similarly the introduction of a statutory minimum wage was no longer specifically mentioned under the heading for women – merely a commitment to 'take action together with the trade unions, against low pay'. Importantly, the intention to introduce a code of practice to control sexism in the mass media and advertising had disappeared altogether.

Moreover, the language used to describe the general conditions of women's lives had become considerably less controversial, declaring that 'domestic skills . . . do not enjoy their proper status' and that women 'should have a genuine choice between staying at home to look after the family or going to work'. Although this can be viewed as a surprising return to an emphasis on the ideology of home and family, and thus in a sense responding to the move to the right of the Conservatives under Thatcher, this more 'balanced' approach also reflected changes within the women's movement which increasingly recognized that some women positively wished the opportunity to spend time as full-time wives and mothers.

However, perhaps as a result of this new emphasis, some specific items had appeared on the agenda, for example, an increase in the maternity grant to at least £100 and in the death grant to at least £200 and an end to VAT on sanitary protection. The intention may have been to offset an impression of vagueness and broad generalizations.

In 1984, Jo Richardson set up an informal working group to consider tentative plans for a Ministry for Women's Rights. At the same time she also began a newsletter, *Labour Party: Women's Action* intended to be a forum for ideas on policies for women and also as a means of overcoming the isolation of women within a male-dominated party.

In early 1986, Jo Richardson published a discussion document, *Labour's Ministry for Women's Rights*. This document gave a comprehensive, analytical background to the requirement for a Ministry for Women, and tackled, amongst other issues, the topic of marginalization: 'commitments on women's rights . . . must have the full public backing of the leadership'. It insisted that a Labour Government, through a women's ministry, should undertake many measures itself. For example:

- The Government's role as a major employer should be used to improve the position of women within the civil service;
- Contract compliance and contract procurement should become an integral part of government's sex equality programmes;
- The Government itself should commission research and inform women of their rights; and
- The findings of formal investigations into sex discrimination should no longer be challengeable in the courts.
(Richardson 1986).

Amongst other radical measures designed to achieve equality (plus an insistence on adequate resources to implement them) the document reasserted the need for a statutory minimum wage. It demanded legislation to provide a shorter, more flexible working week with shorter working days and the provision of better paid parental leave. It demanded a *statutory* requirement on local authorities to make free nursery provision for all three and four year-olds. The document also reasserted the need for action to be taken against the superficial and misleading representation of women in the mass media and advertising.

The tone of Jo Richardson's document was powerful and incisive. It covered a wide range of practical measures, backed up by legislative change, and embodied some of the broader ideological issues to which feminists have been addressing themselves for more than two decades.

## INCORPORATION INTO THE MAINSTREAM

In 1987 the National Executive Committee endorsed the call for a Ministry for Women. Documents on the Ministry for Women which have been produced since then clearly show that the incorporation of women's issues into the mainstream policies of a male-dominated Labour Party resulted in a compromise of both language and content. Emphasis was still placed on opportunities for education, training and gainful employment for women; and attention was drawn to the inequalities of taxation, social security, pensions and superannuation, some of which will be ameliorated by legislation. Contract compliance and contract procurement are encouraged and the statutory provision of child-care facilities for under-fives was endorsed. However, the introduction of a shorter, more flexible working pattern was now only 'actively encouraged' and no longer subject to British legislation. This may be because of the expectation of European Community legislation in line with its social charter. Now sexism was only discussed in the context of schooling and even then only subject to the vague promise that 'action will be taken', and there was no mention of an attempt to influence the mass media's representation of women. Moreover, as is shown later, in the latest document dealing with women, even more concessions are made to moderation.

## THE 1991 POLICY DOCUMENT

The 1991 document *A New Ministry for Women* is the final adaptation into the mainstream. The document makes many pertinent points about the effects of the Thatcher Governments' policies on the lives of women. For example, it noted the existence of the Equal Pay Act but comments:

As time passed, employers have found ways to evade the law. The Conservative government had to be forced to update the law by the European Court to include the idea of equal pay for work of equal value. However, the amended law is so weak as to be of little help. Cases can take up to four years with no less than fifteen stages. In fact, there have only been nineteen successful 'equal value' cases so far.

(Richardson 1991: 6)

The 1991 document set out the agenda for the new Ministry. It will tackle many of the issues previously highlighted by the Party as needing action. The Ministry will look after women's interests in key areas: in the workplace ensuring their safety, working to protect women as consumers and in their roles in public life. The emphasis now placed on women as consumers gave recognition to the heightened concern of many women (in their roles as mothers and carers) about the degradation of the environment and its lasting effects. The involvement of women in environmental issues was reflected in another 1991 publication, *Protecting Our Future: Women and the Environment* which examined air pollution, water pollution and other areas of concern (Labour Party 1991e).

*A New Ministry for Women* once again makes the point that current government legislation, in particular on trade union rights, social security benefits and the structure of education have affected women no less than any members of society. 'This country now lags behind other countries in Western Europe in terms of equal pay; employment and maternity rights; child care; education and training opportunities; and family and social security benefits for women.' But there is no detail or commitment to radical changes to existing legislation such as trade union rights, the Education Act or the drastic reorganization of the National Health Service – all of which have profound effects on women's lives.

Nevertheless, the document sets out the terms of reference for the new Ministry and they meet many of the demands set out by Jo Richardson in 1986. Moreover, in committing itself to a Ministry for Women the Party is, compared to other political parties, setting out a radical agenda.

**The constitution and composition of the Ministry**

In terms of the structure of the Ministry for Women, there will be a Secretary of State for Women supported by a junior minister. This means that the Women's Minister will be a member of the Cabinet and certain Cabinet committees and, hence be able to influence national economic and social policy-making. The remit of the Ministry will be to monitor all government policy for its impact on women and it will also have the power to design policy and initiate legislation which will benefit women. A new select committee on women will be established. This will have the power to cross-examine ministers and senior departmental representatives, with the intention of overseeing and encouraging political debate on women's issues in Parliament.

The Minister for Women will chair a cross-departmental committee to ensure that an equal opportunities perspective is built into the work of all government departments. They, in their turn, will be required to develop their own programmes for promoting sex equality. Each department will produce an annual report detailing both their policies and practices on women (Richardson 1991: 9).

Beyond central government, women's regional advisory commissions will be established as a method of consulting with organizations in each region, and these will represent significant groups of women: voluntary groups, trade union women's organizations, women in industry and local councils.

**A catalyst for change?**

The 1991 document concentrates to a considerable extent on the bureaucratic details of the design of the Ministry for Women (in itself a welcome innovation), but at the expense of a truly woman-centred theoretical framework. The bureaucratic details are important in that they establish the rank and potential effectiveness of the Ministry, which, at Cabinet level, should be in no doubt. But the comprehensive analysis of the 'female condition' is gone; and the language of intent has changed. Phrases such as '*encourages* flexible working patterns', '*promote* fair wages', 'tackle sexual harassment', '*offer* more education and training with child care *if needed*', do not resonate in the same way as 'statutory duty' and 'legislative change', and by comparison with Jo Richardson's 1986 discussion document seem positively flabby. The commitment to increase child benefit and to bring in a national minimum wage are to be welcomed, but are hardly radical.

It seems that, in order to be accepted into the mainstream of party politics, Labour women have had to consign incisive feminist analysis to the back burner and learn the language of compromise. The ideology is undoubtedly still there (despite talk of the post-feminist age) and the achievements to date are considerable. However, it is difficult to avoid the conclusion which Adrienne Boyle reached, that 'male dominated society will attempt to reorganize and co-opt all its major efforts to resist change in the interests of continued male dominance' (Boyle 1991: 47). This brings us back to a dilemma hotly debated by feminists: compromise and achieve something or hold out for radical change. Within the movement there is no real agreement over this, but by their actions women at the top of the Labour Party seem, at least for now, to have accepted the former option. By any standards, women within the Labour Party have pushed forward the cause of women considerably; gaining acknowledgement that women need the support of a Women's Ministry is a radical departure for a political party in contemporary Britain.

It thus seems that the price of inclusion into the mainstream agenda has been high for those pushing the cause of women within the Party. Many of the most pervasive aspects of sexism and inequality are no longer addressed – in part because politics is the art of the possible and legislating to change attitudes is notoriously difficult. More importantly, however, they are not addressed because men within the political process are more willing and able to grasp concrete issues such as pay and child care and shy away from more esoteric issues such as the relationship between the portrayal of women and their role in society. Nevertheless, the Labour Party is still far ahead of other British political parties in its attempts to achieve equality for women through legislation. To end this section on an optimistic note, it is worth repeating Jo Richardson's remarks in her foreword to the 1991 booklet:

> The Ministry for Women will be more than just another Whitehall department. It will be a stimulus to the traditional departments and a catalyst for change. It will shake up the existing establishment. It will tackle the bad, discriminatory practices of the past and departments which resist positive change. The strength of the Ministry will come from pressure from women themselves. . . . I do not expect the first few years to be comfortable or free of controversy. What I do expect is that this voice for women will be a breath of fresh air in the government of this country.
>
> (Richardson 1991: 5)

## INTERNAL PARTY REFORMS

Women have played a role in the Labour Party since its establishment, but that role has essentially been one of support. Women's sections have existed since 1918. They were established with the intention of involving women with the work of the Party. These women's sections are seen as having played two roles: first in helping to develop policies relevant to women and second as support systems to women who were active in the Party. However, this structure meant that the majority of women were kept at a distance from the Party, with a few brave souls venturing into mainstream Labour politics. The majority of women were therefore involved in providing refreshments, fundraising, etc. The 1918 Labour Party constitution laid down that four places on the NEC should be filled by women. Over time, more women became active in the Party, a big boost coming with the Second World War when women were generally allowed to participate more fully in society. Nevertheless, their numbers within the Party have never come close to equalling the 52 per cent of the population as a whole they compose.

In 1972 the Labour Party published an opposition Green Paper, *Discrimination Against Women: Report of a Labour Party Study Group*. This study was initiated by the NEC and looked at education, training, social services, taxation, rights in marriage, politics, law, etc. The aim was to investigate discrimination and recommend policies to further the achievement of equal rights. This study formed the basis of legislation introduced by the Labour Governments of the 1970s. The report's conclusions about women in politics are worth quoting:

> Whilst there is no discernible prejudice against women as volun-tary workers at the grass roots level of political parties (where their fundraising and educational work is much needed and accepted), there are remarkably few women to be found either in Parliament or in the top levels of the party organisations.
>
> (Labour Party 1972: 34)

Although this was explicitly recognized, there does not appear to have been any significant action within the Labour Party in response to this problem.

As noted earlier, in *Labour's Programme 1982* a radical analysis of women's position was set out and an agenda for change established. However, change within the Party itself was slow in coming. In 1982 the party leadership for the first time seriously addressed itself to the role of women within the Party. Advocates of equality had long fought for recognition of the difficulties and barriers faced by women wishing to become politically active within the Party. However, the Party establishment was slow to grasp the significance of this problem and indeed, it was the ascendence of the left within the Party which finally allowed the issue to come to the fore.

In April 1983 the NEC published its *Charter to Establish Equality for Women Within the Party*. Half of this document was devoted to criticizing Tory policies which had affected women and a discussion of Labour's intended remedies. The other half set out steps to fulfil Labour's commitment to 'increasing the involvement of women at all levels, and on all decision-making bodies of the party'. This consisted of nine recommendations.

- Each level of the Party should examine its own structure to determine if women are being discriminated against and prevented from reaching the decision-making bodies.
- Each level of the Party should examine how it can promote women within its own organization.
- An examination should take place to ensure that women are promoted as representatives of the Party on public bodies, etc.
- An examination should take place of the timing of, and venues for, meetings to ensure that they do not deter women's participation.
- Constituency/branch parties should arrange for creche facilities and/or baby-sitting services for all meetings, conferences, etc., and aid with transport if required.
- Special encouragement should be given to women to attend training and policy courses, by provision of child-care support and financial assistance.
- All party material documents and publicity material should be non-sexist in content.
- We should ensure that sexist questions are not asked at selection conferences and on any other occasions when women are being interviewed.
- Each constituency party should appoint a women's officer who would be responsible for coordinating the women's work within the constituency and the promotion of women by the constituency.

(Labour Party 1983d)

The publication of the charter was an important step forward for women within the Party as it explicitly recognized that there were problems, and also set out ways in which they could be tackled. However, as noted, language is very important and throughout the document the word 'should' is used. There was thus no real compulsion behind the document. This meant that the onus was once again on women within the Party to see that the charter was adopted and ensure that the various recommendations suggested were carried out.

This emphasis on women within the Party ensuring that reforms happened indicates that men within the Party were either unwilling to allow women a greater say, or themselves underestimated the hold of the male culture over the Party. The fact that women were left to ensure implementation can be seen as in part reflecting a lack of understanding of the problems which women face. These increase the higher up they climb within traditionally patriarchal organizations.

Generally speaking, the further up an organisation a woman progresses, the more time she has to invest in maintaining her position and proving her worth. The more powerful the position, the greater the competition and the greater the barriers to entry. This can mean that women do not have the political power to advance the cause of other women as their energy has to be invested in survival. Although this is a very stark analysis of what is often a quite subtle process, it does seem to have been at play within the Labour Party.

The details of the 1983 charter are also important because they reflect the fact that even at a time of left-wing ascendency, women in the Party were unable to move it towards positive discrimination.

From the charter's publication in 1983 until 1986, the energy of many women within the Party was invested in the establishment of the Ministry for Women. As shown, the argument for a Ministry for Women was not won overnight and women in the Party, ably headed by Jo Richardson, had to fight all the way for their goal. This meant that little action was taken to advance the position of women within the Party. Nevertheless once the establishment of the Ministry for Women was assured, there was a renewed interest in increasing women's participation. This initially involved a reform of party structures, for example, changing the balance of representation within the women's conference (Labour Party 1988d). This was a time and energy-consuming process and one which did cause some divisions between women in different sectors of the Party.

In late 1988 the Shadow Communications Agency conducted research into women's attitudes towards politics generally and the Labour Party in particular. The research highlighted the fact that although women were in agreement with the values of the Labour Party concerning health, education, pensions, etc., this did not necessarily mean that they voted Labour. Crucially, among the reasons given for not voting Labour was the 'feeling that Labour is the most "male" party. Despite the fact that Labour ha[d] more women MPs than other parties, this is not perceived to be the case.' Interestingly, a random sample of these women thought that the Conservatives were the party with the most women MPs (Labour Party 1990e).

This research had a significant effect on the Labour Party which was attempting to explain its three consecutive election defeats. It was recognized that the Party needed to show to these potential Labour voters that the Party was responsive to their needs. More than that, the Party noted that 'increasing women's representation within party decision-making would not only be fairer, it would also be popular with the electorate at large' (Labour Party 1990e). The party's response was to enhance the profile of the Ministry for Women, women MPs were increasingly brought into the limelight, and there was a renewed interest in making party structures more amenable to women's participation.

Further recognition of the need for internal reforms came in the policy document, *Meet the Challenge, Make the Change* which bluntly stated that the Party should 'take a number of initiatives to ensure greater participation and representation of women . . . at all levels of the party' (Labour Party 1989a: 56).

Great strides forward were made at the 1989 annual conference when in three different contexts members of the Party accepted the principle of quotas for women to ensure fairer representation. Particularly important was the passing of composite resolution 54. The starting point for the resolution was 'that women's representation is inadequate at all levels of the Party and that urgent reforms are needed'. The resolution also acknowledged that *constitutional changes* were required at both national and local levels to ensure that women were fairly represented. Thus, in accepting composite 54, the Party acknowledged the case for affirmative action, something which many members (including some women) had previously rejected.

Composite resolution 54 instructed the NEC to issue guidelines to constituency parties urging that women should be considered when selecting parliamentary candidates. The NEC was also instructed to prepare a list of women interested in a parliamentary career and to circulate this list to all constituency parties. This list is known as the 'W' list and in 1990 there were 163 women on the list (Labour Party 1990d: 1). Composite 54 went on to state:

Conference also recognises that structural changes will not work in isolation and therefore instructs the National Executive Committee to: (a) make women a priority target in the mass membership campaign; (b) look at ways of making the Party more welcoming to women who have joined by providing more training and encouragement; (c) look at the lack of support for women who do stand as parliamentary and council candidates and the long anti-social hours demanded of those who are successful.

(Quoted in Labour Party 1990e: 2)

This was an important innovation as it was an attempt to move away from the traditional 'male' image to an approach which would encourage women's participation.

In sum, composite resolution 54 was further recognition of the fact that the voluntary reforms set out in the 1983 charter had never been fully implemented, and the Party now needed to consider more radical measures. In moving in this direction, the party's policies on women were becoming more radical at a time when on many other issues the Party was moving more towards the centre. The explanation for this mismatch seems to lie with the increased recognition of women as a key group of voters whose support would be necessary for electoral success. The emphasis on removing the 'male' ethos was an important part of this.

Composite 54 also set in motion a consultative exercise designed to elicit the opinions of party members, members of affiliated organizations and women's movements as to the best ways to increase women's participation in the Party. The exercise addressed the question of which bodies were quotas to apply to and at what percentages quotas should be set. The National Conference of Labour Women was also involved in the process and voted on many of the initiatives discussed in the consultation exercise. The results of that exercise were set out in *Representation of Women in the Labour Party*, published as a statement by the NEC for the 1990 conference. This document set out the conclusions and recommendations of the 1989 conference and stated:

These, together with the Labour Party's belief in equality of opportunity, can be combined to form the following statement of principles.
1. There should be equality of representation for women at all levels of the Labour Party.
2. Affirmative action is required to counteract the current imbalance of representation of women.

3. The Labour Women's Organisation has a continuing role in recruiting women to Labour and involving them in party structures.

(Labour Party 1990e)

At the 1990 conference the Party endorsed the aim of attracting a 40 per cent membership level for women in the Party at all levels by the year 2000. It thus accepted that affirmative action was required and also accepted the need to change the party's image to one more 'women-friendly'. By 1990 then, the Labour Party had taken significant steps to ensure that women were to be adequately represented in the Party in the future. This, together with its Ministry for Women, puts Labour far ahead of other British political parties.

However, it has recently been suggested that the aim to have women forming 40 per cent of Labour's MPs by the year 2000 may not be possible because of the constraints imposed by the British electoral system, the nature and organization of Parliament, and the work of MPs. It seems that women are most likely to reach that level of representation in an electoral system based upon multi-member constituencies and that the single-member constituency system used in Britain mitigates against women succeeding in sufficient numbers to satisfy calls for equality (Ellis 1991). Indeed, the Labour Party Campaign for Electoral Reform has consistently pointed this out. Thus, Labour's pathbreaking initiatives may not in themselves be enough to ensure sufficient numbers of women in the most visible area of party activity: the House of Commons. As Marquand pointed out in chapter 4, the Labour Party has begun (albeit slowly) to seriously consider electoral reform. Given the party's attempts to present itself as the political party most responsive to women's needs, there may be a case for moving the issue of electoral reform further up the party's agenda.

In late 1990 Harriet Harman MP produced a discussion document entitled *Time Gentlemen Please The Case For Changing the Sitting Times of the House of Commons*. In this she set out the case for a working day which avoided sittings late into the night.

We need to change to work more effectively. We can hardly tell business and industry that they need to change their patterns of employment if we find it impossible to change our own patterns of work. We will not be believed about recognising the changing role of women in society if Parliament cannot make the necessary changes in response.

(Harman 1990: 1)

Harman set out seven key reasons for a change in working hours. Crucial amongst these was 'Late hours deter women from seeking entry into Parliament and therefore contribute to a situation where only 6.5 per cent of members of parliament are women' (ibid. 2). The other reasons she set out were equally persuasive and likely to appeal to MPs across both party and gender lines. Her initiative met with significant support from women throughout the House of Commons and seems to have been brought into the mainstream as the Leader of the House, John MacGregor, is now planning to act (Wintour 1991c).

## CONCLUSIONS: LABOUR'S POLICIES AND PRACTICES

As this review of Labour's actions on women's issues has shown, over the last decade there have been significant policy changes designed to make the Party more responsive to the needs of women. In the early 1980s the Party produced a radical analysis of the 'women's condition' and its consequences for women and society as a whole. Although much of this radicalism has been lost in the transition to the mainstream, there are still women Labour MPs working on these issues. For example, the 1982 document talked of the need for legislation about the portrayal of women in advertising and the media. Today, Claire Short MP is campaigning to ban pictures of nude women from the pages of tabloid newspapers. Thus, although the majority of women in the Party may have muted their approach, the radical analysis of the women's position has not completely disappeared.

The 1982 programme also established an agenda for action, which is largely still in place today. Since the early 1980s the Party has been consistently committed to action on health, social security, education, employment, safety and child care. However, the way that these issues are to be tackled has varied somewhat and as we noted earlier, in many cases the Party has moved from a full commitment on issues to a promise to work towards particular aims. This is in part a reflection of the swing away from the left which has occurred since the early 1980s, but is more fundamentally a recognition of the costs involved in fulfilling the agenda for women. However, although the Party has lost some of its early radicalism – particularly its analysis of women's position in society – it has maintained promises to act on issues which affect the lives of the majority of women.

This is in stark contrast to the Conservative Party who seem to have, rather belatedly, discovered that there is discrimination against women. The Conservative Party seems to have suddenly woken up to women as a voting group and in 1991 began an initiative designed to win their votes (Cope 1991; Beavis and Watson, 1991). John Major's Opportunity 2000 programme to bring women into management is to be welcomed; however, it fails to do anything to affect the lives of the majority of women. Although the Labour Party does deal with bringing women into management (Labour Party 1991g), their programme also works at other levels of society, and thus has a much greater chance of achieving the equality women are seeking.

In implementing their agenda for women, the Labour Party will undoubtedly face problems, particularly concerning the costs of some initiatives; for example, in improving support services for carers, providing nursery places, etc. However, the chances of success are increased by the fact that many of the policies to be gathered under the Ministry for Women are in line with EC policies. This may provide aid for their implementation and also political support for their fulfilment.

The plans for a Ministry for Women undoubtedly makes Labour the most forward looking British political party. As we have shown, the fight to instal a Shadow Ministry for Women took over four years of work and women in the Party have been fighting for internal reforms for decades. Their voice has been strengthened, however, by the rediscovery of the power of women voters.

## ACKNOWLEDGEMENTS

The authors would like to thank Adrienne Boyle of Sheffield City Council's Women's Unit for her help at the outset of this project. They would also like to thank the Labour Party Library for their help in gathering information.

# Part III

# 12 The European Community

## Stephen George and Ben Rosamond

In few areas can the change in the policy of the Labour Party have been as dramatic as in the case of the European Community. The 1983 manifesto made a commitment to withdrawal from EC membership; the 1987 manifesto said virtually nothing about the EC; by the 1989 elections for the European Parliament, Labour was successfully presenting itself as the more pro-European of the two major parties.

Significant signs of the conversion were the party's embrace of the European social charter and its acceptance that sterling should be included in the exchange rate mechanism (ERM) of the European monetary system (EMS). By 1991, in the context of discussion around the two intergovernmental conferences (IGCs) on monetary union and political union, Labour had come to support the deepening and widening of the EC, adopting the principle of 'subsidiarity'[1] as the basis for delineating national competences from Community competences, the extension of qualified majority voting in the Council of Ministers to such areas as social and environmental policy, and greater powers of scrutiny for the European Parliament (EP) to ensure democratic accountability (Labour Party 1989a, 1990a).

Also, all of the Policy Review documents claimed to have a European dimension, suggesting that the leadership saw the EC not only as a separate policy area, but also as a factor in the formulation of all other policy.

## LABOUR AND BRITISH MEMBERSHIP OF THE EC

To understand the extent of the change in Labour policy on the issue it is important to recall the background to the 1983 manifesto commitment. In the 1970s opposition to membership of the EC had been one of the key planks in the strategy of the left wing of the Party (Bilski 1977; George 1990: 76–7). It had been a useful issue around which to organize opposition to the social democratic element in the leadership because it had attracted support from a wider cross-section of the party's members than any other issue. Not only the left were opposed to membership; the trade unions were against it, and so were some figures who would generally be thought to be on the right of the Party, such as Peter Shore.

Despite losing the referendum on the issue in 1975, the opponents of British membership of the EC continued their attack, and eventually this negative attitude was one of the reasons for the departure of some of the leading figures of the Party in 1981 to form the Social Democratic Party. This defection was presented by the left as a betrayal, and it became extremely difficult in the aftermath of the split for anybody to raise their voice in favour of the EC without having the same accusation levelled at them.

The 1983 manifesto commitment to withdrawal was made in this atmosphere of rampant anti-EC sentiment. It was also made in the context of an economic policy based on what was known as the Alternative Economic Strategy (AES) which advocated the regeneration of the British economy on the basis of introducing selective controls on imports and then implementing a reflationary strategy. This was deemed to be incompatible with continued membership of the EC. Indeed, in some versions of the AES withdrawal was seen as the vital prerequisite for the 'socialist' regeneration of the British economy (see Gamble, chapter 5).

It should be noted, though, that some members of the parliamentary party privately made no bones about their feeling that this line of policy was misconceived. Publicly, however, they kept their own counsel and waited for the tide within the Party to turn.

Defeat in the 1983 election led to a change of leadership and the beginnings of a reappraisal of policy generally. The issue of membership of the EC had never been high on the list of voters' concerns, but the 1983 manifesto commitment had been successfully presented by Labour's opponents as one piece of evidence in a picture of the Party as out of touch with the realities of the modern world, and therefore unfit to govern.

In the 1987 manifesto little attention was given to the EC. There was some evidence that the leadership was moving to a more accommodating position between 1983 and 1987. For example, in 1984 Neil Kinnock published an article called 'A New Deal for Europe' (Kinnock 1984a) in which, while criticizing various aspects of the EC, he argued for its reform from within rather than reiterating the calls for withdrawal. It was really only after the 1987 election, though, that rapid evolution began in the party's public attitude. Indeed, Judge (1988: 452–3) has pointed out that Labour's opposition to the ratification of the Single European Act (SEA) in 1986 was still based on a fundamentally nationalist perspective. The first significant public sign of a shift came in the autumn of 1988 over the social dimension to the 1992 project, which the Conservative Government refused to accept was necessary.

On 8 September 1988 Jacques Delors, the President of the European Commission, addressed the annual conference of the Trades Union Congress at Bournemouth. He called for a social Europe that would not just be for employers but would benefit each and every citizen of the Community. This meant it was necessary to improve workers' living and working conditions and to provide better protection for health and safety at work. He received a standing ovation (George 1990: 193).

In October 1988 Margaret Thatcher implicitly attacked Delors in a speech at the College of Europe in Bruges, in which she asserted, 'We have not successfully rolled back the frontiers of the state in Britain, only to see them reimposed at a European level, with a European super-state exercising a new dominance from Brussels' (Thatcher 1988: 4). Labour ridiculed her charges, and defended the concept of the social dimension and the harmonization of social legislation across the EC.

In the course of 1989 the Commission produced several successive drafts of what it called a 'social charter', a general declaration of the principles of a social dimension to the 1992 programme. The whole concept was rejected by the British Government, and Mrs Thatcher was outvoted by 11 to 1 on the acceptance of such a charter at the Madrid meeting of the European Council in June, and on the acceptance of a much modified version of the charter at the Strasbourg European Council in December. It was to coincide with the latter meeting that Labour produced its policy paper, *The Social Charter: How Britain Benefits* (Labour Party 1989c).

Throughout that year Labour leaders had made much more positive statements about the EC. On 28 April 1989, Neil Kinnock told the Welsh TUC:

We need a Government in Britain that will participate in the development of Europe; that will play a direct, influential role in fashioning the institutions and relationships of the market within which our economy must work in order to prosper. Mrs Thatcher's failure to accept cooperation . . . is creating the threat of a two-tier Europe, with Britain firmly in the second rank . . . a second speed Britain will not generate the wealth which is essential to sustain and enhance the prosperity and to expand the justice and freedom of the British people.

(*The Independent*, 29 April 1989)

The following month, launching the Labour manifesto for the elections to the European Parliament, Kinnock argued that Labour were 'better Europeans' than the Conservatives (*The Independent*, 19 May 1989).

This claim appeared to be vindicated to some extent by the negative campaign that the Conservatives ran in the elections, featuring strong attacks on the Commission as a body that was intent on interfering in British affairs and dictating to the British people. The campaign, about which several leading Conservatives expressed concern, preceded the worst Conservative result and the best Labour result in any nationwide election since 1979. How far this was a reflection of the public's verdict on the relative 'Europeanness' of the two parties is open to doubt. Domestic issues, and especially the unpopularity of the community charge, probably had more influence on the outcome. However, the Labour 'victory' in the election was treated by the party's leadership as vindication of the more pro-EC line that had been adopted in the aftermath of Delors' speech to the TUC, and which had been evolving since Kinnock became party leader.

If the social dimension was the pivotal issue which led Labour to align itself with the Commission against the anti-EC attitudes of the Prime Minister, monetary union was the more serious problem internally within the Conservative Party, and the more obvious basis for Kinnock's claim that Thatcher's policies would leave Britain in the slower lane of a two-speed Europe. The credibility of the Labour position, and its ability to exploit the divisions within the Conservative ranks, therefore required that a clear position be adopted on this issue.

The first question concerned British entry to the ERM of the EMS. James Callaghan, as Prime Minister in 1978, had declined to include sterling in the ERM, largely, it was thought by some observers, because of opposition within the Labour Party, which was forcibly expressed by several speakers at the October annual conference. For her own reasons, Thatcher had pursued the same line, and had continued to do so even after a majority of industrial and financial interests in Britain had begun to advocate entry. Indeed, by the end of 1989 it seemed that Thatcher was the only high ranking member of the Cabinet still opposed to entry to the ERM.

In October 1989 a furore arose over remarks made by Professor Alan Walters, the Prime Minister's personal adviser on economics, in an article in the journal *The American Economist*, in which he called the EMS 'half-baked', and maintained that Mrs Thatcher agreed with his view. This incident precipitated the resignation of the Chancellor, Nigel Lawson.

Fortuitously for Labour, the whole incident blew up just after Kinnock had reiterated his party's position on entry to the ERM, and while John Smith was actually in Brussels consulting with Delors on the question. This consolidated the image of Labour as the Party that was clear on the issue, and the Conservatives as badly divided.

Labour's conditions, as set out in the run-up to the European elections and restated by Kinnock in October 1989, were that sterling should enter the ERM once the EC member states had agreed a coordinated strategy to promote economic growth, enhanced regional support, and adequate arrangements for central banks to swap currencies in the context of support operations. There was also a need for entry to be at a competitive rate. Such far-reaching conditions were hardly a headlong rush to surrender national sovereignty, but they did mark a coherent position, which was more than the Conservatives had, and they also echoed the demands that other European socialist parties were making for the evolution of the EMS.

Qualifications were still present in Labour's response to the British alternative to the Delors plan for moving to monetary union.[2] The 'Major plan' for a 'hard Ecu', was described by John Smith as nothing but a diversion and, in an echo of Alan Walters, as 'half-baked'. However, he also made it clear that Labour was not yet ready to accept stages 2 and 3 of the Delors plan, and did not accept that binding fiscal or budgetary rules were necessary for monetary union.

Labour's image as a pro-EC party was further enhanced during the summer of 1990 when the Commission started to produce proposals for legislation to implement the social charter. In June 1990 the Commission produced a draft directive on the rights of part-time workers, which would give them the same protection as full-time workers. The Conservative Government predictably attacked the proposals, whilst Labour's Tony Blair defended them as a major advance in protecting part-time workers. In September 1990, the Commission's plans for guaranteed rights for expectant mothers were rejected by the Government; Blair described the response as 'backward-looking and isolated, anti-European and dogmatically opposed to giving a decent quality life to modern working women' (*The Independent*, 13 September 1990).

By October, membership of the ERM was again to the fore, with John Smith at the party conference advocating early entry as a means of bringing down inflation and interest rates. On the last day of the conference the Government suddenly announced that it was taking sterling into the ERM, although at a higher level than advocated by Labour, and was cutting interest rates immediately by one per cent.

Labour responded to this stealing of its clothes by moving the debate quickly onto the next issue: the creation of a European single currency and a European central bank to administer it. This was due to be discussed at the European Council meeting in Rome in October 1990, and there were clear signs that Britain would again be isolated. On 15 October, Chris Smith, a member of the opposition Treasury team, stated that Labour would be prepared to accept a single currency and a European bank, provided that the bank was democratically accountable and worked to a remit that included economic growth and a stronger regional policy (*The Independent*, 18 October 1990). Again the qualifications echoed the demands of other European socialist parties, and the clear statement contrasted with the obvious divisions within the Conservative Party.

Rome marked the beginning of the end for Mrs Thatcher, and the Labour Party was able to sit back and enjoy the carnage precipitated within the Conservative Party by her passionate and uncompromising opposition to monetary union. Shortly after the Conservative leadership issue was settled, however, senior figures in the party outlined to the press the position on the issues that were about to come under negotiation in the two IGCs.

On monetary union, the subject of one of the IGCs, a statement from the National Executive Committee in December (Labour Party 1990c) indicated that Labour would support a politically accountable European bank and a single currency, and accepted that this would require coordination of tax and budgetary policies. This position gave a rather different gloss to John Smith's statement in November 1989 that binding rules for fiscal and budgetary policy were not necessary. The December 1990 statement also linked monetary union to the achievement of the party's supply-side strategy for economic recovery.

On political union, the subject of the other IGC, Gerald Kaufman said that Labour supported a stronger European Parliament, and the extension of qualified majority voting in the Council of Ministers to cover social policy and the environment, and possibly other areas if the European level seemed the most appropriate at which to handle them (*The Independent*, 14 December 1990).

These represented quite advanced pro-EC positions, in line with those of other European socialist parties, and well out in front of those of the Conservative Party even under the new leadership of John Major. Most remarkable, though, is the distance that the Labour Party had travelled in only a little over two years; a journey the extent and speed of which need to be explained.

## THE CAUSES OF CHANGE ON EUROPE

Although the change of Labour policy towards the EC appears to have happened remarkably quickly, the speed of change in 1989–90 could not have occurred unless a longer period of evolution in thinking and attitudes had been going on in the preceding years.

The election defeat in 1983 started the reassessment, but initially it was a slow process. Perhaps it was fortunate for Labour that the EC was not an issue in the 1987 election; the budgetary dispute having been resolved, and the SEA, although signed, having yet to hit the headlines in Britain. This lull in interest in the issue allowed the Party to hide how little progress had been made in changing attitudes and policy.

The continuing negativism of some sections of the party presumably explains why change was slow. However, it seems likely that the Labour leadership was as affected as every other socialist party in Europe by the experience of the 1981–4 experiment in France. The socialist Government that was elected there in 1981 attempted to reflate the French economy to alleviate high unemployment, in fulfilment of its manifesto pledge, but in the context of continuing policies of non-expansion by France's major trading partners, and especially the Federal Republic of Germany. The result was a massive balance of payments deficit, soaring inflation and three devaluations of the French franc within the ERM, forcing an eventual reversal of policy to embrace the anti-inflationary priorities of the other members of the EC (Machin and Wright 1985; Ross *et al.* 1984).

From this experience European socialists generally drew the conclusion that a new strategy had to be devised which would operate on a European scale. It was necessary to counter the spread of neo-liberal ideas by accepting the interdependence of national economies, and of financial markets, and construct an approach that would reaffirm the idea of social consensus as the basis of economic progress, but would also acknowledge that jobs could not be created by unilateral national reflations. The corollary to this was the need to bring about some degree of convergence between the economic performance of states, to form a basis for economic management at the European level; and in order to maintain the confidence of financial markets it was necessary to base this on a low initial level of inflation. Labour leaders were actively involved in discussions with other European socialist parties throughout the 1970s, and were fully aware of the development of this strategy.

In the same period, and for much the same reasons, intellectual opinion on the British left was shifting away from support for the AES, and towards advocacy of coordinated European-wide strategies for growth. There was a general recognition of the impotence of national governments in the face of multinational capital and the consequent need for the transnationalization of the 'socialist struggle'. On this basis some elements of the Labour left actually made an input into the European debate mentioned previously (Holland 1983; Coates 1986).

The Labour group of Members of the European Parliament (MEPs) also emerged in the 1970s as an increasingly important link between the national party and European socialist thinking. Whereas the 1979 intake of Labour MEPs had all come from solid traditional Labour areas, and had been selected for their hostility to the EC, the 1984 intake was more diverse. Because the election was held in the first year after a national election, when the Government was going through a period of post-election unpopularity, Labour won more seats than in 1979, and in many cases the new MEPs were less anti-EC and more open minded. Also, some of the older MEPs gradually lessened their hostility after experiencing the reality of working with socialist colleagues in the European Parliament. The ability of MEPs to play the game of 'pork-barrel politics' and help local authorities in their constituencies to benefit from the European Regional Development Fund increased their influence at local level, and helped the image of the EC when its support for development projects was contrasted with the lack of support from the British Government.

At the same time there was an important learning process about the EC going on independently within the leadership of the trade unions (see Rosamond, chapter 7). This also resulted from the practical experience of working in Europe alongside colleagues from other member states, in forums such as the Economic and Social Committee. At a time when trade unions were being attacked and denied a voice in national decision-making, the trade union officials found that their opinions were still sought and sometimes acted upon at the level of the EC.

Generational change and response to the challenge of Thatcherism also brought a new type of trade unionist to the fore, people like John Edmonds of the GMB, who were more pragmatic in their outlook than the older guard, and more open minded about the benefits of working through the EC. At the same time, experience began to change the attitude of some of the longer-established figures, like Clive Jenkins.

Initially this change in attitude did not extend fully to the rank and file. Nevertheless, some union leaderships realized that it was necessary to re-evaluate the oppositional stance to the EC, and this led to attempts to convert the membership. A look at successive GMB conferences in the mid-1980s, for example, indicates that rank and file hostility to the EC was being managed out of the agenda by the union's leadership. In 1988 the TUC produced an excellent report on 1992, prior to its annual conference, which was entitled *Maximising the Benefits, Minimising the Cost* (TUC 1988), and which presented 1992 as a package which could be reconciled with trade union interests. Overall, a lot of groundwork was done to effect a shift in policy, with Delors' speech to the 1988 TUC conference marking the public conversion.

It is difficult to exaggerate the importance of this speech as a turning point in the evolution of opinion on the EC within the TUC. Delors spoke to the delegates about the things for which they were working and in which they believed: a say in economic and social policy-making; better protection for the rights of their members and increased rights for vulnerable groups such as the unemployed. Whereas the prospect of achieving these objectives had been set back yet again at national level by the re-election of Thatcher, Delors held out the prospect of achieving them through action within the EC. This is what so pleased delegates that they gave him a standing ovation, and so displeased Thatcher that she felt obliged to launch a counter-attack in Bruges a few weeks later.

At this point the issue of the EC became entwined with the fundamental party-political division over the future of the British economy and society, with support for the EC having the connotation of being the 'progressive' side of the argument, and opposition appearing to involve alignment with the Thatcherite vision. Just as it had been virtually impossible in the early 1980s to raise a loud voice within the Labour Party in favour of the EC without seeming to be in sympathy with the SDP, so the whole debate around the social charter made it very difficult in the early 1990s to raise a loud voice within the Labour Party against the EC without appearing to be in sympathy with the social policies of Thatcherism.

For the Labour leadership the issue of the social dimension therefore provided the ideal vehicle to carry the Party as a whole into a more positive stance towards the EC. Was the Delors speech, then, part of a coordinated strategy? Perhaps it was, because there were reasons why the Labour leadership would be feeling the urgency of carrying the Party into a firmer commitment at this time. On the other hand, Delors did not state his position only at the TUC conference: it was one of a series of speeches and interviews that he gave throughout the EC in an attempt to rally the support of trade unionists behind his proposals for a social dimension. Partly the aim of this series of statements was to gain support for the Commission's social programme. More importantly it was part of a campaign, of which the social charter itself was also a part, to ensure that trade unions would be prepared to support the 1992 programme.

The freeing of the internal market was fundamental to the Commission's hopes of reviving the economy of the EC, which had been in recession throughout the 1970s. There had already been a remarkable surge in investment in anticipation of the single market. But the single market would inevitably involve losers as well as winners, and the costs would in part have to be carried by trade unionists in various member states, who might prove active in mobilizing the unions in defence of their jobs. Delors' speech was, then, part of a wider campaign rather than a deliberate and isolated intervention in British domestic politics. On the other hand, undermining the obstructionist stance of the British Government was central to that campaign; and the speech did provide the ideal focal point for an acceleration of the Labour leadership's move to embrace EC membership, which had become more important by 1988 for a number of reasons.

First, the signing of the SEA in 1986 marked a considerable step away from national economic sovereignty. If anybody within the Labour leadership had held onto the idea that a national economic programme was still feasible, the SEA destroyed the last vestiges of that hope. The introduction of majority voting into the Council of Ministers on all matters concerned with the freeing of the internal market signalled an acceleration of economic interdependence beyond that already existing.

Second, the pace of events in the EC was also accelerating rapidly. It was becoming increasingly evident that the Conservatives would not be easily able to accept several aspects of the 1992 programme that were considered by other member states and by the Commission to be fundamental. These included the social dimension, but much more significantly monetary union. It became imperative for Labour to take up a positive position on monetary union for two reasons: because it would not be in a position to exploit the potentially devastating splits within the Conservative Party if it was open to the accusation of being itself indecisive and divided; and also because it was necessary in order to fill the gap in its economic policy left by the effective demise of incomes policies as a weapon against inflation.

The latter policy objective related to the credibility of Labour as a party of government. The Conservative victory in 1987 on the basis of little more than 40 per cent of the vote indicated that Labour still had to win the confidence of a large number of anti-Thatcher voters. Even after eight years the Conservatives were still able to present Labour as the Party that had tolerated rampant inflation and bullying trade unions. This had the effect of sustaining support for the centre parties amongst those who rejected Thatcherism but still could not forget the Wilson–Callaghan years.

Membership of the ERM, and ultimately European monetary union, provided a way of alleviating some of these concerns, although the social dimension was a much easier way into converting the Party as a whole to Europeanism, and also allowed one important step to be taken away from the old Labour orthodoxy. After some hesitation, the party's leadership accepted the social charter in full in December 1989 (Labour Party 1989c), including the guarantee of the right of workers not to join a trade union as the corollary of their right to join a union (*The Independent*, 7 December 1989). This in itself marked a retreat from the defence of the closed shop that had once been Labour policy. Helpfully for the leadership, the position of the social charter on this issue coincided with the development of Labour's own policy on industrial relations, so that embracing the European policy provided a useful means of making a controversial switch in domestic policy.

Much more significant, though, was the acceptance of membership of the ERM. The external discipline that membership imposed would ensure that a Labour Government would have to follow anti-inflationary policies even in the face of persistently high levels of unemployment. In the 1987 document *New Jobs for Britain*

(Labour Party 1987e), the Party had already accepted that control of inflation rather than economic expansion would be the top priority for a Labour Government. The problem was getting voters, and the financial markets, to take this seriously. All previous Labour Governments had rewarded their loyal constituency upon return to office with expansionary policies that had immediately stored up problems for the future. If outsiders were to believe the new policy orientation, a positive step such as embracing the discipline of the ERM was necessary. It would also tie a Labour Government into commitments that would provide a perfect excuse for resisting the calls of its supporters for immediate expansionary policies. In this way Labour could use the obligations of EC membership in the same way that continental parties had been using them for years, as a weapon in internal party politics.

Persuading the Party to go along with the commitment to the ERM, and eventually to monetary union under certain conditions, was made inestimably easier for Labour by Thatcher's adamant opposition to both steps, and the trouble that this caused within the Conservative Party and the Government. If Edward Heath's staunch support for membership of the EC had helped the anti-EC faction within the Labour Party in the early 1970s, Thatcher's increasingly shrill attacks on the ERM and the plans for monetary union made it much easier for the leadership at the start of the 1990s to swing the Party into line behind the strategy of the external constraint on inflation, and also behind the European socialist programme.

## CONCLUSION

Labour travelled a remarkable distance from its position of opposition to membership of the EC in the early 1980s to an apparent full embrace of a European socialist strategy, involving increased powers for the EC, at the start of the 1990s. The change came about in response to both European developments and domestic political considerations. Adopting a pro-EC stand on the social charter helped the Labour leadership to move away from a commitment to the trade union closed shop in its industrial relations policy, and gave it a convenient weapon with which to beat the Conservative Government. Early adoption of a commitment to membership of the ERM, and qualified acceptance of monetary union, allowed Labour to exploit serious divisions within the Government, and potentially provided a future Labour Government with a useful excuse not to repeat the mistakes of the French socialist Government of the early

1980s by adopting disastrous national reflationary policies to reward its core constituency in the aftermath of an election victory.

There are grounds, though, for questioning how deep the conversion to European policy has gone even within the leadership. In June 1991, Neil Kinnock disappointed a majority of Labour MEPs and many of his EC counterparts by refusing to accept the formation of a European socialist party which would have bound national parties into adopting joint policies on matters coming under the competence of the EC, and a single manifesto for the 1994 elections to the EP. The sticking point appeared to be that policies would have been decided by majority vote, ruling out the use of a Labour veto on policies with which the national leadership could not agree. Only Kinnock spoke against the proposal at a special socialist summit in Luxembourg, and only his Danish counterpart supported him (*The Independent*, 4 June 1991).

Examination of the Policy Review as a whole also indicates that, although it claimed to possess a European dimension, it was still entirely premised on the achievement of a Labour majority at Westminister. It was interesting in this respect that Labour's leaders did not join in the chorus of European socialist criticism about the watering down by the Commission of the provisions of the social charter, on the grounds that a majority Labour Government would enact the provisions of the original charter anyway. In other words, the Party was not formulating its policy with implementation at the level of the EC in mind, which perhaps cast some doubt on the acceptance in the Policy Review of the principle of subsidiarity.

It is also probably true that there were more divisions within the Party than members allowed to emerge during a period when there was a premium on winning the next election. While traditional opponents like Tony Benn made no secret of their doubts about the EC, in the interests of party unity they did not attack the leadership on the issue. The suspicion remained that once Labour formed the Government, some of these divisions might come to the fore, and that doubts about the policy of the leadership might prove to be more widespread than had appeared.

On the other hand, it has to be said that the Party as a whole underwent a considerable process of learning about the EC in the 1980s, which was continuing in the 1990s, and seemed likely to accelerate if there were a Labour Government in the future. The road that Labour was travelling had already been travelled by other European socialist parties, and given the momentum of the development of the EC in a more federal direction it seemed unlikely in the early 1990s that Labour would not arrive at the same destination as its EC counterparts eventually.

## ACKNOWLEDGEMENTS

Stephen George would like to acknowledge the contribution made to his thinking on this subject by papers presented to the 1991 conference of the European Community Studies Association (North America) by David M. Andrews (Massachusetts Institute of Technology), John Gaffney (Aston University) and Manfred McDowell (Southeastern Massachusetts University).

# 13 The Labour Party and foreign policy

*Joanna Spear*

## INTRODUCTION

This chapter focuses on the overall thrust of foreign policy and highlights other important elements, particularly the relationship with the United States, relations with the Third World and attitudes towards international organizations. It begins with an overview of Labour's foreign policy. The following sections analyse each phase of policy in detail. The final section of the chapter examines the implementation of Labour's foreign policy in the 1990s, highlighting some of the prospects and problems involved.

In order to assess Labour's chances of implementing its foreign policy, it is necessary to examine the international context within which they will have to operate. The international system has changed markedly in the last five years with the end of the Cold War and talk of a New World Order. More broadly, four major trends can be discerned which are affecting the position of Britain in the international system. First, the international system is becoming much more interdependent with national economies becoming evermore enmeshed. Consequently, it is difficult for any one state to successfully act alone. In the contemporary system concerted action is often required for successful policy implementation. Britain has recognized this by joining multilateral organizations, particularly the European Community (EC), which indicates the second major change in the international system. This is the trend towards regionalism in the aftermath of the Cold War. With the end of bipolarity, the system seems to be evolving into a multipolar arrangement based upon regions. Necessity is forcing Britain closer to Europe and making the coordination of foreign and security policy an increasing priority. A final trend clearly identifiable is the emergence of a new international agenda which encompasses issues such as the transition to democracy and market-based economies of ex-communist states, economic recession and environmental pollution and degradation. What is important about this new agenda is that it is not of any one state's making and that the issues cannot be tackled by individual sovereign states.

Together these four trends form the constraints within which a Labour Government's foreign policy would be created and implemented. Britain has responded to these trends by becoming more involved in multilateral institutions such as the EC, the North Atlantic Treaty Organisation (NATO), the Western European Union (WEU) and other regional arrangements. However, all of these have the effect of cutting down the ability of a government to pursue an independent foreign policy. One of the major implications of this is that the differences between British political parties over foreign policy will become more apparent than real, as the menu for choice continues to diminish. Thus a new type of consensus may be emerging, one based upon necessity. These points will be returned to in the final section of this chapter.

**OVERVIEW**

In Britain from 1945 to about 1981 a bipartisan consensus existed concerning foreign policy. The basis of this consensus was a belief that the possession of nuclear weapons was a necessity given Britain's position in the international system and the responsibilities she faced as a great power.

However, in 1981 the Labour Party broke away from the consensus. With the ascendancy of the left in the Party, the foreign policy agenda was transformed. Between 1981 and 1984 the Party advocated a radical re-orientation of British foreign policy designed to facilitate the establishment of socialism at home. The overall thrust of the policy was neutralist, anti-American, isolationist and opposed to the use of force. However, one area of continuity with past policy was the continued advocacy of multilateral diplomacy as the means to solve international problems.

From 1986 onwards there were indications that the party's foreign policy was beginning to edge back towards the centre. Although the Party fought the 1987 election on a unilateralist platform there was no longer a commitment to withdraw from the EC and the emphasis on neutralism was gone. After the electoral defeat in 1987 the Policy Review was initiated. The review of foreign policy was justified on the basis of changes taking place in the international system, specifically the end of the second Cold War; however, it also reflected the fact that Labour's radical foreign policy had been unpopular with British voters.

The period 1987 to date has seen the Party move more towards the centre in foreign policy. The Labour Party is now very supportive of the European Community and no longer anti-American in tone. In terms of relations with the Third World, although support remains strong, the aim is now to pragmatically work through existing organizations such as the International Monetary Fund (IMF) to achieve change, as opposed to championing radical reform. In the post-review period faith in multilateral diplomacy has remained, and indeed has been strengthened by its conversion to a pro-EC stance and its increased enthusiasm for NATO in its new role as a political organization.

## POST-WAR LABOUR FOREIGN POLICY

In the early post-war period, foreign policy was seen as something different from the everyday stuff of politics. Due to its importance to the survival of the British State, there was a general perception that foreign and defence policy should be insulated from the normal pushing and pulling of party politics. This is best expressed by the aphorism 'politics stops at the water's edge' and indeed, until 1981, major disputes over British foreign and defence policy between British parties were few and far between. What disputes there were tended to centre on the means of foreign policy, rather than the ends. This is not to say that there were not factions within both major parties who sought to move away from this apolitical approach to foreign policy, merely to indicate that they were unsuccessful.

As Barber has noted, in the pre-war period Labour's Clement Attlee had said that Socialist and Conservative foreign policies were quite distinct, based upon different views about the nature of society. However, once in power in 1945, Attlee eschewed 'ideological abstractions' in favour of the 'national interest' which he declared did not vary with the political hue of the party in power (Barber 1976: 26).

This bipartisanship was in part a consequence of the two parties having worked together in the wartime coalition Government. However, it also reflected a more general situation in British politics where often shadow ministers have had recent experience in government and have a common perception of the foreign policy problems to be tackled. This led quite often to a discernible 'national view' of an issue. The bipartisanship was also a consequence of Britain's position as a power in decline in the international system. In such a situation foreign policy is more than ever about attempting to maintain and maximize power and influence.

Soon after the Second World War, Winston Churchill remarked that British foreign policy interests lay in three interlocking 'circles' or spheres of interest; Europe, the Empire and the 'special relationship' with the United States. Churchill said that these spheres were of equal importance. However, trying to maintain interests in all three against a background of economic problems led to a gradual recognition that Britain was experiencing 'overstretch'. Foreign policy then came to focus on how to scale down commitments without losing influence.

One solution pursued by both parties was decolonization and the transformation of the Empire into the Commonwealth. This was completed in three major phases: under Labour in 1947–8, under the Conservatives in the late 1950s following Macmillan's 'wind of change' speech, and again under Labour from 1968 onwards with the retreat from east of Suez. Britain's withdrawal was carefully undertaken so as to avoid the creation of a power vacuum and in many instances the United States took over Britain's defence commitments. The move from Empire to Commonwealth marked a downgrading of the importance of relations with the Third World and a concomitant upgrading of relations with the United States and Europe. It was also recognition that Britain was no longer a great power.

In the post-war period relations with the United States – the so-called 'special' relationship – were given a high priority. There was great interdependence between the two in the areas of security and economics. However, as Northedge noted, this closeness also engendered frictions (Northedge 1974: 170–85). The British Empire was a prime source of friction between the US and Britain. The process of decolonization removed this in large part, but both the left within the Labour Party and the US urged that the process be completed with haste. This was an ironic congruence in that later the left would be criticizing US neo-imperialism in the Third World.

One of the major post-war disputes between Labour and the US was over British rearmament in the early 1950s and its effects on the British economy. The US insisted that Britain rearm to a tune of £1,500 million per annum. This led to disputes within the Labour Cabinet as the cost had to be financed by charging for some NHS services. The result was the 1951 resignations of three cabinet ministers, the most prominent of whom, Bevan declared, 'we have allowed ourselves to be dragged too far behind the wheels of American diplomacy' (quoted in Northedge 1974: 181). Bevan's predictions about the economic effects of giving way to US demands appeared to come true when the Labour Government was unseated as a result of the economic crisis precipitated by rearmament. Bevan headed a splinter group within the Party for the next six years which provided a platform for Labour critics of the US. However, in 1957, Bevan was reconciled with the leadership and anti-Americanism within the Party receded.

Other disputes with the US concerned trade with the Soviet Union and communist China, and more fundamentally, over economic policy. The two western powers had very different economic policies; the US favouring free trade whilst the British, particularly under Labour, sought to avoid the 'anarchy' of an unrestricted market place. This led to some disputes within the General Agreement on Tariffs and Trade (GATT) and COCOM (the inter-alliance organization formed to monitor trade with the Eastern bloc). There were also disputes in the relationship during the years of the Cold War, particularly over the status of ex-colonies who now declared themselves neutral (for example, India). Whereas the US was unable to tolerate this – considering that it made these new states easy prey to the communists – the British were more sanguine, regarding these states as capable of maintaining their neutral status (Northedge 1974: 187–8).

The warmth of the 'special relationship' has always very much depended upon personal relations between President and Prime Minister, and an element of this was obviously political affinity. Thus, the times when there has been a Democrat in the White House and a Labour Prime Minister have seen the Labour Party being particularly supportive of US policies. The last such conjunction was when Jimmy Carter was President and James Callaghan was Prime Minister. During the period 1977–9 the two leaders cooperated on a range of issues, not least on policies towards 'hot spots' such as Southern Africa, and on policies such as arms transfer control and the prevention of missile proliferation (Spear 1990).

Relations with Europe are dealt with more fully in chapter 12 of this volume. However, it is important to note that initially both Labour and the Conservatives were opposed to membership of the EC. This was in part because joining the EC could be seen as an admission that Britain was no longer able to stand alone as a great power. The decision to seek membership thus had symbolic importance which went beyond the act itself. Indeed, the debate over entry caused intra-party disputes for both Labour and the Conservatives and the hostilities engendered were never fully assuaged. Nevertheless, by 1974 the party leadership was in favour of EC membership.

According to Northedge 'a strong case can be made out for saying that the British Labour Party since 1945 has on the whole shown greater sensitivity to UN opinion and charter obligations than have the Conservatives' (Northedge 1974: 313). There are several reasons for this. The basic philosophy of the Party is that conflict is a result of removable conditions and that the role of the international organization is to work to eradicate the inequalities and poverty which provoke conflicts. The UN was also regarded as the right forum in which to negotiate multilateral arms control – another priority for the Party. Moreover, the Party has always been more internationalist in focus than has the Conservative Party. Finally, the party membership has remained more committed to the UN in the post-war period than has the population as a whole. Together these conditions add up to an idealistic streak in the Labour Party's approach to international organizations.

In summary, the period 1945–81 saw Labour Party policy committed to the possession of nuclear weapons, and involved in three different spheres of interest: the Third World, the Atlantic Alliance and Europe and supportive of multilateral diplomacy.

**LABOUR'S FOREIGN POLICY 1979–1987**

As has been set out by Smith (see chapter 1), in the aftermath of the 1979 election defeat there was a significant change in the balance of power within the Labour Party. The left achieved a greater degree of dominance and, although not in complete control, was in many areas able to set the agenda for the Party. This is certainly true in the area of foreign policy where the moderate tone of the Callaghan Government was replaced by a more radical approach. The primary reason for the change was the desire to have a foreign policy which would facilitate socialism at home and abroad. More generally there was a perception that the old policies had not worked as the world had slipped into the Second Cold War and a deep economic crisis. There were thus fears for the future of the international system.

The new radicalism resulted in the Party committing itself to nuclear disarmament, withdrawal from the EC and advocating a radical restructuring of the international economic system through a New International Economic Order (NIEO). This new radicalism was an attempt to build a socialist foreign policy and provide Britain with the independence from other states in the system to institute socialism at home.

At the 1982 party conference a motion achieved the two-thirds majority necessary to make unilateral nuclear disarmament official Labour Party policy. Although there had long been support within the Party for unilateralism, this was a radical departure from the traditional bipartisan approach to British defence policy. The policy remained controversial within the Labour Party, to the point where ex-Prime Minister James Callaghan was accused of having sabotaged Labour's chances at the 1983 general election by his statements in opposition to unilateralism.

Alongside the move to unilateralism there were attempts within the Party to ensure that Britain would leave NATO and would remove all US military bases from Britain. These moves were seen as the logical corollaries to unilateralism. Nevertheless, the left was unable to triumph on these issues. The party leadership declaring that it would remain within NATO, but stressing that it would work to change that organization (Dunn 1991: 13).

In opting for unilateralism the Labour Party declared itself to be reflecting the concerns of ordinary people about what has been termed the 'Third World War Scare' (Sabin 1986). Nevertheless, the policy was very controversial, particularly as it was being proposed during a period of extreme tension between East and West. The political debate which ensued has been described as fundamentally a debate about Britain's role in the world as much as a discussion of British possession of nuclear weapons (Dunn 1991). Although the Conservatives publicly scorned Labour's unilateralism as unworkable and undesirable, the Government felt sufficiently threatened to produce in the 1983 statement on the defence estimates a comprehensive case for the possession and modernization of British nuclear forces.

It is important to note that alongside the Labour Party's policy of unilateralism was a commitment to increase spending on conventional defence. Although in part a 'sweetener' intended to placate the defence establishment, it was also evidence of the party's commitment to an activist foreign policy. The Party also laid stress on Britain's role as a catalyst for further disarmament and its unilateral action as a means of implementing the Nuclear Non-proliferation Treaty's commitment to vertical disarmament (Labour Party 1982a: 247).

The aim to re-order relations with the Third World was also reflected in a continued interest in arms transfer restraint (Labour Party 1982a: 250 and 259; Labour Party 1987d), something which had been practised by the Callaghan Government (Spear 1990).

In 1982 the Falkland Islands were invaded by Argentina. This incident served to underline divisions within the Party over the use of force. Despite Michael Foot's statement to the House of Commons pledging Labour's full support to the Government in its handling of the crisis and the strong statements issued by the NEC, there was vocal opposition from party members to the Government's favouring of military over diplomatic solutions (Labour Party 1982a: 52–4). The depth of divisions is illustrated by a vote taken in the House of Commons on 20 May 1982. Thirty-three Labour MPs defied a three-line whip and voted against the use of force in the crisis (House of Commons 1982). This opposition to the Labour Party line led to the dismissal of three front-bench MPs (Faulds, Tilley and Dalyell) on 24 May. This hostility to the Thatcher Government's actions in the Falklands did not cease with the end of the conflict. Indeed, MPs such as Tam Dalyell continued to investigate British actions in the conflict, such as the sinking of the Argentinean ship, the General Belgrano (Dalyell 1982), and the Party consistently called for an independent inquiry into its sinking (Labour Party 1984e). Like the NATO vote before it, the Falklands crisis served to underline the gap between the party leadership and the membership. The leadership was driven by the need to support the perceived 'national interest' and thus be seen as fit to govern, and by the knowledge that Thatcher would seize any opportunity to discredit Labour. However, this inevitably brought the leadership into dispute with the left of the Party.

Another indication of the increasing radicalization of Labour Party foreign policy in the early 1980s was the swing away from support for the EC. There had always been a section of the Party opposed to membership of the Community and they took every available opportunity to re-state this opposition (see, for example, Labour Party 1977b). The 1983 manifesto included a commitment to withdraw from the EC. This was justified as necessary because the Community would hamper the party's economic programme and also desirable because the Community did not include all European states (Labour Party 1983c: 32–3; Labour Party 1984c). Together with the move to unilateralism this re-orientation of policy away from the EC amounted to the first break with the post-war British consensus on foreign policy.

In contrast to past foreign policy, the party's policies in the early 1980s were openly anti-American. The reason for this was that the party's new orientation to a socialist, anti-imperialist foreign policy made the US the natural enemy standing in the way of progress towards a more just international system and as an obstacle to development in the Third World. Although the degree of anti-Americanism initially reflected the different positions of those in the Party *vis-à-vis* the new orientation of foreign policy, concern was generally heightened after the election of Ronald Reagan as President. Indeed, in many ways this was a reflection of opinion more generally. Reagan's bellicosity and strident championing of the US role as both the policeman of the system and the means by which communism was to be 'rolled back' caused unease throughout Europe and in political parties of all complexions. The US commitment to European security was increasingly doubted and there was concern that the US would use Europe as a nuclear battlefield in its confrontation with communism. Indeed, as Dunn has noted, in the debate over the purchase of Trident missiles by Britain: 'one of the ironies of this entire episode [was] that it was precisely this concern over the American security guarantee that bolstered the support for the continued possession of an independent deterrent' (Dunn 1991: 14).

There was also strident opposition to US foreign policy in Central America. Labour Party policy towards the region was spurred and supported by the various solidarity campaigns with links to the Party. These campaign groups provided expertise and information and kept these issues to the fore of the party's foreign policy agenda. From the early 1970s onwards the Labour Party had stressed its commitment to democracy in the region and concern over human rights, and in this context had opposed US support for authoritarian regimes (see, for example, Labour Party 1978). From 1979 on, there was great sympathy for the Sandinista Government of Nicaragua in its struggle to build a socialist society on the ashes of the Somoza dictatorship and in the face of 'a US financed counter-revolution and direct military intimidation from the United States of America' (Labour Party 1983c). This is a reference to the Reagan Doctrine directed against Central American left-wing parties (Labour Party 1981b). The President's chosen sight for the battle against the forces of the 'evil empire' was Central America and he set about systematically undermining these parties via the Reagan Doctrine (Labour Party 1984b)

Opposition to the United States' foreign policy and its emphasis on anti-communism did not necessarily mean that the Labour Party did not accept that there was, in some sense, a Soviet threat; rather there was a belief that the threat was exaggerated out of all proportion and that because of this the US was primarily responsible for the demise of *détente* and the onset of the Second Cold War. Labour Party thinking on this was clearly set out in *Baiting the Bear*, produced in 1984 which noted, 'The new policy of the Reagan Administration is to "prevail" over the Soviet Union to reverse its external and internal policies through the wide application of political, economic and military pressure' (Labour Party 1984b: 27).

In the 1980s, Labour Party foreign policy also paid particular attention to relations with the Third World. This was a consequence of the move to establish a socialist, neutralist foreign policy and an attempt to build new relations with other states who attempted to stand apart from the superpower confrontation. Another factor which led Labour to conclude that relations with the Third World needed to be restructured was the international debt crisis (Labour Party 1984c). The Party also recognized the destabilizing effects of poverty and injustice in the world as highlighted by the influential Brandt Report (Brandt 1980). As Labour's 1982 programme stated:

> We are committed to stand side by side with those people and governments fighting to break out of the vice of oppression and poverty . . . the world is an unjust and unequal place, and we are determined to radically alter the status quo.
>
> (Labour Party 1982)

This was to be achieved by reconstructing the world's financial institutions (i.e. the IMF, World Bank, GATT) so that they worked in favour of the whole international community, that is, a commitment to a NIEO (Labour Party 1986d). The Party also focused on the issue of British development aid and consistently highlighted the Conservative failure to meet the United Nations target of aid amounting to 0.7 per cent of gross national product (Labour Party 1982b, 1983c, 1985d, 1987a; Kinnock 1986). The Party also criticized the Thatcher Government's decision to leave the United Nations Educational and Cultural Organization (UNESCO) which was seen by Labour as a vital element of relations with the Third World (Foulkes 1985).

A major issue for the Party throughout the 1980s was South Africa, where it consistently campaigned for full sanctions to be instituted against the apartheid state (Labour Party 1984c, 1985b, 1986d). The Party also criticized Thatcher's policy of 'constructive engagement' (Labour Party 1985e).

## INDICATIONS OF CHANGE, 1986–1987

By 1986 there were signs that changes in policy were on the way. In part this was a response to the changing international system, but also to the problem of the 1983 electoral defeat. A key international development was the accession to power of President Gorbachev whose commitment to disarmament, although in a sense vindicating Labour's policy, ironically came at a time when there was new debate in the Party over the merits of unilateralism (Carvel, 1986). Moreover, Neil Kinnock had shown increasing flexibility over the timetable for nuclear disarmament (Perry, 1986; Withrow and Hughes, 1986). In the absence of a clear change in direction, but aware of the electoral target unilateralism presented to the Conservative Party, the Labour Party became a vocal advocate of accepting Soviet arms control proposals, hoping that they could thus avoid the issue (Labour Party 1986b). Other signs of policy change include those noted by George and Rosamond (see chapter 12), concerning the party's attitude to EC membership. The party's enthusiasm for the Community increased as it came to be seen as a means for protecting the rights of individuals and for improving working conditions, workers rights, etc. Kinnock also made determined attempts to improve the party's relationship with the Reagan administration (Ball, 1986; DeYoung, 1986).

The 1987 election manifesto, *Britain Will Win*, paid comparatively little attention to foreign policy, reflecting the fact that some issues were once again the subject of intense debate. As a consequence, the manifesto concentrated more upon ideas and concepts than concrete policies, talking about human rights, freedom and peace. The only real policy pledges concerned sanctions for South Africa – a major bone of contention with the Thatcher Government – and development. A reflection of the changing attitudes was that the manifesto made no mention of withdrawal from the EC, but maintained elements of the previous attack on its interference in national economic management (Labour Party 1987c). On the issue of disarmament the manifesto stressed the party's preference for negotiated multilateral disarmament, but pledged to unilaterally disarm if negotiations failed. In the run up to the election the debate about defence policy raged and Kinnock was forced to call upon the Party to stop bickering in public about the unilateral policy (Cassell and Riddell, 1987; Bevins and Brown, 1987). Although the commitment to achieving UN aid targets remained, there was a more conciliatory attitude towards the major economic institutions: 'We will promote international action to lift the burden of Third World debt and improve the trading conditions of the developing countries' (Labour Party 1987c: 16). The party's election platform also stressed the need for multilateral action to solve problems such as terrorism, and advocated confidence-building measures between East and West (Labour Party 1987b; *Financial Times*, 23 March 1987). The manifesto also stressed the role of international organizations such as the UN, the Commonwealth, NATO and the EC (Labour Party 1987c; Labour Party 1987d).

## THE POLICY REVIEW AND POST-REVIEW FOREIGN POLICY

The Policy Review was formally initiated at the 1987 Labour Party conference. The team examining foreign policy was convened by Gerald Kaufman, MP and Tony Clarke of the NEC under the title *Britain and the World*. The first indications of the policy changes under consideration came in the 1988 report to the NEC conference. The report presented there talked of the best means to the desired end: a socialist foreign policy. The document stressed Labour's commitment to multilateral diplomacy (and stressed Britain's prime position to act as a motivator in various forums), Third World development and support for Southern Africa. The document emphasized that Labour would work for the reform of the EC from within, and stayed on the fence over defence policy, blandly stating that nuclear weapons create hostility, but deliberately not providing any solutions to this problem (Labour Party 1988b). The debate on foreign policy at the party conference provided further amplification of the review group's thinking. However, overall the debate concentrated on defence policy and a motion on unilateralism (opposed by the leadership) was passed by a clear majority (Labour Party 1988b).

The full report from the review group, *A Power For Good*, was presented to conference in 1989 and contained detailed policies as well as aims and values. Importantly, there was no mention of socialism in this document – the word was no longer connected with foreign policy. Again there was a stress on multilateralism and this was reinforced by its positive attitude to the European Community. The report looked at various international trouble spots: the Middle East, Southern Africa, Cyprus, the Falklands, Central America, etc. In each of these areas the stress was on multilateral diplomacy and Britain's role as a key player in international institutions.

In terms of policies on aid and development, the Party maintained its commitment to action. However, all mention of the NIEO had disappeared and in its place was an emphasis on the positive role that Britain could play in working for change through existing institutions.

Thus, the policy was still interested in change, but was no longer radical. That is, the Party now calculated that the best way to ensure a better deal for the Third World was by pragmatically working for reform from within, rather than advocating a radical transformation of the whole economic system. One new element of the party's approach was an emphasis on ensuring that development was environmentally responsible. This was in part a linking of foreign to domestic policies and reflected interdependence between the two, but it was also a recognition of the popularity of the issue with the British electorate.

Croft (see chapter 14) discusses in detail the Policy Review's statements on defence. What is worth noting is the continued emphasis on arms control and Britain's role as a motivator for the process. Interestingly, there was also discussion of NATO's role as a political organization, in part reflecting the emerging debate in Europe but also serving to make continued membership more palatable to peace campaigners within the Party. NATO was therefore positively presented as a means through which to secure desirable ends.

Continuing the trend noted from 1986 onwards, there was a significant move away from anti-Americanism to an emphasis on the need to cooperate with the US to achieve positive outcomes. This cooperative attitude was obvious during the 1991 Gulf War against Iraq where the party leadership went out of its way to stress support for the US-led alliance. This was legitimized by the UN endorsement of the alliance's actions, but was nevertheless in stark contrast to pre-review attitudes to US interventions in the Third World.

The Gulf War also served to highlight the changed attitude of the Labour Party to the use of force. Kinnock was able to claim with confidence that the Party supported the use of force if diplomacy failed. This was in contrast to Michael Foot's position during the Falklands conflict, arguably a dispute in which Britain had a much more immediate interest. The new professionalism of the Party was also illustrated by the way in which dissent from party policy was handled. It was made clear that there was no room for dissent by members of the front-bench team. This led to two resignations from the front-bench – Claire Short and Tony Banks – but added to the perception of the Party as supportive of the war (Wintour, 1991; *The Guardian*, 13 March 1991). It was also the case that many of the Labour MPs opposed to the war were those marginalized on the left of the Party; for example, Tony Benn and Tam Dalyell

(*The Guardian*, 13 March 1991). Their opposition, then, did not overly detract from the perception of a party ready to fight to defend British interests. Moreover, the Conservative Party under John Major chose not to exploit the divisions that did exist in the Party – restraint which Margaret Thatcher would have been unlikely to have shown. This again allowed Labour to present itself as a party fit and ready to take over the management of Britain's foreign policy.

Labour's 1991 publication, *Opportunity Britain*, continued the emphasis on multilateralism and declared the alliance's success in the Gulf War as a triumph for multilateral action. The report again scanned international hot spots and stressed the role which the UN should play, but noted that the organization needed to be strengthened to effectively fulfil this mandate. There was also mention of a New World Order, but little discussion of what its principles were or how it would work – except for an increased role for the UN (Labour Party 1991b).

Interestingly, the document noted that when *A Power For Good* was released with its emphasis on NATO's political role it was scorned by the Conservatives. Yet by 1991 the NATO agenda was almost exactly that advocated by Labour (Labour Party 1991b: 51). The Party also continued to stress its support for the political development of the EC and contrasted its approach with that of the Conservatives. There was also stress on the desirability of expanding the Community to include other European Free Trade Association (EFTA) countries and central and eastern European states. The EC was also stressed as a stepping stone for the achievement of common security; a recognition that non-military aspects of security are of increasing importance in the international system.

In summary then, post-Policy Review foreign policy was based on the principles of multilateralism through institutions such as NATO, the EC, the Conference on Security and Cooperation in Europe (CSCE) and the UN. The emphasis was on cooperative action to achieve desired results and on working with other states in the system to achieve this. The key changes in post-review foreign policy were the changed attitude towards the EC, the more positive attitude to working with the United States and the move away from unilateralism. Gone was the radicalism of the early 1980s which broke the traditional bipartisan consensus and in its place was a reformist agenda and a promise to work with others to achieve the best for Britain and the international system.

## IMPLEMENTATION OF LABOUR PARTY FOREIGN POLICY

To entitle this section implementation is in a sense over ambitious. Foreign policy in the 1990s will consist primarily of reacting to events in the international system as there is little room for independent action.

Particularly important is the ever increasing interdependence of the international system and the consequent blurring of the boundaries between domestic and foreign policies. These trends have been evident since the 1970s but have been accelerated by British entry into the EC and the moves from a bipolar international system to a multipolar system based upon regional blocks. The increasing need to coordinate actions with European partners and to consider the likely impact on other states of both foreign and domestic policies serves to curtail the range and scope of policy choices.

The changes in the international system present both opportunities and problems for a future Labour Government. Several of the seemingly more intractable problems in the system are currently under negotiation; for example, disputes in South Africa, Cambodia, the Middle East and Cyprus and this removes several potential problems from the Labour's international agenda. However, as recent events in Yugoslavia have shown, new problems are emerging in the new system. Issues of Balkanization, nationalism, ethnicity and fostering democracy will have to be dealt with by a future Government (*The Guardian*, 26 August 1991).

However, a Labour Government will not be alone in facing these problems, and it is here that the party's commitment to multilateral diplomacy may pay off as the CSCE, NATO, UN and EC become forums for problem solving (*Independent on Sunday* 21 April 1991). These international organizations are increasingly being viewed as the mechanisms for coping with such problems, and in this sense the international system is increasingly coming to parallel the Labour Party's foreign policy agenda. Congruence between the two has never been greater.

Another aspect of the issue is that the majority of foreign policy is reactive, that is, responding to events in the international system, rather than initiating policies. This means that the party in government could only hope to have general principles as a framework for responding to events, and maybe initiate policy change on one or two issues. This is particularly true given the increased emphasis on multilateral diplomacy, which leaves even less room for national initiatives.

Nevertheless many questions over Labour Party policy remain, particularly over how to achieve the changes it envisages. These are issues currently also being discussed internationally. Questions under discussion include 'How is the United Nations to be strengthened?' (Kaufman, 1991) and 'How will other international organizations function in new roles, for example, NATO as a political structure?' (*The Guardian*, 27 August 1991). Labour has, as yet, given little indication of its response to these and other questions about making multilateral diplomacy work, but research on these questions is currently in progress.

Importantly, the Labour Party is no longer alone within Britain in strongly advocating multilateral diplomacy, placing emphasis on development, environmental aid, and linking aid to human rights (see Labour Party 1991c and 1991d; *The Guardian*, 19 August 1991). The post-Thatcher Conservative Party is increasingly expressing faith in international organizations as a means of problem solving – a radical departure from the Thatcher years (Mayall 1990: 86). This dovetailing of the foreign policies of British political parties is almost inevitable given the changing international system and the fact that states in decline have fewer options available to them. In the past the two major parties wished to achieve the same end: maximization of British power and leverage in the international system, but their routes were different. Increasingly though, the route for the two parties is the same. Although foreign policy is rarely in Britain a prime election issue, the task for the Labour Party at the next election may be to define its foreign policy as different to that of the Conservatives.

In examining the Labour Party's foreign policy in the past it seems clear that there will remain some differences between them and the Conservatives. Specifically, throughout the post-war period there has been an element of idealism running through party policy and this is unlikely to disappear. Moreover, despite the Conservative Party's conversion to multilateral diplomacy and the re-ordering of the system, their agenda is more nationalistic, more concerned with military security and less concerned with advancement for the Third World.

## ACKNOWLEDGEMENTS

The author would like to thank the Labour Party Library staff for their help in the research for this chapter.

# 14 The Labour Party and the nuclear issue

*Stuart Croft*

## INTRODUCTION

Throughout the 1980s, the debate over nuclear weapons and nuclear deterrence was an incredibly bitter one for the Labour Party. There was a clash of philosophy, of policy and of loyalty, all of which added to an image of a Party hopelessly divided. Those who supported Britain's retention of a nuclear deterrent, who might be termed the traditionalists, fought and lost in the early 1980s against those who argued for unilateral nuclear disarmament. This chapter will seek to ask whether the new traditionalists have defeated the unilateralists in the late 1980s and early 1990s as Labour's defence commitments have dramatically altered once more.

On the one side of this debate were the traditionalists, those who believed that Labour's first duty was to the security of the United Kingdom and, in a nuclear world, argued that this meant possessing nuclear weapons, basing American nuclear forces in Britain and supporting the NATO alliance strategy of Flexible Response which included an intrinsic threat of the first use of nuclear weapons. For the traditionalists, the challenge made to their line on policy was a rejection of much of what the Labour Party had achieved in the past for British security. After all, it was the Labour Government of Clement Attlee and Ernest Bevin who took the decision to produce an atomic bomb in January 1947; for Bevin, there had to be a bomb with 'a bloody union jack flying on top of it' (Bevin quoted by Hennessy, in Wheeler 1990). Later, it was the Wilson Governments which carried through the decision to purchase the Polaris system and, in the 1970s, decided to develop the Chevaline warhead (at a cost of some £1 billion) to ensure that the Polaris system could successfully defeat developing Soviet strategic defences. Finally, the Callaghan Government had, along with the rest of NATO, taken the decision to pursue the deployment of INF systems – the Ground Launched Cruise Missile in Britain – in order, as it was seen, to strengthen NATO against a developing Soviet challenge. In many ways the traditionalists argued that it had been the Labour Party and not the Conservatives that had taken the most significant decisions regarding Britain's nuclear development over the previous thirty-five years, and that this was a tradition with which they were entirely comfortable. Despite the upheaval of the early 1980s some figures within the Party – such as the MPs Bruce George and John Gilbert, prominent figures on the House of Commons Defence Committee – maintained a public commitment to these arguments. For this group, the unilateralist challenge would make Labour unelectable, Britain undefendable and NATO untenable.

In contrast, the unilateralists openly rejected Labour's nuclear past. For the unilateralists, the Labour leadership of the past had colluded with the Tories to produce a security policy for Britain which had actually undermined British and international security; further, that policy was also immoral. The danger was not the threat posed by Soviet aggression, but rather the imminent danger posed by the nuclear arms race and by nuclear strategies that relied upon short-warning time and deep strikes. Accidental nuclear war could be envisaged; indeed, many believed it was almost inevitable. Ill-conceived talk in the Reagan administration about limited nuclear war and prevailing in a nuclear war simply acted to give the movement a strong anti-American edge. Thus, the unilateralists attacked the two fundamental pillars of traditionalist post-war British security policy: nuclear deterrence and the Anglo-American alliance. The unilateralists also argued that they too had important historical links within the Labour Party; that they were not, in any sense, an 'entryist' movement, an argument Joan Ruddock, in particular, sought to refute. After all, there had been the bitter debates in the late 1950s within the Party over unilateralism, culminating in the 1960 party conference at which Labour had first committed itself to a policy of nuclear unilateralism (Driver 1964). Indeed, the strand of radicalism within the Party could be traced back to the period before the nuclear age, even to the opposition to the First World War. The unilateralists were able therefore to argue that they had a legitimate prescription for Labour and, given the deterioration in East–West relations, an urgent prescription for the United Kingdom and indeed the world.

The political battle between the two groups was intense, and split the Party dramatically at all levels: in Parliament, at conference, in constituencies and in wards. From 1981, it was clear that the unilateralists were in the ascendancy. The Labour Party divided with the formation of the Social Democratic Party (SDP), as many of the traditionalists at all levels of the Labour Party moved over to the SDP. Indeed, it was the protest campaign itself that 'affected the Labour Party sufficiently to influence many not of this persuasion [i.e. traditionalists] to leave and join the new SDP' (Freedman 1986: 81). This inevitably left those supporting unilateralism in a stronger position within the Labour Party, but probably also reflected that on the nuclear issue, the traditionalists had already been defeated. Michael Foot, a life-long proponent of the unilateralist cause – and indeed one of its most inspirational supporters – became leader of the Labour Party, and the Party fought the 1983 General Election on a manifesto that in its prescription for defence was arguably the most radical put forward by any major party in the twentieth century in terms of challenging a pre-existing consensus. This chapter will examine the development of Labour's defence policy from this point. In the first section, it will examine the movement in defence policy from the high-water mark of the unilateralist tide in 1983. The second section will then examine the culmination of Labour's defence changes in 1991, and will ask whether the Labour Party has rejected unilateralism in order to return to traditionalism in its nuclear policy.

## 1983–1987: THE APPLICATION OF UNILATERALISM?

Labour fought the 1983 election on a radical manifesto which called for a non-nuclear defence policy for the United Kingdom within the lifetime of the forthcoming Parliament. This meant that the Trident system had to be cancelled, that the existing Polaris system had to be entered into arms control talks with a clear view to negotiating the system away completely within five years, that all American nuclear bases in the United Kingdom had to be closed, that Britain had to work to turn NATO into a non-nuclear alliance, and in addition that Britain's defence spending had to be brought down to the European average. Yet despite – or perhaps because – of its radical nature, these policies apparently fell on an unreceptive electorate. Labour's defence strategy did not prevent Labour from suffering a serious electoral defeat at the hands of the Conservatives; indeed, it seemed to many to have contributed to the scale of that defeat. According to one source, the Conservative lead over Labour on the issue of defence stood at

67 per cent, the largest ever lead on any political issue (see Byrd 1988: 166).

Naturally, there was a great deal of analysis of the reasons for the defeat within the Labour Party in the aftermath of the election. On the contribution of the nuclear issue to Margaret Thatcher's second term of office two schools of thought emerged or perhaps re-emerged. The traditionalist view was that the whole policy of unilateralism was at fault. Labour's last Prime Minister, James Callaghan argued at the 1983 party conference that:

> What the movement has failed to understand is that it reversed the traditional policy of the Labour Party on which we fought eleven successive elections without any real attempt to convince the British people that what we were doing was right . . . you make a fundamental mistake by believing that by going on marches and passing resolutions without any attempt to tell the British people what the consequences were, you could carry their vote. And you lost millions of votes.
>
> (Quoted in Baylis 1990: 96)

However, this traditionalist analysis – although widely supported amongst the SDP – was deeply unpopular with the broad mass of the Labour Party, and contributed to the intensification of the vilification of Labour's last Prime Minister within the Party itself. Clearly it was too early for traditionalism to be reasserted amongst the membership. In contrast to the traditionalists, the unilateralists argued that it was not the message that was at fault, but rather it was the presentation. Most disastrous, it was felt, was the disagreement between Labour's leader, Michael Foot, and its foreign affairs spokesperson, Denis Healey. During the height of the election campaign Healey argued that if a Labour Government was unable to obtain a bilateral arms control deal with the Soviet Union – trading off a proportion of the Soviet arsenal for Britain's entire force – Britain's strategic nuclear forces would have to remain in operation; to say otherwise would make the negotiations little short of a farce. Yet in contrast, Foot argued that the Polaris system had to be disarmed regardless of whether a deal was struck with the USSR or not; the elimination of one nation's entire nuclear arsenal was the prime point, not some trade-off. Thus the task of the new leader, Neil Kinnock – a committed unilateralist – was to devise ways of explaining the unilateralist logic to the British electorate and to avoid damaging splits within the Shadow Cabinet during election preparations.

The tactics selected to achieve this were to provide a more precise definition of Labour's unilateralist position applied in terms of the specific circumstances of the mid-1980s. For Kinnock and the leadership, one of the key problems of the defence strategy at the 1983 election had been the success of the Conservatives – undoubtedly helped by the 'Falklands Factor' – at defining Labour's defence policy in unflattering terms. The Labour position was presented by their political enemies as being weak on defence: suggestions ranged from being in league with the KGB at worst, to, at best, naïvely misunderstanding the threatening nature of the Soviet Union and the hostility of international politics. Thus, Labour sought to address those criticisms, and the first clear sign of that new presentation was in an NEC document issued in 1984 entitled *Defence and Security for Britain*. The unilateralist argument was kept: British nuclear weapons were still to be eliminated, American nuclear bases would still be closed, INF systems – Cruise – were still to be withdrawn, a Labour Government would urge NATO to move to a policy of no first use of nuclear weapons, and there should be a European nuclear weapons free zone. However, there were two new harder-line elements reflecting the attempt to defuse the 'weak on defence' label. First, the NEC argued for an increase in investment in British conventional capabilities, paid for by the savings from the nuclear budget. By arguing that more had to be spent on the army, navy and air force, rather than stressing the need to reduce Britain's defence expenditure (representing a higher percentage of GDP than that of its allies), it was hoped to attract some credibility and possibly even support from the armed services, given the fears of a financial squeeze on new conventional equipment caused by the purchase of the Trident system. Second, the Party emphasized very strongly its commitment to NATO, which previously had seemed to be rather ambivalent. When in 1983 the Party had argued that NATO must become a non-nuclear alliance, critics suggested that when NATO Governments refused to comply, Labour would withdraw Britain from NATO. Given the popularity of the alliance in opinion polls, and the fact that few if any in the leadership could really envisage a withdrawal from NATO, this was clearly an issue which demanded clarity. In this manner, the Party leadership hoped to be seen to be taking seriously the size of the Soviet armed forces. This emphasis also did much to move the Party away from other unilateralist groups such as the Campaign for Nuclear Disarmament (CND) and the Alternative Defence Commission (ADC), both of which argued for an end to NATO (see, for example, Alternative Defence Commission 1987). The close association of Labour with CND was seen by some in the Party to be of questionable utility, at best limiting the autonomy of the Labour Party leadership to make policy.

Thus, there appeared to be movement in Labour's position. However, it was limited movement, designed to clarify and make the next election easier to fight, rather than actively aiming to change the nature of Labour's defence commitment. The theme was clearly that of applying the unilateralist logic to the specific national and international circumstances of the day. This trend became clear over the next two years, and was made explicit at the end of 1986. On 12 November 1986, Kinnock argued in the House of Commons that it would be quite immoral to rely upon the nuclear umbrella. This confirmed rejection of the American nuclear guarantee to Britain and Western Europe – and therefore of NATO strategy – was followed in December by the publication of the Party's major pre-election document, *Modern Britain in the Modern World* (Labour Party 1986a). The manifesto confirmed the lines of *Defence and Security for Britain*: Trident was to be cancelled; INF systems were to be withdrawn; NATO had to move to a policy of no first use of nuclear weapons; and there should be a European nuclear weapons free zone and a move to defensive defence. In addition, the commitment to NATO was reinforced, as was the commitment to improve conventional forces. In a letter attached to *Modern Britain in a Modern World*, Kinnock wrote 'Britain must face a choice between nuclear weapons and effective conventional forces: we cannot have both'. Britain could most effectively contribute to NATO, it was suggested, through providing modern conventional forces, which could not be achieved while purchasing the Trident system. Thus, in a clever inversion of the traditionalist logic, it would actually be in the interests of NATO for Britain to elect a Labour Government. Unfortunately for the Party, no major NATO Government was even slightly convinced of this, least of all the Government of the United States.

The Labour leadership spent the period prior to the election 'clarifying' its defence policy, partly in order to avoid the mistakes of the 1983 election campaign. In March, Kinnock flew to the United States to explain Labour's position to President Reagan (Cassell 1987). Kinnock's assertion that he and Reagan were in fact allies since both sought a non-nuclear world, and that it was Mrs Thatcher who was in fact isolated, was roundly rejected in Washington. Kinnock also softened Labour's position on INF systems; instead of removing them in the aftermath of an election victory, 'as long as talks aimed at removing intermediate range nuclear forces from Europe continue, we would take no action regarding US cruise missiles' (Kinnock 1987);[1] while in the manifesto, the commitment to close American nuclear bases in the United Kingdom was also made dependent upon the progress of the INF negotiations (Evans 1987). Such changes were made late and did not have the effect of clarifying Labour's position in the election campaign. The attempt to eliminate the errors of the 1983 campaign failed miserably. Two mistakes stood out. In a television interview, Kinnock allowed himself to be drawn into discussing how he would respond as Prime Minister to a hypothetical Soviet attack. He suggested that the best defence would be 'to use all the resources you have to make any occupation totally untenable' (*Sunday Times* editorial, 31 May 1987). Admitting to advocating a defence policy that could lead to occupation was never going to endear Kinnock to the British electorate. When later that week John Smith was asked in a radio interview how a non-nuclear British Army of the Rhine was supposed to fight against a nuclear armed enemy he was reduced to confusion (Keegan 1987).

The obvious conclusion, pointed out repeatedly by the Conservatives, was that Labour had no defence policy; the Conservative's election poster, of a soldier with his hands raised in surrender with the slogan 'Labour's policy on arms', was well judged in the light of the Labour leadership's confusions, all of which added to the difficulties of canvassing at local level. In just a few days Labour's newly-found and hard-worked for credibility on defence issues simply vaporized, handing the Conservative Party an overwhelming advantage in the electoral battle.

Labour had entered the 1983 election on a unilateralist platform, and fought the 1987 election on what might be described as applied unilateralism. Yet this, too, failed the Party as the Conservatives again swept to a large-scale victory. Labour's own estimates reportedly calculated that defence had cost it 3 per cent of the vote (Hoggart 1987). Later evidence of polling from July 1987 seemed to indicate an even deeper failure. Only 26 per cent had been persuaded to support unilateralism; but, even more lamentably, it appeared that Labour had failed to attract the support of 50 per cent of even this group (Jones and Reece 1990: 47). Indeed it appeared that 'whilst the party political consensus may have broken down, the views of the electorate as a whole on the subject of British nuclear weapons have not changed appreciably for some considerable time' (Ibid: 1990: 64).

Argument again raged throughout the Labour Party in the aftermath of the election over the degree to which the defence policy had failed and contributed to the scale of the defeat. All agreed that altering policy in the few months before the election had been an error; it was vital, in order to avoid confusion, to be clear well before the campaign began. Clearly this was a major incentive to begin the Policy Review process well ahead of the next general election. Some sought to go further in their analysis and prescriptions. They felt that the failure of 'applied unilateralism' to attract support – this became clear in a series of detailed qualitative polls carried out by the Party after the election – meant that unilateralism itself could never win support. As Denis Healey reportedly said about the 1983 election, 'it wasn't the confusion, it was the unilateralism that was the damaging thing' (see Jenkins 1987b). Thus unilateralism had to undergo major modifications, and the term itself had to be avoided as a vote-losing term (much as the American Democratic Party sought to avoid the term 'liberal'). For others in the Labour leadership, however, the fault had been in moving from the original unilateralist doctrine to its less convincing, applied comrade. They argued that the policy had itself been a poor compromise lacking principle and conviction, and they fought a strong rearguard action at the 1987 Party Conference, achieving the adoption of two composite resolutions affirming the commitment to a non-nuclear defence policy. In the immediate aftermath of the election, Kinnock maintained a public loyalty to the unilateralist creed (Hoggart 1987). However, a majority of the Party leadership, including Kinnock himself, clearly inclined towards the position opposing unilateralism and in the next few years brought about a significant change in Labour's defence policy, culminating in the elimination of the unilateralist approach. The degree to which this group reverted to the positions of the traditionalists will be examined in the next section.

## THE POLICY REVIEW PROCESS:
## THE RETURN OF TRADITIONALISM?

In addition to its electoral defeats, there was an additional reason for a reconsideration of Labour's defence policy: the attitude of the Soviet Union under Mikhail Gorbachev. In 1983 it had appeared that the Soviet leadership was more inclined towards Labour than the Conservatives, although electorally this had not proved an advantage. Four years later Labour had again offered a much more benign view of the Soviet Union than had the Conservatives, yet prior to the 1987 election it became clear that Moscow would support the Conservatives over Labour. Gorbachev probably calculated that a

Labour victory would cause trouble within NATO which could upset the improving East–West relationship, while it would also damage Anglo-American relations and thus weaken Britain's role as a broker between the superpowers which at that particular moment Thatcher seemed able to play (Dunn 1991; Wheeler 1991). In any case, Gorbachev's warm welcome of Thatcher on her visit to Moscow in the spring of 1987 undoubtedly helped the Conservatives electoral prospects, particularly when compared to Kinnock's cool reception in Washington at the same time (see Jenkins 1987b: 308–11). Lukewarm Soviet support had not helped Labour electorally in 1983; implied Soviet criticism damaged the Party's electoral prospects in 1987. For the Labour leadership, it seemed quite clear that despite the advent of perestroika and glasnost in Moscow, the Soviet Union had rejected the utility of the Labour Party's policy of applied unilateralism. In addition, the emergence of East–West *détente* offered new possibilities.

The redefinition of Labour's stance on defence began early in the new Parliament. In November 1987, Gerald Kaufman began the process by arguing that:

Labour has led the world in arguing for nuclear weapon reductions. During the period in which no progress was made internationally in achieving such reductions, Labour's non-nuclear defence policy had by definition to be unilateralist. We were proposing to make nuclear weapon reductions when no-one else was doing so. Now, however, nuclear weapon reduction is a policy adopted and about to be implemented by the two nuclear superpowers. . . . The unilateralist nature of our non-nuclear defence policy has been overtaken by other countries doing what in the past we would do alone if necessary.

(Labour Party Campaign and Communications Directorate, ref. PR/285/87)

The implication was clear: whereas in the past only unilateralism could have achieved Labour's aims, world developments – notably the INF Treaty – meant that in the future multilateralism would again be a credible policy. This theme was taken up by Martin O'Neill, who argued that 'to have decommissioned Polaris . . . was to some extent the politics of gesture'; most importantly that'the logjam has been broken' making other, non-unilateralist routes to security again worthy of consideration (*END* 1988: 7).

This process continued throughout early 1988, with Kinnock himself using the arguments and phrases introduced by Kaufman and

O'Neil (see, for example, Wintour and McKie 1989). With the ground prepared, changes began to be revealed. In May, Kaufman – the central figure in the defence review – declared that Labour accepted the American nuclear guarantee. In a television interview on 5 June 1988, Kinnock felt sufficiently comfortable with the pace of change, and the relative passivity with which the Party was responding to change, to repudiate unilateralism itself. However, that was probably a misjudgement. That television interview led directly to the resignation of Denzil Davies, the Parliamentary Defence Spokesperson, which provided a focus for criticism within the Party on the nuclear changes. Davies complained that Kinnock was making up policy without informing his Defence team; worse still, that he was making up policy without the consultation that was supposed to be central to the review process. The pressure became so intense that Kinnock felt compelled to repudiate his own televised comments and suffered, in Michael Cassell's words, 'an apparent temporary attack of faint-heartedness' (Cassell 1989). However, this was to be a mere tactical setback rather than a strategic reverse, since policy changes were still planned. Indeed, from the perspective of the reformist leadership, such a hiatus in publicity on the defence issue was possibly beneficial, for two reasons. First, with the Policy Review process about to be concluded, there seemed to be little purpose in discussing in public issues that could only be contentious in private. Second, with the belief that the defence issue had damaged the Party's electoral prospects in 1983 and 1987, it seemed to be a good tactic in the run-up to the 1992 election to neutralize defence as a major political issue and focus instead upon the economy and health service.

By the time of the Party Conference in October 1989, the leadership was able to gain endorsement for the Policy Review document – a manuscript that failed to make reference to unilateral action, and stated that Britain's nuclear capability would be placed into international arms control negotiations. The fundamental shift in policy was therefore made in 1989. At the following year's conference, a unilateralist motion was comfortably beaten by 3.57 million votes to 1.96 million. By the time of the launch of the revised policy document in April 1991, *Opportunity Britain*, the final acts of the elimination of unilateralism were almost complete. The document stated that 'We have at no stage . . . made a commitment to getting rid of all nuclear weapons for as long as others have them' (Stevens 1991). Kaufman was more specific: 'There is no commitment whatever by the Labour Party, by a Labour Government, to divest Britain of nuclear weapons where others retain them' (Jones 1991). In an article in *The Guardian* on 10 July 1991, Kaufman made it clear that a Labour Government would not consider eliminating its own force while the Soviet Union was still armed: a very far cry from the position of 1983. But the implications were rather more than that; given the limited nature of Britain's nuclear force, such a policy would give a Labour Government almost no scope for reductions within an international arms control treaty, grounds upon which Labour defence spokespersons have criticized the Conservative Government over in the 1980s.

Labour's Policy Review process has therefore produced a number of dramatic changes from the manifestos of 1983 and 1987. Unilateralism has been eliminated, with Polaris and Trident to be entered into a START II arms control process (on this, see Scott 1991). The abolition of battlefield nuclear weapons has been continually called for, but in the aftermath of German unification this seems in any case inevitable. The abandonment of Flexible Response as NATO strategy remains important, but with the end of the Cold War NATO has already engaged in a Strategic Review. The American nuclear umbrella guarantee to Britain and Europe and US nuclear bases, formerly to be rejected, are now instead to be kept. Indeed, in another reversal of positions, it is now the United States that is closing its own bases in the United Kingdom as part of its post-Cold War cost cutting.

The broad public political justification for these changes has been related to the changing international environment. Interestingly, this argument was already being used at the end of 1987, before the end of the Cold War, before the collapse of communism in east and central Europe and the Soviet Union itself, well before German unification, before the Paris Conference on Security and Cooperation in Europe and before the conventional arms control agreement. Thus, as time has passed, international events have assisted the Labour leadership in putting their arguments across. As the fear of war has receded, the heat has gone out of the defence debate, and Labour's changes of policy have therefore been less controversial than they were in the early 1980s. This is something of an irony, for at a time when the Soviet Union was ruled by hard line communists, Labour was prepared to eliminate Britain's own nuclear force in a blaze of public controversy, whereas from the time when the threat became minimal at most, Labour has insisted on negotiations over those weapons amid public indifference. It is certainly somewhat ironic that these changes in international relations have had the effect of weakening the arguments of the unilateralists dramatically. As late as

March 1988, the Parliamentary Labour CND argued that 'A Labour Government should eliminate all British nuclear weapons systems within the lifetime of the first Parliament and should ensure the removal of remaining US nuclear weapons within the same period . . . independent of responses . . .' (Parliamentary CND 1988: 4). With major nuclear arms control agreements now signed and with Washington's closure of many of the United States' military bases in Britain, the political push for such change is weak. Indeed, the argument that such a unilateralist policy would upset some of the positive movements in international politics – a view long associated with the traditionalists and discredited within the Labour Party for much of the 1980s – has now been reasserted.

Given the reversion of Labour's defence policy, does this imply that the traditionalist arguments are once again dominant within the Party on the nuclear question? Clearly, from the analysis presented in this chapter, the Labour Party in the early 1990s began to prescribe policies with a greater similarity to those of the traditionalist Governments of the past, than to the unilateralist opposition of the early 1980s. Yet, despite this, traditionalism probably has not been fully embraced by the Party. The Labour Party still has some of its earlier unilateralist policy direction, albeit now extremely muted. There is, for example, some ambivalence to the whole issue of nuclear deterrence that stands in contrast to the view of the Conservative Party. Further, Labour is committed to negotiate Trident away in arms control negotiations. The goal of a non-nuclear world therefore remains, and stands in contrast to the traditionalist position.

Thus in two important areas – deterrence, and the future of the British bomb – the Labour Party in the early 1990s finds itself still with something in common with the position of the Party in the early 1980s. Nevertheless, the degree of change has been enormous, and it is certainly conceivable that even these limited associations with the past will be forgotten in the near future. The primary reason for this change probably relates to prioritizing political motivations. It is unlikely that the leadership have become committed believers in the traditionalist approach in such a relatively short period of time, perhaps with a few exceptions. The rationale for the changes in policy do not seem to have stemmed from an intellectual repudiation of unilateralism; rather they seem to come from a strong desire to neutralize the defence issue. Defence lost Labour many votes in 1983 and 1987, preventing the Party from implementing its economic and social policies which at almost any time are closer to the heart of the Party. In other words, neutralizing the defence issue seems to be seen as one of the prices that has to be paid for having an opportunity to introduce change in other areas. As Neil Kinnock said in a speech in May 1989,

> I'm not asking anyone to stand on their head. I am asking everyone to stand up and face the future. I'm not asking anyone to give up what they have thought was right for the past 30 years. I am asking them to do what is right for the next 30 years. *In your fidelity to your own views, be certain that you are not leaving all those who need us to a fate of interminable Thatcherism.*
>
> (emphasis added, Wintour and Hetherington 1989)

This theme of neutralizing the defence issue is probably so important for the Labour Party that one can expect it to continue into government, certainly as far as nuclear forces are concerned. Further change of policy would therefore come as a result of a future Labour Government following movement in the newly-reformed bipartisan defence consensus, rather than from the Government leading the initiative.

# Part IV
# Conclusions

# 15 Continuity and change in Labour Party policy

*Martin J. Smith*

The chapters in this book demonstrate the scale of the changes that have occurred in Labour Party policy since the 1987 election. Some of these reforms are directly the result of the Policy Review whilst others have a much longer history. The reform of Labour Party policy raises a number of questions. First, how much has Labour policy changed? Has it changed more in some areas rather than others and to what extent is it a return to Labour Party policy of the 1960s and 1970s? Second, is there any coherence and ideological consistency in the post-review policy? Do these changes place Labour within a post-Thatcherite consensus? Third, what do these policy changes mean for a potential Labour Government and what will they mean in the light of a fourth Labour defeat? This chapter suggests some answers to these questions in light of the preceding analysis.

## HOW HAS LABOUR CHANGED?

In certain areas – defence, economic policy and the European Community – Labour has completely reversed its position since 1983. For instance, economic policy is now based on fundamentally different principles. As Gamble (see chapter 5) pointed out, the policy proposed in the 1982 programme and the 1983 manifesto was based on national protectionism, whilst in the review the leadership recognized the need to integrate Britain into the world economy. The policy outlined in 1982 was within the tradition of reformist socialism. This is the belief that socialism can be achieved through democratic means by gradually increasing state ownership and control of the means of production. Therefore, the policy in the 1982–3 period was intended to initiate the transition to socialism.

With the Policy Review the Labour leadership has made a clear break with reformism. Labour's goal is no longer a publicly owned and controlled economy. Rather its aim is to use the market economy, with state assistance and intervention where necessary, to provide economic growth, increasing wealth for all and a just society. The goal is not to abolish capitalism but to run it in a humanitarian way without an unquestioning faith in either the market or state intervention.

In defence and foreign policy, and attitudes to the European Community there have also been substantial changes. The unilateralist, anti-American, anti-EC and isolationist position adopted in the early 1980s has been replaced by a strong commitment to Europe, an acceptance of multilateral disarmament and a much more sympathetic view of the United States. The policy shift over Europe has been particularly striking, as George and Rosamond outlined in chapter 12, with Labour accepting the ERM, monetary union and greater political union. At the Party's 1991 conference, Labour was happy to accept European policy in a wide range of areas and, according to Hugo Young (1991), 'sovereignty was not even a footnote'.

However, despite these changes since the early 1980s, there is a degree of consistency between the policy post-review and policy before the 1980s. The Labour leadership, at least in the 1970s, had been revisionist in terms of economic policy, supportive of Britain's relationship with the USA and accepted membership of the EC. Yet, as several chapters have demonstrated, it would be simplistic to see post-review policy as a return to Wilsonism. Although economic policy may be called revisionist in its acceptance of the market and of capitalism, this is not a replica of the revisionism of Crosland or its adaption by Wilson. As we have seen, supply-side policies and industrial strategy are much more central to economic management than they were in the past. As Guiver demonstrated (see chapter 6), this commitment to the supply-side has, for example, resulted in Labour taking a much greater interest in small business.

Labour's attitude to nationalization has also changed. Whilst Wilson and Callaghan did not favour greater nationalization, they were prepared to use it as part of their economic strategy and because of pressures from within the Party. The Kinnock leadership has almost completely removed nationalization from the agenda, accepting that in most areas it is now inappropriate, and maintaining only a loose commitment to the renationalization of certain 'natural' monopolies. At present the only absolute proposal for renationalization is for the National Grid, with water also being a priority (Harrison 1991). Instead, the leadership has placed greater emphasis on regulation. They accept that the market has to be policed and have therefore made proposals for greater regulation in areas such as the environment, energy, industrial relations and the privatized industries.

Perhaps the most substantial changes in policy have occurred in the area of what might be called the new agenda: the social quality of life issues that relate to post-material values (Heath *et al.* 1990). Environmental policy, women's policy and constitutional reform have all changed markedly from the party's position in both the 1970s and the 1980s. Carter (chapter 9) outlines how both before 1983 and between 1983 and 1987 Labour paid lip service to environmental policy but tended to keep it low on the agenda. By contrast Labour is now taking environmental policy seriously. The Party proposes quality growth, an Environmental Protection Executive and the use of taxes to encourage environmentally friendly activities. A similar change has also occurred in relation to women's equality. Previous Labour Governments have passed anti-discrimination and equal pay legislation but the Party is now committed to moving beyond legalistic attempts at equality with a number of positive measures and the establishment of a Ministry for Women.

More surprising is the change on constitutional reform. Traditionally Labour has had a very conservative view of the need to reform the State. The actions of a Labour Government have been perceived as more important than the mechanisms and procedures of the State (see Marquand chapter 4). The Party is, however, becoming increasingly aware of the need for constitutional reform. The leadership is reconciled to devolution and a Bill of Rights and has even accepted proportional representation for an elected second chamber to replace the House of Lords. Marquand makes clear that this commitment to constitutional reform is relatively limited in scope, but compared to Labour's dismissal of constitutional reform in the past this is a significant change of direction.

The developments which might be of the greatest significance and of long-term impact are the reforms concerning party organization and the party's relationship with the trade unions. Unlike previous leaders, Kinnock has been successful in changing the organization of the Party in a way which will make it much more susceptible to control by the leadership (Seyd and Whiteley, chapter 3). The 1991 conference demonstrated the degree to which the leadership now controls policy-making. There was only one major issue – the size of defence spending cuts – on which the leadership was defeated in a conference vote. Even then Kinnock made it clear that he would ignore the decision in government. Despite the changes of policy and the growth of central policy-making, the Party appears to be more unified in its support for the leader than it has been for many years.

The reforms relating to the Party and the trade unions have two dimensions. First, Kinnock intends to transform the party–union relationship by reducing the significance of the block vote and by reforming the way policy is made. Second, the Party is proposing changes in industrial relations. The leadership's commitment to trade union reform is a substantial shift from both the position in 1982–3 and the 1970s. After the failure of *In Place of Strife*, Labour leaders in the past have not been prepared to tackle the union question. However, under Kinnock the leadership is using the Conservative employment laws as the basis of a new Labour view of industrial relations (see Rosamond, chapter 7).

In contrast to these areas of policy change, there has been a significant degree of continuity in welfare policy. Welfare has always remained central to Labour's ideology and policy (see Alcock, chapter 10). The creation of the welfare state after the Second World War remains in Labour's collective mind, its greatest achievement. Labour continues to distinguish itself from the other parties by its commitment to equality and the universal provision of welfare. Labour's most definite and costed spending commitments are to increase pensions and child benefits. In addition, a consensus exists throughout the Party that the provision of all aspects of welfare should be state-centred. Alcock demonstrates a certain consistency in Labour's welfare policy throughout the 1970s and 1980s in the wish to expand the universal welfare state. Labour has retained its commitment to state education, a free and public health service, improvements in public housing and increased welfare benefits.

However, even in this policy domain, faced with the reality of constraints on spending and the new agenda established by the Thatcher Governments, Labour has been forced to rethink some of its policies. Consequently the Party has accepted the right to buy council houses, has increasingly come to recognize the rights of consumers, as well as producers, of welfare, and has started to consider the limits on the universal provision of welfare. Nevertheless much of Labour's policy in health, social security and education is similar to past policy. Labour is committed to increasing spending, to public provision and to bringing opted-out schools and hospitals back into local and health authority control.

Labour, in most policy areas, has undergone remarkable changes since 1983 when it appeared unelectable. Even in the view of defectors to the SDP, like David Owen and Shirley Williams, the Labour Party

is now a serious contender for government. But these changes have
occurred in different ways and for different reasons in each policy
area. In some areas the influence of Thatcherism is noticeable such
as welfare and trade union reform. In others – constitutional reform
and women's policy – it is clearly absent. In the area of the 'new agenda'
pressure for change has come more from the constituency parties,
Labour local authorities, outside pressure groups and perceived
changes in the views of voters in general. The degree of change also varies from area to area. Economic
policy is more in line with Labour's traditional policy, whilst environ-
mental policy and women's policy are developing in new directions.
It appears that Labour is becoming increasingly economically conservative whilst maintaining some radicalism on issues within the
'new agenda'. Yet some commentators suggest that these changes
are not much more than the Downsian logic forcing Labour and the
Conservatives into a new centre ground consensus. To what extent
does a new consensus exist between the major parties?

## LABOUR, CONSERVATIVES AND THE
## LIBERAL DEMOCRATS: A NEW CONSENSUS?

It is being increasingly suggested that there is now a post-Thatcherite
consensus, with the three main parties sharing the fundamentals of
policy and disagreeing only on details. Hence all three parties are
committed to maintaining the market economy with Labour accepting
that capitalism is here to stay and the Conservatives under John
Major moving from a dogmatic belief in the benefits of *laissez-faire*.
Likewise, the three main parties are committed to a strong public
sector for the provision of welfare services which they believe should
be made more responsive to the consumer. There is a high level
of agreement on the need to protect the environment through
increased environmental regulation. On Europe and foreign policy
the consensus seems even greater. All three parties are committed to
ERM and EMU with differences existing on the timing of monetary
union and the question of greater political union. They all accept the
commissioning of Trident and the need for multilateral disarmament
and all want a responsible cut in defence spending in line with Britain's
commitments in the post-Cold War world.

Yet this view of a cosy consensus is too simplistic. With the collapse
of communism and the increasing importance of new issues like
the environment and constitutional reform, the traditional right/left
political axis is changing. The ideological consistency which previously

delimited the parties is disappearing and is being replaced by distinctions on new criteria which change from issue to issue. The Labour Party now has little alternative but to reconcile itself to the existence of the market. Events in Eastern Europe mean that there is no sign of a viable alternative. This does not mean that Labour is moving into a Conservative defined economic consensus. Major differences continue to exist over the relationship of the State to the market and the degree of intervention which is desirable (see chapters 2 and 5).

The Labour leadership, despite its policy shifts, still believes a high level of state intervention is necessary to assist economic transition, to encourage particular areas of the economy, to assist certain regions, to ensure that certain skills are available and to enable the market to operate in the most efficient and socially just way. The Liberal Democrats and post-Thatcherite Conservatives adopt a more social market position while accepting that state intervention is necessary in particular instances. However, on other issues the alignments between the parties change. In the case of constitutional reform, the Democrats adopt the most radical position, followed by Labour's hard left with the Labour leadership accepting a degree of reform and the Conservatives and Thatcherites more supportive of the *status quo*.

Although there is certainly more consensus in the 1990s than there was during the Thatcher years, the relationship between the parties varies from issue to issue. The traditional consistency that existed within parties has disappeared. The Conservatives may be radical on privatization but they are conservative on family policy and constitutional reform. Labour is radical on women's policy while being conservative in its fiscal policy. Although there is a consensus on certain issues and on particular criteria – for example, the existence of the market – policies on how to deal with the market and achieve the best economic results contain great differences. The Democrats are increasingly claiming that they are the only radical party in British politics, but there is great difficulty in defining radicalism – is it increased or reduced intervention in the economy, leaving the EC or supporting federalism? – and, moreover, parties are likely to be radical on some issues and not on others.

What do these policy changes and new alignments mean for socialism? Is Labour now a socialist party? This, of course depends on how socialism is defined. David Owen claimed he was a socialist after he left the Labour Party; both Neil Kinnock and Roy Hattersley call themselves democratic socialists. If socialism, however, means state planning and public ownership it is clear that the Labour Party is a long way from this position. If the basis of socialism is equality, Labour would claim that its belief in equality is still strong. Yet, the Party is not committed to absolute economic equality and its promises on taxation and welfare would suggest that Labour is not even proposing a radical redistribution of wealth.

In accepting the market, the continuation of capitalism, income inequality and a limited role for the State, Labour is moving into the tradition of European Social Democracy and is clearly distinguishing itself from reformist and revolutionary socialist parties such as the French Communists or the position of Labour's hard left. Many commentators, whether critics or supporters, would argue that Labour has always been revisionist and social democratic (Coates 1975; Miliband 1961; Minkin and Seyd 1977). Labour is at last admitting that it is a social democratic party with no pretentions of attempting to achieve a socialist society. Labour has for the first time broken completely with its socialist tradition and sided firmly with its social democratic tradition. It is a social democracy based on capitalism, economic growth and social justice (see M. Young 1991).

However, this commitment to social democracy does not solve Labour's problems. The confidence, coherence and attractiveness of social democracy has suffered because of the collapse of 'actual existing socialism', the difficulties and failures of social democratic Governments during the 1970s and the problems of defining a distinct social democratic programme for the 1990s.

The failure of social democratic Governments to deal with the economic crises of the 1970s without abandoning some of their key commitments to full employment and expansion of the welfare state created a crisis of confidence. During the 1980s social democratic Governments have stayed in power by moving to the right – to some degree in France, even further in Spain and a long way in Australia and New Zealand. Alternatively, social democratic parties have had long periods in opposition as in Britain and Germany (or they have done both). Even in Scandinavia, where social democracy apparently survived the crisis of the 1970s and the New Right backlash in the 1980s, social democratic Governments are facing increasing problems. In Sweden the social democrats have lost power after finding it increasingly difficult to maintain economic growth and to deal with the growing pressures to cut public expenditure and taxation.

With governmental and electoral failure producing changes in policy, there is a question over what is distinctive about social democracy. If social justice is the main feature of British social democracy in the 1990s it is not clear what distinguishes it from the Liberal Democrats or even the Conservatives. Labour can no longer guarantee full employment and increased public expenditure. The governmental failures of the 1970s and the electoral failures of the 1980s have made Labour increasingly defensive.

However, what appears to distinguish Kinnock's Labour Party from both the Conservatives and the Democrats is a continuing faith in both the State and the public sector. Despite the commitment to fiscal responsibility, the Party is still committed to providing welfare and modernizing the economy through state intervention. Neil Kinnock said in his 1991 conference speech, 'Britain needs a government with a sense of purpose that will provide the country with a new sense of direction'. This direction is towards the modernization of the economy through state-sponsored training, education and supply-side reforms which will provide the economic growth for higher welfare provisions (*The Guardian*, 2 October 1991). While Hatersley claimed, 'it is the hope and belief in equality that drives us on to victory . . . the vision of the more equal society has not faded, and it will be the ideal we choose to put into practice the day we are elected to power'.

Labour's social democracy is based on the commitment to welfare and state intervention as a means of creating a society with greater social equality. These beliefs clearly distinguish Labour from the Conservative's distrust of the State and their faith in the negative freedom of the individual. Nevertheless, the Labour leadership talks of an 'enabling' state to create a society of greater social justice but this is to be achieved with limited increases in expenditure, little redistribution of wealth, no attempt to tackle financial or multinational capital and few democratic reforms. Labour's insecurities – fear of defeat and internal conflict – have limited the radicalism of its policies. The contradictions between Labour's vision of a socially just world and the need to come to terms with the financial constraints of the real world could cause real problems for a future Labour Government.

## LABOUR IN GOVERNMENT

If Labour does, either despite or because of its caution, form a government, many problems are likely to develop. Inconsistencies within the policies and internal and external constraints are liable to present a Labour Government with great hurdles to implementation. As a BBC *Panorama* programme pointed out, all past Labour Governments have faced tremendous difficulties once in power and it seems likely that some of these constraints will re-emerge for a future Labour Government (BBC 1991). What problems might a Labour Government have to face?

First, every previous Labour Government has faced a sterling crisis and been forced to devalue as a result of the City's lack of confidence in its economic programme. Recently Labour's economic team has spent much time trying to reassure the City that its policies will not harm City interests. However, if a Labour Government is to avoid pressure on sterling, it will have to be very cautious in its fiscal and spending policies and may, despite its industrial strategy, be forced into raising interest rates. Therefore Labour's hopes of a growth dividend could be thwarted and this would greatly limit its options on economic, social and industrial policy.

Second, these economic constraints will be increased by Labour's commitment to the ERM and monetary union. Despite the Labour Party's calls for reductions in interest rates, if Labour is to remain within the ERM, interest rates will be determined by EC interest rates and currency values. Moreover, Labour is committed to not devaluing within the ERM, and maintaining sterling at its current value is likely to require relatively high interest rates. If monetary union occurs, the levels of public expenditure and taxation will be linked even more closely to our European allies. Without the advantage of a cheap currency, in order to remain economically viable, Britain will have to achieve German levels of competitiveness. This will further constrain economic and social policies. It is clear that membership of the ERM has important implications for the level of unemployment and Labour has not said how it will deal with this problem. Labour has not yet reconciled its commitment to Europe with its industrial strategy and its goals in social and welfare policy.

Third, despite Labour's attempt to appear financially responsible by making only two firm spending commitments to increase pensions and child benefits, many of Labour's policies for health, education, training and welfare will require extra spending. In addition, a number of groups in the public sector will possibly support Labour in the hope of increased public expenditure. Consequently, there will be tremendous pressure on a Labour Government for increased spending from various constituencies and failure to meet these demands could produce a high level of disillusionment. The leadership argues that it can meet demands for increased spending through a growth dividend, but Bob Rowthorn has suggested that this growth dividend has already been committed by the Conservatives whilst what is left will disappear on Labour's commitment to increasing pensions (BBC 1991). Despite the constraints on spending, there will be pressure both internal and external on a Labour Government for extra spending. Labour is yet to reconcile its fiscal conservatism with its desire to expand the welfare state.

Fourth, trade union and Labour leaders have worked very closely over recent years and Kinnock has depended on the trade unions for achieving many of his key policy and organizational changes. It is possible that the unions will expect rewards for their support and will relish the opportunity to regain access to the corridors of power. Hence unions are likely to place particular demands on a Labour Government, which given the constraints will not easily be met. One potential area of conflict is pay. Labour is opposed to an incomes policy. Instead there will be a National Economic Assessment which will provide a forum for discussion between unions, employers and government over what the country can afford in terms of pay increases. It remains unclear what will happen if trade unions are not prepared to accept the findings of the NEA. Will increasing wages force Labour into a formal incomes policy with all the pitfalls and crises that has created for previous Governments? The potential for conflict between trade unions and a Labour Government is high.

Fifth, in addition to union pressure, a Labour Government is also likely to face demands from constituency parties and left-wing MPs for more radical policies. Seyd and Whiteley in chapter 3 indicate that Labour members are more left wing than Labour voters. Should a Labour Government fail to meet some of its spending promises and back down on other policies like the minimum wage, dissent within the CLPs and the PLP will increase and create extra pressures on the Government and increased conflicts within the Party.

Sixth, many of the chapters in this book indicate the importance of the EC in terms of policy-making and implementation. The Community has an increasing role in economic policy, environmental policy, social policy, industrial relations, women and even foreign and defence policies. Consequently, a large number of policies will be determined at the European level rather than domestically. This will again limit the options available to a Labour, or any, Government.

Seventh, despite some consideration of constitutional reform, Labour has paid little attention to the State in an administrative sense. The British State, and especially the Treasury, is extremely conservative. The Party has paid little attention to the internal obstacles it might face. As Hutton points out:

> when it comes to managing credit flows, coordinating Treasury policy with the DTI to launch an industrial strategy or, say, regionalising commercial banks, the opposition will be intense. For example, the permanent secretary to the Treasury and the chief economic adviser can hardly be expected to disown personal beliefs that financial deregulation is irreversible – or that government intervention always ends in tears.
>
> (Hutton 1991)

More importantly, the Party has considered neither the impact that thirteen years of Conservatism will have had on the State, nor how the administration could be reformed in order to implement Labour's policies. The Thatcher Governments created certain institutional structures, for instance, the hiving off of a number of government agencies and privatization, which will affect the capabilities and options of a future Government. Even the Thatcher Governments, despite having clear goals and a determined leadership, failed to achieve many of its aims. The reasons for this included the failure to control the implementation process, the nature of the pre-existing policy communities, unintended consequences of policy implementation and external constraints (Marsh and Rhodes 1992). Labour has paid almost no attention to overcoming these problems.

This ignorance of state organization is apparent in two areas. In the Policy Review it is proposed that the DTI be made equal if not superior to the Treasury (see Gamble, chapter 5). In the 1960s Labour tried a similar policy with the Department of Economic Affairs. The DEA was effectively destroyed through the Treasury denying it information, maintaining control over the levers of economic policy and not relating fiscal and monetary policy to the industrial strategy (see Rodgers 1985). Despite this lesson, the leadership has not considered how the DTI is to be provided with the capabilities to overcome the dominance of the Treasury. The Treasury is a key coordinating ministry as well as the central economic ministry, but there are no proposals for reducing its powers. Indeed, the dominance of Labour's Treasury team in opposition demonstrates the difficulties that might exist in reducing the powers of a Labour Chancellor of the Exchequer.

A second area is the departmental nature of British Government. British Government is very strongly departmental with most policy being made within departments with only nominal coordination by

Cabinet (Jordan 1981). As a consequence, government strategies are often undermined by departments pursuing their own interests rather than the goals of the Government. Despite the commitment of the Thatcher Governments to reducing expenditure, public expenditure often increased because none of the spending ministries were prepared to see their own budgets cut. A future Labour Government is likely to face this problem to an even greater extent. It has a commitment to increased, but controlled, expenditure. Yet there is no consideration of how the Cabinet will control departmental demands for increased expenditure in areas like health, education and social security.

Guiver (see chapter 6) in outlining Labour's small business policy talked of Labour's diminishing options. In all areas of policy the factors outlined above will limit the options available to a future Labour Government. The constraints on Labour from the 'real world' explain to some extent the changes that have occurred in party policy. The review was an attempt to recognize the constraints. At the same time the party's organization, ideology, membership, trade unions and even past policy create an alternative set of demands. As Guiver highlighted, the leadership is caught between the options presented by the external world and the demands presented from within the Party. The Policy Review and subsequent policy reforms have been an attempt to reconcile these two forces. But Labour's plans for spending and economic policy suggest that it has yet to come to terms with the constraints it faces from Europe and the economy. Hence, Labour demands cuts in interest rates whilst acknowledging that the ERM determines the scope for change. It maintains a policy of increased spending on education, training, health and pensions but commits itself to fiscal conservatism and limited taxation increases. Moreover, considering the record of past Governments, both Labour and Conservative, a large question mark hangs over the ability of Labour to overcome the inherent problems of low growth, high imports and high inflation that persist within the British economy. If Labour fails to solve these problems what will it mean for Labour's social programme? The Policy Review has produced change but also contradictions which will create great difficulties in government. Nevertheless, Labour's problems may be greater should it fail to win a fourth time.

## LABOUR IN OPPOSITION?

It is impossible to predict what will happen to the Labour Party should it fail to win a fourth election. The possibilities are infinite, presumably Neil Kinnock will no longer remain as leader, the Party may split again and there could be a realignment of British politics. However, two scenarios seem more probable than others.

One view is that the left has been prepared to remain quiet during the 1980s in order not to rock the boat and so give Kinnock the chance to win the election. Should Labour lose, members of the left in the constituencies, the PLP and the unions are likely to blame the reforms for the defeat and so call for a return to 'socialist' policies. With trade union support, the left could again become dominant. From this point endless possibilities exist with the right either biding their time, fighting to maintain control of the Party or spliting the Party. This could raise the possibility of the Liberal Democrats challenging Labour as the second party.

An alternative view is that during the Kinnock years the left has been well and truly routed. The hard left has been isolated, with no one emerging to replace Tony Benn as unofficial leader of the left and it has no real alternative policies. Moreover, Militant is being further weakened by more purges and by conflicts within its own camp over whether it should stay in, or leave to fight, the Labour Party. If this is true, it seems probable that Kinnock will be replaced by a leader of the centre left or the right who after a fourth defeat will have the authority to take the Kinnock reforms even further. This might include cutting the links with the trade unions completely and accepting the need for electoral reform.

All this is, of course, speculation. What is true is that Labour has undergone profound changes in policy and organization in recent years. The reasons for these changes are complex. They cannot be simply reduced to monocausal explanations like the impact of Thatcherism or a Downsian model of party competition. The reasons for change and the degree of change have varied in each policy area. In addition, this change has not occurred in a vacuum. Change within Labour reflects changes within other parties and is part of the response of all the political parties to a changing world. For Labour, the shock of electoral defeat and the economic constraints have made it increasingly cautious and therefore economically conservative. It has attempted to retain its radicalism through the new agenda and through its vision of social justice, but whether this establishes a distinctive social democratic Labour Party which can achieve its goals in government remains to be seen.

# Notes

### 3 LABOUR'S RENEWAL STRATEGY

1 One of the rare opportunities to distinguish members' and activists' viewpoints came in the 1988 elections for party leader and deputy leader. Local parties were more likely to cast their votes for the incumbents (i.e. Kinnock and Hattersley) after a ballot of all members rather than after a vote of the General Committee delegates only. Furthermore, constituency parties voting for the incumbents after a ballot of all members were then more likely to go and vote for 'hard left' candidates in the NEC elections when the decision was taken solely by General Committee delegates.

2 Neil Kinnock claims in his introduction to the final report of the Policy Review, *Meet the Challenge, Make the Change*, that many constituency parties and branches discussed the issues and submitted their views. The Party, however, made no systematic attempt to consult the members and feed their opinions into the Policy Review. See Hughes and Wintour 1990: 101.

3 A random sample of party members in England, Scotland and Wales, drawn in such a way as to reflect the regional composition of the individual membership, was conducted in late 1989/early 1990. Postal questionnaires were sent to one in every thirty members: 8,075 were dispatched and 5,065 were returned – a response rate of 63 per cent. A random sample of non-respondents was asked to complete a two-page questionnaire comprising basic social background questions. Slight biases in the sample were uncovered in terms of occupation and trade union membership and these were corrected by constructing appropriate interlocking weights for those two variables. All statistics cited are based on the analysis of the weighted data set.

4 Assuming respondents answered all ten questions a minimum score of 10 and a maximum of 50 was possible. We classified respondents scoring 26 and under as 'traditionalists', between 27 and 34 as 'intermediates', and 35 and above as 'modernizers'.

5 We asked members whether they had engaged in a range of political activities over the past five years (displaying an election poster, signing a party petition, donating money to the Party, delivering party election leaflets, canvassing voters, attending party meetings, standing for party office, or standing for local or national elections

as a party representative). Their responses ('not at all', 'rarely', 'occasionally' and 'frequently') were scored from 1 to 4 on each activity and the 'inactive' ranged from 1 to 13, the 'occasionally active' from 14 to 19, the 'fairly active' from 20 to 25 and the 'very active' from 26 to 32.

6 Members were asked to rate on a thermometer scale ranging from 0 to 100 a wide range of Labour personnel.

7 The percentage distribution of opinions from Left to Right was as follows (NB. rounding up has occurred):

| *Left* | | | | | | | | *Right* |
|---|---|---|---|---|---|---|---|---|
| 1 | 2 | 3 | 4 | 5 | 6 | 7 | 8 | 9 |
| 18 | 25 | 25 | 11 | 11 | 3 | 2 | 2 | 6 |

8 We define 'cold' as those members who rank Kinnock and Benn from 0 to 25, 'cool' from 26 to 50, 'warm' from 51 to 75 and 'hot' from 76 to 100.

9 More than 40 per cent of our respondents felt they were less active in the Party than five years before, and these outnumber the respondents who felt they were more active than before by more than two to one.

10 We are grateful to Lewis Minkin for these terms.

## 7 THE LABOUR PARTY, TRADE UNIONS AND INDUSTRIAL RELATIONS

1 The reason for the failure of this composite was its claim that the Party had accepted some of the Thatcherite anti-trade union law. The motion in support of the 'People at Work' document, sponsored by the TGWU and the GMB, also called for the repeal of all anti-trade union law.

## 9 THE 'GREENING' OF LABOUR

1 This paper is based on a number of personal interviews with Labour politicians, party workers and representatives from pressure groups.

2 The Joint Policy Committee was probably exceptional in obtaining direct pressure group representation on a Labour Party body. Normally the pressure groups eschew such institutional links for fear of becoming too involved and thus being tainted by party politics.

## 12 THE EUROPEAN COMMUNITY

1 'Subsidiarity' is a complex and contested concept. It is usually used to denote the division of competence between national, regional and supranational levels of government. In the words of the Policy Review: 'Labour believes that decisions should be made at the level [European Community, national, regional or local] where the maximum democratic control and effectiveness is ensured and that is the basic criterion which a Labour Government will apply' (Labour Party 1989a: 80). But this does not necessarily imply a willingness to surrender national sovereignty in particular areas by devolving power either upwards to the EC level or downwards to the regional or local level. As Adonis and Tyrie

have noted, 'subsidiarity' can be used as justification for extending the competence of the EC into new areas, in defence of national sovereignty against a further Community encroachment, or as a basis for a full-scale federalism (Adonis and Tyrie 1990: 5).

2 The Delors report on monetary union, which was presented to the June 1989 European Council meeting in Madrid, proposed a three-stage process. In the first stage the EMS currencies that remained outside of the ERM (those of Britain, Greece, Portugal and Spain) would join, and the wider band of fluctuation between currencies would disappear. In the second stage economic policy would be closely coordinated, the band of fluctuation between currencies in the EMS would be narrowed, and the Governors of Central Banks would meet as a committee to prepare for the institution of a European Monetary Cooperation Fund. In the third stage national currencies would be irrevocably locked together, and the European currency unit (the Ecu) would become a currency in its own right, managed by the European Monetary Cooperation Fund.

## 14 THE LABOUR PARTY AND THE NUCLEAR ISSUE

1 At the superpower summit at the end of 1986 in Reykjavik, Reagan and Gorbachev had come close to agreeing the elimination of all INF category weapons.

# Bibliography

Adonis, A. and Tyrie, A. (1990) *Subsidiarity: As History and Policy*, London: Institute of Economic Affairs.

Alternative Defence Commission (1987) *The Politics of Alternative Defence*, London: Paladin.

Anderson, B. (1986) 'Neil gets his "nukes" in a twist', *Sunday Telegraph*, 7 December.

Anderson, V. (1991) 'Labour has a chance to seize the green initiative', *Samizdat*, 13/14, 37–9.

Andrews, G. (1991) (ed.) *Citizenship*, London: Lawrence & Wishart.

Bacon, R. and Eltis, W. (1976) *Britian's Economic Problem: Too Few Producers*, London: Macmillan.

Ball, I. (1986) '"Young Kinnock" claims he is attuned to the US', *Daily Telegraph*, 24 November.

Barber, J. (1976) *Who Makes British Foreign Policy?*, Milton Keynes: Open University Press.

Barratt-Brown, M., Emerson, T. and Stoneman, C. (1976) *Resources and the Environment: A Socialist Perspective*, Nottingham: Spokesman.

Barry, N. (1990) *Welfare*, Milton Keynes: Open University Press.

Bassett, P. (1988) *People at Work*, London: Fabian Society.

Baxter, S. (1991) 'Quietly Towards 2000', *New Statesman and Society*, 24 May.

Bayliss, F. (1991) *Making a Minimum Wage Work*, London: Fabian Society.

Baylis, J. (1990) *British Defence Policy*, London: Macmillan.

Beavis, S. and Watson, C. (1991) 'Industry to push top jobs for women', *The Guardian*, 13 August.

Beer, S. (1982) *Britain Against Itself*, London: Faber & Faber.

Benn, T. (1981) *Arguments for Socialism*, London: Jonathan Cape.

Bevins, A. and Brown, C. (1987) 'Kinnock acts to get the party back into line', *The Independent*, 12 March.

Bilski, R. (1977) 'The Common Market and the growing strength of Labour's left wing', *Government and Opposition*, 12, 306–31.

Bogdanor, V. (1979) *Devolution*, Oxford: Oxford University Press.

Bolton, J.E. (1971) *Report of the Committee of Inquiry on Small Firms*, London: HMSO.

Bosanquet, N. (1980) 'Labour and Public Expenditure' in N. Bosanquet and P. Townsend (eds) *Labour and Equality*, London: Heinemann.

Boyle, A. (1991) *From Solidarity to Action: Can Public Policy be an Effective Way of Progressing Radical Change for Women in Society?*, unpublished MSc thesis, University of Southampton.

Brack, D. (1990) 'David Owen and the social market economy', *Political Quarterly*, 61, 463–76.

Brandt Report (1980) *North South: A Programme for Survival*, London: Pan.

Brett, E.A. (1986) *The World Economy Since the War*, London: Macmillan.

British Broadcasting Corporation (1991), *Panorama* 8 July.

Bromley, S. (1991) *American Hegemony and World Oil*, Cambridge: Polity Press.

Brundtland, G. (1987) *Our Common Future*, United Nations: Oxford University Press.

Burns, A., Newby, M. and Winterton, J. (1985) 'The restructuring of the British coal industry', in *Cambridge Journal of Economics*, 9.

Butler, D. and Kavanagh, D. (1984) *The British General Election of 1983*, London: Macmillan.

Butler, D. and Kavanagh, D. (1988) *The British General Election of 1987*, London: Macmillan.

Butler, D. and Marquand, D. (1981) *European Elections and British Politics*, London: Longman.

Butler, D. and Rose, R. (1960) *The British General Election of 1959*, London: Macmillan.

Byrd, P. (1988) (ed.) *British Foreign Policy Under Mrs Thatcher*, London: Philip Allen.

Cameron, P. (1983) *Property Rights and Sovereign Rights*, London: Academic Press.

Campbell, B. (1990) 'Working together for women', *The Guardian*, 6 October.

Cannell, W. and Chudleigh, R. (1983) *The PWR Decision*, London: Friends of the Earth.

Carvel, J. (1986) 'Labour misgivings over defence policy', *The Guardian*, 5 December.

Cassell, M. (1989) 'Kinnock braces himself for rough ride on defence', *Financial Times*, 24 March.

Cassell, M. and Riddell, P. (1987) 'Kinnock steps in to defuse Labour defence policy row', *Financial Times*, 12 March.

Coates, D. (1975) *The Labour Party and the Struggle for Socialism*, Cambridge: Cambridge University Press.

Coates, D. (1980) *Labour in Power?*, London: Longman.

Coates, D. (1989) *The Crisis of Labour*, Oxford: Philip Allan.

Coates, K. (1986) *Joint Action for Jobs: A New Internationalism*, Nottingham: New Socialist/Spokesman.

Coates, K. and Topham, T. (1986) *Trade Unions and Politics*, Oxford: Basil Blackwell.

Cole, G.D.H. (1920) *Guild Socialism Re-stated*, London: Leonard Parsons.

Cook, R. (1984) 'Towards an alternative ecological strategy', *New Ground*, 2.

Cope, N. (1991) 'A gender for the nineties', *The Guardian*, 13 August.

Crewe, I. (1982) 'The Labour Party and the electorate', in D. Kavanagh (ed.) *The Politics of the Labour Party*, London: George Allen & Unwin.

Crewe, I. (1983) 'Why Labour lost the British elections', *Public Opinion*, July, 7–9 and 56–60.

Crewe, I. (1986) 'On the death and resurrection of class voting: some comments on *How Britain Votes*', *Political Studies*, 34, 260–8.

Crewe, I. (1987) 'A new class of politics', *The Guardian*, 15 June.

Crewe, I. (1989) 'The decline of labour and the decline of Labour: social and electoral trends in post-war Britain', *Essex Papers in Government and Politics*, No. 65.

Crosland, A. (1956) *The Future of Socialism*, London: Jonathan Cape.

Crosland, A. (1971) *A New Social Democratic Britain*, London: Fabian Society.

Crosland, A. (1974) *Socialism Now*, London: Jonathan Cape.

Crouch, C. (1986) 'Conservative industrial relations policy towards labour exclusion', in O. Jacobi *et al.*, (eds) *Economic Crisis, Trade Unions and the State*, London: Croom Helm.

Crouch, C. (1989) 'The Conservatives and the trade unions. Is the struggle over?', Paper presented to the annual conference of the Political Studies Association, April, University of Warwick.

Crowther-Hunt, Lord and Peacock, A.T. (1973) 'Memorandum of dissent', *Report of the Royal Commission on the Constitution*, Vol. II, Cmnd 5460–1, London: HMSO.

Curran, J. (1984) (ed.) *The Future of the Left*, Oxford: Polity Press.

Curran, J. (1987) 'Can Tribune end Labour's civil war?', *The Times*, 10 September.

Curran, J. and Downing, S. (1989) 'The State and small business owners: an empirical assessment of consultation strategies', Paper given at the 12th National Small Firms Policy and Research Conference, November.

Curran, J. and Stanworth, J. (1981) 'Size of workplace and attitudes to industrial relations in the printing and electronics industries', *British Journal of Industrial Relations*, 19 (1), 14–25.

Dahrendorf, R. (1988) *The Modern Social Conflict*, London: Weidenfeld & Nicolson.

Dalyell, T. (1982) *One Man's Falklands*, London: Cecil Woolf.

Department of Employment (1991) *Small Firms in Britain 1991*, London: HMSO.

Department of Trade and Industry (1991) *Constraints on the Growth of Small Firms*, London: HMSO.

Devereux, M. and Morris, C. (1983) 'North Sea oil taxation', *Institute for Fiscal Studies*, Report Series, No. 6.

DeYoung, K. (1986) 'Labor's Kinnock leaves for US to bolster image, explain policy', *Washington Post*, 24 November.

Donnison, D. (1991) 'Sinking with the tide', *The Guardian*, 21 August.

Downs, A. (1957) *An Economic Theory of Democracy*, New York: Harper.

Driver, C. (1964) *The Disarmers*, London: Hodder & Stoughton.

Drucker, H. (1984) 'Intra-party democracy in action: the election of the leader and deputy leader by the Labour Party in 1983', *Parliamentary Affairs*, 37, 283–93.

Dunn, D. (1991) 'Challenges to the nuclear orthodoxy' in S. Croft (ed.) *British Security Policy*, London: HarperCollins.

Dyson, K. (1980) *The State Tradition in Western Europe*, Oxford: Martin Robertson.

Ellis, G. (1991) 'Out for the count', *The Guardian*, 6 November.

END (1987) 'Labour: "serious about defence"', *END Journal*, December–January.

Epstein, L. (1967) *Political Parties in Western Democracies*, London: Pall Mall.

Evans, M. (1987) 'Labour shifts on defence strategy', *The Times*, 20 May.

Ferris, J. (1985) 'Citizenship and the crisis in the welfare state' in P. Bean, J. Fereis and D. Whynes (eds) *In Defence of Welfare*, London: Tavistock.

Fletcher, M. (1987) 'Tories to spoil Kinnock's defence trip', *The Times*, 9 March.

Flynn, A. and Lowe, P. (1991) 'The party politicisation of the environment in Britain: a preliminary survey', Paper presented to a conference on green politics, University of Exeter, March.

Foote, G. (1985) *The Labour Party's Political Thought*, London: Croom Helm.

Foulkes, G. (1985) 'Letter to the Right Honourable Margaret Thatcher', 4 December.

Franklin, M. (1985) *The Decline of Class Voting in Britain*, Oxford: Oxford University Press.

Freedman, L. (1986) *The Price of Peace*, London: Macmillan.

Gallup (1990) *Gallup Political Index*, London: Gallup.

Gamble, A. (1988) *Free Economy and Strong State*, London: Macmillan.

George, S. (1990) *An Awkward Partner: Britain in the European Community*, Oxford: Oxford University Press.

Geroski, P.A. and Knight, K.G. (1991) *Targeting Competitive Industries*, London: Fabian Society.

Gibbon, P. and Bromley, S. (1990) '"From an institution to a business"? Changes in the British coal industry 1985–89', *Economy and Society*, Vol. 19.

Gill, S. and Law, D. (1988) *The Global Political Economy: Perspectives, Problems and Policies*, Hemel Hempstead: Harvester Wheatsheaf.

Glennester, H. (1983) (ed.) *The Future of the Welfare State*, London: Heinemann.

Goss, D. (1991) *Small Business and Society*, London: Routledge.

Gough, I. and Doyal, L. (1991) *A Theory of Human Needs*, London: Macmillan.

Gough, I. *et al.* (1989) 'Socialism, democracy and human needs', in P. Alcock *et al.*, *The Social Economy in the Democratic State*, London: Lawrence & Wishart.

Gould, B. (1989) *A Future for Socialism*, London: Jonathan Cape.

Graham, C. and Prosser, T. (eds) (1988) *Waiving the Rules: The Constitution Under Thatcher*, Milton Keynes: Open University.

Gray, J. (1990) 'Conservatism, individualism and political thought of the New Right', in J.C.D. Clarke (ed.) *Ideas and Politics in Modern Britain*, London: Macmillan.

Bibliography 237

Hadley, R. and Hatch, S. (1981) *Social Welfare and the Failure of the State*, London: Allen & Unwin.
Haines, J. (1977) *The Politics of Power*, London: Hodder & Stoughton.
Hakim, C. (1989a) 'Identifying fast growing firms', *Employment Gazette*, January, 29–44.
Hakim, C. (1989b) 'New recruits to self-employment in the 1980s', *Employment Gazette*, June, 286–97.
Hall, S. (1985) 'Authoritarian populism: a reply', *New Left Review*, 151, 115–24.
Hall, S. and Atkinson, F. (1983) *Oil and the British Economy*, London: Croom Helm.
Hall, S. and Held, D. (1989) 'Citizen and citizenship', in S. Hall and M. Jacques (eds).
Hall, S. and Jacques, M. (eds) (1989) *New Times*, London: Lawrence & Wishart.
Hamilton, M.B. (1989) *Democratic Socialism in Britain and Sweden*, London: Macmillan.
Harman H. (1990) *'Time Gentlemen Please' The Case for Changing the Sitting Times of the House of Commons*, London: Labour Party.
Harman, H. and Richardson, J. (1989) *Health Care for Women: The Impact of the NHS White Paper*, London: Labour Party.
Harris, R. (1984) *The Making of Neil Kinnock*, London: Faber & Faber.
Harrison, M. (1960) *Trade Unions and the Labour Party Since 1945*, London: Allen & Unwin.
Harrison, M. (1991) 'Can business win the next election?' *Independent on Sunday*, 29 September.
Haseler, S. (1969) *The Gaitskellites: Revisionism in the British Labour Party 1951–64*, London: Macmillan.
Haseler, S. (1980) *The Tragedy of Labour*, London: Basil Blackwell.
Hatfield, M. (1978) *The House the Left Built*, London: Gollancz.
Hattersley, R. (1987) *Choose Freedom*, London: Penguin.
Hayek, F.A. (1960) *The Constitution of Liberty*, London: Routledge & Kegan Paul.
Hayek, F.A. (1978) *A Tiger by the Tail: The Keynesian Legacy of Inflation*, London: Institute of Economic Affairs.
Hayek, F.A. (1979) *Law, Legislation and Liberty Vol. III*, London: Methuen.
Heath, A., Jowell, R. and Curtice, J. (1985) *How Britain Votes*, Oxford: Pergamon Press.
Heath, A., Jowell, R., Curtice, J. and Evans, G. (1990) 'The rise of the new political agenda?', *European Sociological Review*, 6 (1), 31–48.
Heffer, E. (1986) *Labour's Future: Socialist or SDP Mark 2?*, London: Verso.
Hills, J. (ed.) (1990) *The State of Welfare*, Oxford: Oxford University Press.
Hine, D. (1986) 'Leaders and followers: Democracy and manageability in social democratic parties of Western Europe', in W.E. Paterson and A.A. Thomas (eds) *The Future of Social Democracy*, Oxford: Clarendon Press.
Hirst, P. (1989) *After Thatcher*, London: Collins.

HMSO (1977) *Policy for the Inner Cities*, Cmnd 6845, London: HMSO.
HMSO (1990) *Encouraging Citizenship: Report of the Commission on Citizenship*, London: HMSO.
Hobsbawn, E. (1981) 'The forward march of Labour halted?', in M. Jacques and F. Mulhurn (eds) *The Forward March of Labour Halted?*, London: New Left Books.
Hodgson, G. (1981) *Labour at the Crossroads*, Oxford: Martin Robertson.
Hoggart, S. (1987) 'Kinnock: we're sticking to our guns on defence', *Observer*, 28 May.
Hogwood, B. and Keating, M. (eds) (1982) *Regional Government in England*, Oxford: Clarendon Press.
Holland, S. (ed.) (1983) *Out of Crisis: A Project for European Crisis*, Nottingham: Spokesman.
House of Commons (1982) *The Falklands Campaign: A Digest of Debates in the House of Commons*, April–June, London: HMSO.
Howell, D. (1976) *British Social Democracy*, London: Croom Helm.
Hughes, C. and Wintour, P. (1990) *Labour Rebuilt: The New Model Party*, London: Fourth Estate.
Hurd, D. (1988) 'Citizenship in the Tory democracy', *New Statesman*, 29 April.
Hutton, W. (1991) 'Tide in Labour's affairs again at the flood?', *The Guardian*, 30 September.
Ignatieff, M. (1991) 'Citizenship and moral narcissism', in G. Andrews (ed.) *Citizenship*, London: Lawrence & Wishart.
Jenkins, P. (1987a) 'Grasping the nettle of deterrence', *The Independent*, 28 May.
Jenkins, P. (1987b) *Mrs Thatcher's Revolution: The Ending of the Socialist Era*, London: Cape.
Jenkins, P. (1988) *The Thatcher Revolution: the Post-Socialist Era*, London: Cape.
Jenkins, P. (1990) *New York Review of Books*, 25 April.
Jessop, B., Bonnet, K., Bromely, S. and Ling, T. (1987) *Thatcherism*, London: Polity Press.
Johnson, N. (1990) *Reconstructing the Welfare State: A Decade of Change*, Hemel Hempstead: Harvester Wheatsheaf.
Johnston, P. (1986) 'Reagan does deal with Kinnock: US to stay out of nuclear defence', *Sunday Times*, 28 September.
Jones, G. (1991) 'Kinnock abandons Labour's commitment to unilateral nuclear disarmament', *Daily Telegraph*, 17 April.
Jones, P. and Reece, G. (1990) *British Public Attitudes to Public Defence*, London: Macmillan.
Jordan, A.G. (1981) 'Iron triangles, woolly corporatism and elastic nets: images of the policy process', *Journal of the Policy Process*, 1, 95–123.
Judge, D. (1988) 'Incomplete sovereignty: the British House of Commons and the completion of the internal market in the European Community', *Parliamentary Affairs*, 41, 4.
Katz, R. (1990) 'Party as linkage: a vestigial function?', *European Journal of Political Research*, 18 (1), 143–61.
Kaufman, G. (ed.) (1983) *Renewal: Labour's Britain in the 1980s*, Harmondsworth: Penguin.

Kaufman, G. (1987) Speech in Rhyl, 27 November, Labour Party Campaign and Communication Directorate, Reference PR 285/87.

Kavanagh, D. (1990) *Thatcherism and British Politics*, Oxford: Oxford University Press.

Keane, J. (1988) *Democracy and Civil Society*, London: Verso.

Keegan, J. (1987) 'Kinnock's only weapon', *Daily Telegraph*, 28 May.

Kellner, P. (1989a) 'The party's review that may extinguish socialism', *The Independent*, 8 May.

Kellner, P. (1989b) 'Marching towards the same ideals', *The Independent*, 20 February.

Kelly, R. (1991) 'Party organisation', *Contemporary Record*, 4 (4) 6–8.

King, A. (1977) *Britain Says Yes*, Washington DC: American Enterprise Institute.

King, A. (1982) 'Whatever happened to the British party system?', *Parliamentary Affairs*, 35, 241–51.

Kinnock, N. (1984a) 'A new deal for Europe', in J. Curran (ed.) *The Future of the Left*, Cambridge: Polity Press.

Kinnock, N. (1984b) 'Message to the anti-apartheid movement', 21 March, London: Labour Party.

Kinnock, N. (1985) 'Message to the anti-apartheid movement', 16 June, London: Labour Party.

Kinnock, N. (1986) 'Speech to the South Wales NUM gala', 14 June, London: Labour Party.

Kinnock, N. (1987) 'Labour's plan for the no-nuclear defence of Britain', *New York Times*, 28 March.

Kinnock, N. (1989) 'A hand on the tiller – and the till', *The Guardian*, 10 April.

Kinnock, N. (1991a) 'Statement following meeting with President De Klerk of South Africa', London: Labour Party.

Kinnock, N. (1991b) 'Statement following meeting with Nelson Mandela', London: Labour Party.

Klein, R. (1980) 'The welfare state: a self-inflicted crisis', *Political Quarterly*, 51, 24–34.

Klein, R. and O'Higgins, M. (eds) (1985) *The Future of the Welfare State*, Oxford: Blackwell.

Kogan, D. and Kogan, M. (1982) *The Battle for the Labour Party*, London: Kogan Page.

Labour Party (1972) *Opposition Green Paper: Discrimination Against Women: Report of a Labour Party Study Group*, London: Labour Party.

Labour Party (1973) *Labour's Programme 1973*, London: Labour Party.

Labour Party (1974) *Let Us Work Together*, London: Labour Party.

Labour Party (1977a) *Regional Authorities and Local Government Reform*, London: Labour Party.

Labour Party (1977b) *The EEC and Britain: A Socialist Perspective*, London: Labour Party.

Labour Party (1978) 'Statement on Nicaragua', *National Executive Committee*, London: Labour Party.

Labour Party (1981a) 'Statement on US policy in Central America and the Caribbean', *National Executive Committee*, London: Labour Party.

240  *Bibliography*

Labour Party (1981b) 'The struggle in El Salvador', *Labour Party International Department Information Paper*, 23, London: Labour Party.

Labour Party (1982a) *Labour's Programme 1982*, London: Labour Party.

Labour Party (1982b) 'Development cooperation', *Labour Party Discussion Document*, London: Labour Party.

Labour Party (1982c) 'Report of the National Executive Committee of the 81st annual conference of the Labour Party', 27 September to 1 October, London: Labour Party.

Labour Party (1983a) *The New Hope for Britain*, London: Labour Party.

Labour Party (1983b) *Labour Party Policy Towards Small Businesses*, Research Note 29, London: Labour Party.

Labour Party (1983c) 'NEC statement', October, London: Labour Party.

Labour Party (1983d) 'Charter to establish equality for women within the party', London: Labour Party.

Labour Party (1984a) *Defence and Security for Britain*, London: Labour Party.

Labour Party (1984b) 'Baiting the bear: the foreign policy of President Reagan', *Labour Party International Department Information Paper*, 63, London: Labour Party.

Labour Party (1984c) 'The EEC and the Third World: towards a socialist perspective', *Labour Party International Department Information Paper*, 64, London: Labour Party.

Labour Party (1984d) 'The international debt crisis', *Labour Party International Department Information Paper*, 67, London: Labour Party.

Labour Party (1984e) 'NEC statement to conference on the Falklands', *Foreign Policy NEC Statements*, London: Labour Party.

Labour Party (1985a) *Labour's Charter for Co-ops*, London: Labour Party.

Labour Party (1985b) *Labour's Charter for Local Enterprise*, London: Labour Party.

Labour Party (1985c) *Bosses' Freedoms, Workers Burdens*, London: Labour Party.

Labour Party (1985d) *For the Good of All: Labour's Plans for Aid and Development*, London: Labour Party.

Labour Party (1985e) 'Statement by the NEC on South Africa to the annual conference', London: Labour Party.

Labour Party (1986a) *Modern Britain in the Modern World*, London: Labour Party.

Labour Party (1986b) *Statement on the Environment*, London: Labour Party.

Labour Party (1986c) 'Mikhail Gorbachev's disarmament proposals: Labour's response', *Press Release*, 29 January, London: Labour Party.

Labour Party (1986d) *Overseas Aid: Britain's Place in the World*, London: Labour Party.

Labour Party (1987a) *Britain Will Win*, London: Labour Party.

Labour Party (1987b) 'East–West relations', *Background Briefing*, CH5, London: Labour Party.

Labour Party (1987c) 'International cooperation', *Background Briefing*, 4, London: Labour Party.

Labour Party (1987d) 'The war in the Gulf', Statement by the National Executive Committee to the annual conference, London: Labour Party.

Labour Party (1987e) *New Jobs for Britain*, London: Labour Party.
Labour Party (1988a) *Democratic Socialist Aims and Values*, London: Labour Party.
Labour Party (1988b) *Report of the Eighty-Seventh Annual Conference of the Labour Party*, London: Labour Party.
Labour Party (1988c) *Social Justice and Economic Efficiency*, London: Labour Party.
Labour Party (1988d) *Report of the Consultation on the National Conference of Labour Women*, London: Labour Party.
Labour Party (1989a) *Meet the Challenge, Make the Change: A New Agenda for Britain*, London: Labour Party.
Labour Party (1989b) *Report of the Eighty-Eighth Annual Conference of the Labour Party*, London: Labour Party.
Labour Party (1989c) *The Social Charter: How Britain Benefits*, London: Labour Party.
Labour Party (1989d) *Working with Women for a Safer Environment: Consultation Document Labour's Ministry for Women*, London: Labour Party.
Labour Party (1989e) *A New Future for Women, Labour's Programme for Women*, London: Labour Party.
Labour Party (1990a) *Looking to the Future*, London: Labour Party.
Labour Party (1990b) *An Earthly Chance*, London: Labour Party.
Labour Party (1990c) 'NEC statement on economic and monetary union', *Tribune*, 14 December.
Labour Party (1990d) *Representation of Women in the Labour Party: Consultative Document*, London: Labour Party.
Labour Party (1990e) *Representation of Women in the Labour Party: Report of the Consultative Process*, London: Labour Party.
Labour Party (1991a) *Modern Manufacturing Strength*, London: Labour Party.
Labour Party (1991b) *Opportunity Britain*, London: Labour Party.
Labour Party (1991c) 'The 1988 deal and the Toronto summit', *Labour Party News Release*, 17, June 1991, London: Labour Party.
Labour Party (1991d) 'Chalker steals Labour's clothes', *Labour Party News Release*, 25, June, London: Labour Party.
Labour Party (1991e) *Protecting Our Future: Women and the Environment*, London: Labour Party.
Labour Party (1991f) *Women's News*, London: Labour Party.
Labour Party (1991g) *The Missing Culture: Labour's Plans for Women in the Arts and the Media*, London: Labour Party.
Lansman, J. and Meale, A. (eds) (1983) *Beyond Thatcherism: the Real Alternative*, London: Junction Books.
Lash, S. and Urry, J. (1987) *The End of Organised Capitalism*, Oxford: Polity Press.
Lawson, K. and Merkl, P. (eds) (1988) *When Parties Fail*, Princeton: Princeton University Press.
Leadbeater, C. (1987) *The Politics of Prosperity*, London: Fabian Society.
Lipsey, D. (1981) 'Crosland's Socialism', in D. Lipsey and D. Leonard (eds), *The Socialist Agenda: Crosland's Legacy*, London: Jonathan Cape.
Longstreth, F. (1988) 'From corporatism to dualism? Thatcherism and

242   *Bibliography*

the climacteric of British trade unions in the 1980s', *Political Studies*, 36, 413–32.

Low Pay Unit (1988) *Britain Can't Afford Low Pay: A Programme for a National Minimum Wage*, Low Pay Unit.

Lowe, P. and Goyder, J. (1983) *Environmental Groups in Politics*, London: George Allen & Unwin.

McCarthy, M. (ed.) (1990) *The New Politics of Welfare*, London: Macmillan.

McCreadie, R. (1991) 'Scottish identity and the constitution', in B. Crick, C. Crouch and D. Marquand (eds) *National Identities. The Constitutions of the United Kingdom*, Oxford: Basil Blackwell.

Machin, H. and Wright, V. (eds) (1985) *Economic Policy and Policy-making Under the Mitterand Presidency 1981–1984*, London: Frances Pinter.

MacInnes, J. (1987) *Thatcherism at Work*, Milton Keynes: Open University.

McKee, V. (1991) 'Fragmentation on the Labour right', *Politics*, 11, 23–9.

McKenzie, R. (1955) *British Political Parties*, London: Heinemann.

Marquand, D. (1988) *The Unprincipled Society*, London: Fontana.

Marsh, D. and Rhodes, R.A.W. (1992) *Implementing Thatcherite Policies: Audit of An Era*, Milton Keynes: Open University.

Marsh, I. (1990) 'Liberal priorities: The Lib–Lab pact and the requirements for policy influence', *Parliamentary Affairs*, 43 (3), 292–321.

Marshall, G., Rose, D., Newby, H. and Vogler, C. (1988) *Social Class in Modern Britain*, London: Unwin Hyman.

Marshall, T.H. (1950) *Citizenship and Social Class and Other Essays*, Cambridge: Cambridge University Press.

May, J.D. (1973) 'Opinion structure of political parties: the spatial law of curvilinear disparity', *Political Studies*, 21 (2), 135–51.

May, T.C. and McHugh, J. (1991) 'Government and small business in the UK; the experience of the 1980s', Paper presented to the annual conference of the Political Studies Association, University of Lancaster, April.

Mayall, J. (1990) 'Britain and the Third World', in R. O'Neill and R.J. Vincent (eds) *The West and the Third World*, London: Macmillan.

Meadows, D. *et al.* (1972) *The Limits of Growth*, London: Earth Island.

Merkel, W. (1990) 'After the golden age: is social democracy doomed to decline?', Paper to the Institut de Ciencies i Politiques Conference in Socialist Parties in Western Europe, Barcelona.

Miliband, R. (1961) *Parliamentary Socialism*, London: Merlin.

Milward, N. and Stevens, M. (1986) *British Workplace Industrial Relations 1980–1984*, Manchester: Manchester University Press.

Minkin, L. (1978) *The Labour Party Conference*, London: Allan Lane.

Minkin, L. (1980) *The Labour Party Conference*, 2nd Edition, Edinburgh: Edinburgh University Press.

Minkin, L. and Seyd, P. (1977) 'The British Labour Party', in W.E. Paterson and A.H. Thomas (eds) *Social Democratic Parties in Western Europe*, London: Croom Helm.

Mitchell, A. (1983) *Four Years in the Death in the Labour Party*, London: Methuen.

Mitchell, A. (1989) *Beyond the Blue Horizon*, London: Bellew.

Mitchell, N. (1987) 'Where traditional Tories fear to tread: Mrs Thatcher's trade union policy', *West European Politics*, 10, 33–45.

MORI and the Joseph Rowntree Reform Trust Limited (1991) *The State of the Nation*, London.

NALGO (1990) *NALGO, the European Community and 1992*, London: Nalgo.

Neustatter, A. (1987) 'Labour moves on Women's Ministry', *The Guardian*, 7 April.

Neustatter, A. (1991) 'Labour's positive steps', *The Guardian*, 26 March.

Norman, M. (1987) 'Should there be a Ministry for Women?', *The Daily Telegraph*, 7 April.

Northedge, F.S. (1974) *Descent from Power: British Foreign Policy, 1945–73*, London: George Allen & Unwin.

Olson, M. (1982) *The Rise and Decline of Nations*, New Haven: Yale University Press.

Panitch, L. (1988) 'Socialist renewal and the Labour Party', *Socialist Register*.

Parliamentary CND (1988) *Britain in the World – Labour's Role in Defence*, Submission to the Labour Party's Policy Review.

Parry, G. and Moyser, G. (1990) 'A map of political participation in Britain', *Government and Opposition*, 25, 147–69.

Pelkman, J. and Winters, A. (1988) *Europe's Domestic Market*, London: Routledge.

Pepper, D. (1986) 'Radical Environmentalism and the labour movement', in J. Weston (ed.) *Red and Green*, London: Pluto.

Perry, J.M. (1986) 'Kinnock vows to remove nuclear weapons from UK but appears to modify timetable', *Wall Street Journal*, 21 November.

Pinder, J. (1989) 'The single market: a step towards European union', in J. Lodge (ed.) *The European Community and the Challenge of the Future*, London: Pinter.

Piore, M.J. and Sabel, C.F. (1984) *The Second Industrial Divide*, New York: Basic Books.

Plant, R. (1981) 'Democratic socialism and equality', in D. Lipsey and D. Leonard (eds) *The Socialist Agenda: Crosland's Legacy*, London: Jonathan Cape.

Plant, R. (1988a) 'Citizenship and society', *New Socialists*, December.

Plant, R. (1988b) *Citizenship, Rights and Socialism*, London: Fabian Society.

Pocock, J.G.A. (1975) *The Machiavellian Moment*, Princeton: Princeton University Press.

Porritt, J. and Winner, D. (1988) *The Coming of the Greens*, London: Fontana.

Porter, A., Spence, M. and Thompson, R. (1986) *The Energy Fix*, London: Pluto.

Punnett, R.M. (1990) 'Selecting a leader and deputy leader of the Labour Party: the future of the electoral college', *Parliamentary Affairs*, 43, 179–95.

Raban, C. (1986) 'The welfare state: from consensus to crisis', in P. Lawless and C. Raban (eds) *The Contemporary British City*, London: Harper & Row.

Richardson, J. (1986) *Labour's Ministry for Women's Rights: A Discussion Document*, London: Labour Party.

244    *Bibliography*

Richardson, J. (1991) *A New Ministry for Women*, London: Labour Party.
Rodgers, W. (1985) 'Blurred vision from the commanding heights', *The Guardian*, 12 April.
Rosamond, B. (1990) 'Labour and the European Community: learning to be European', *Politics*, 10 (2), 41–8.
Rose, C. (1991) *The Dirty Man of Europe*, London: Simon & Schuster.
Rose, R. and Mackie, T. (1988) 'Do parties persist or fail? The big trade-off facing organisations', K. Lawson and P. Merkl (eds) *When Parties Fail*, Princeton: Princeton University Press.
Ross, G., Hoffman, S. and Malzacher, S. (eds) (1984) *The Mitterand Experiment, Continuity and change in Modern France*, Cambridge: Polity Press.
Rothwell, R. (1986) 'The role of small firms in technological innovation', in J. Curran, J. Stanworth and D. Watkins (eds) *The Survival of the Small Firm Vol. 2*, Aldershot: Gower.
Royal Commission on the Distribution of Income and Wealth (1980) *An A to Z of Income and Wealth*, London: HMSO.
Rutledge, I. and Wright, P. (1985) 'Coal worldwide: the international context of the British miners' strike', *Cambridge Journal of Economics*, 9.
Ryle, M. (1988) *Ecology and Socialism*, London: Radius.
Sabin, P.A.G. (1986) *The Third World War Scare in Britain*, London: Macmillan.
Sage, A. (1990) 'Owen and Kinnock: are they by any chance related?', *The Independent on Sunday*, 20 May.
Samuels, R. (1987) *The Business of the Japanese State*, New York: Ithaca.
Sanders, D., Ward, H. and Marsh, D. (with D. Fletcher) (1987) 'Government popularity and the Falklands War: a reassesment', *British Journal of Political Science*, 17, 281–314.
Scarrow, S, (1990) 'The decline of party organisation? Mass membership parties in Great Britain and West Germany', Paper to the annual meeting of the American Political Science Association, San Francisco.
Schumacher, E.F. (1973) *Small is Beautiful*, London: Blond & Briggs.
Scott, L. (1991) 'Targeting Trident in arms negotiations', *Arms Control*, 12 (1).
Seyd, P. (1987) *The Rise and Fall of the Labour Left*, London: Macmillan.
Seyd, P. (1990) 'Party renewal: The British Labour Party', Paper presented to workshop on the European socialist parties, University of Barcelona, October.
Seyd, P. and Whiteley, P. (1992) *Labour's Grassroots: The Politics of Party Membership*, Oxford: Oxford University Press.
Seyd, P., Whiteley, P. and Broughton, D. (1991) 'Labour's reorganisation down at the grassroots', in I. Crewe, P. Norris, D. Denver and D. Broughton (eds) *British Parties and Elections Yearbook 1991*, London: Harvester Wheatsheaf.
Shaw, E. (1988) *Discipline and Discord in the Labour Party*, Manchester: Manchester University Press.
Shaw, E. (1989) 'The Labour Party and the Militant Tendency', *Parliamentary Affairs*, 42, 180–96.
Shaw, E. (1990) 'Before the Policy Review: the evolution of Labour's economic strategy 1979–1987', Paper presented to the annual conference of the Political Studies Association, April, University of Durham.

Shaw, G.B. (1962) 'The transition', in A. Briggs (ed.) *Fabian Essays*, London: George Allen & Unwin.

Sheffield Group (1989) *The Social Economy and the Democratic State*, London: Lawrence & Wishart.

Shutt, J. and Wittington, R. (1984) 'Large firm strategies and the rise of small units. The illusion of firm job generation', *Working Paper Series No. 15*, University of Manchester: School of Geography.

Skidelsky, R. (1989) 'Partnership of freedom and fairness', *The Guardian*, 10 April.

Simpson, B. (1973) *Labour: the Unions and the Party*, London: Allen & Unwin.

Spear, J. (1990) 'Britain and conventional arms restraints', in M. Hoffman, (ed.) *UK Arms Control in the 1990s*, Manchester: Manchester University Press.

Spear, J. (1991) 'Relations with the south' in S. Croft (ed.) *British Security Policy*, London: HarperCollins.

Steel, D. (1980) *A House Divided: The Lib-Lab Pact and the Future of British Politics*, London: Weidenfeld & Nicolson.

Stephenson, H. (1982) *Claret and Chips*, London: Michael Joseph.

Stevens, P. (1991) 'Labour drops n-arms stand', *Financial Times*, 17 April.

Storey, D.S. and Johnson, S. (1987) *Are Small Firms the Answer to Unemployment?*, London: Employment Institute.

Strange, S. (1986) *Casino Capitalism*, Oxford: Basil Blackwell.

*Sunday Times* (1987) 'Editorial', 31 May.

Sweet, C. (1983) *The Price of Nuclear Power*, London: Heinemann

Szarka, J. (1990) 'Networking and small firms', *International Small Business Journal*, 4 (4), 29–46.

Taylor, A.J. (1987) *The Trade Unions and the Labour Party*, London: Croom Helm.

Taylor Gooby, P. (1985) *Public Opinion, Ideology and State Welfare*, London: Routledge & Kegan Paul.

Taylor Gooby, P. (1991) 'Social welfare: the unkindest cuts', in R. Jowell, S. Witherspoon and L. Brook (eds) *British Social Attitudes*, Aldershot: Gower.

Teague, P. (1989) *The European Community. The Social Dimension. Labour Market Policies for 1992*, London: Kogan Page.

Thatcher, M. (1988) *Britain and Europe: Text of speech delivered in Bruges by the Prime Minister*, 20 September, London: Conservative Political Centre.

Therborn, G. (1984) 'The prospect of Labour and the transformation of advanced capitalism', *New Left Review*, 145.

Thompson, G. (1986) *The Conservatives' Economic Policy*, London: Croom Helm.

Townsend, P. (1991) *The Poor are Poorer*, University of Bristol.

Townsend, P. and Bosanquet, N. (1972) *Labour and Inequality*, London: Fabian Society.

Travis, A. (1991) 'Poor families poorer during Thatcher era, says Meacher', *The Guardian*, 30 August.

TUC (1988) *Maximising the Benefits. Minimising the Costs*, London: TUC.

TUC (1989) *Towards a Charter for the Environment*, London: TUC.

TUC (1990a) *Environmental Issues and Policy Implications: Towards the White Paper*, London: TUC.

TUC (1990b) *Congress Annual Report*, London: TUC.

Tyler, R. (1987) *Campaign*, London: Grafton.

Walker, A. (1984) *Social Planning: A Strategy for Socialist Welfare*, Oxford: Blackwell.

Ward, H. and Samways, D. (1992) 'From blue to green? Environmental policy and policy implementation under Thatcherism', in D. Marsh, and R. Rhodes (eds) *Implementing Thatcherite Policies*, Milton Keynes: Open University.

Webb, S. and Webb, B. (1920) *A Constitution for the Socialist Commonwealth of Great Britain*, London: Longmans Green.

Weiner, M.J. (1987) *English Culture and the Decline of the Industrial Spirit*, Harmondsworth: Penguin.

Wheeler, N. (1990) 'The dual imperative of Britain's nuclear deterrent', in M. Hoffman, (ed.) *UK Arms Control in the 1990s*, Manchester: Manchester University Press.

Wheeler, N. (1991) 'Perceptions of the Soviet threat', in S. Croft, (ed.) *British Security Policy*, London: HarperCollins.

Whitehead, P. (1985) *The Writing on the Wall*, London: Michael Joseph.

Whiteley, P. (1983) *The Labour Party in Crisis*, London: Methuen.

Williams, F. (1989) *Social Policy: A Critical Introduction*, Cambridge: Polity Press.

Wilson, H. (1974) *The Labour Government 1964 to 1970*, Harmondsworth: Penguin.

Wilson, H. (1979) *The Financing of Small Firms*, Cmnd 7503, London: HMSO.

Wilton, I. (1990) 'Labour Policy Review: Is it a break with the past', *Contemporary Record*, 4 (1), 14–15.

Wintour, P. (1991a) 'Kinnock beats challenge from anti-war MPs', *The Guardian*, 28 February.

Wintour, P. (1991b) 'Major hopes world kudos will net votes', *The Guardian*, 7 September.

Wintour, P. (1991c) 'Commons morning sitting plan to save midnight oil', *The Guardian*, 5 November.

Wintour, P. and Hetherington, P. (1989) 'Kinnock bows to deterrent', *The Guardian*, 3 May.

Wintour, P. and McKie, D. (1989) 'Kinnock vows shift on defence', *The Guardian*, 10 February.

Withrow, J. and Hughes, D. (1986) 'Kinnock welcomes nuclear warships', *Sunday Times*, 23 November.

Wright, P. (1986) 'The changing market for coal and the relationship between the NCB and the electricity supply industry', Paper presented to the Coalfields and Community Conference, Sheffield.

Young, H. (1990) 'Labour's song for Europe plays at no. 10', *The Guardian*, 15 May.

Young, H. (1991) 'Making a virtue of piety', *The Guardian*, 3 October.

Young, M. (1991) 'Socialist chance of a lifetime', *The Guardian*, 10 September.

# Index

economic management 62–3,
68; and nuclear issues 201; and
Policy Review 18–20; and small
businesses 77, 87; and welfare
policies 133
Wilton, I. 87
Winner, D. 120–1, 123
Winter of Discontent 4, 7, 91
Winters, A. 21
Wintour, P. 9–11, 92, 125, 166, 197,
210, 213
Withrow, J. 195
Wittington, R. 86

women 151–67; and continuity
and change in Labour Party 219;
early initiatives 153–6; internal
reforms of party 159–66; 1991
Policy document 156–9; policies
toward 152–3
working class: support for party 15
World Bank 194
Wright, P. 103, 113
Wright, V. 177

Young, H. 23, 218
Young, M. 223